TEACH YOURSELF

TRACING YOUR FAMILY HISTORY

Stella Colwell

KU-160-218

Hodder & Stoughton

A MEMBER OF THE HODDER HEADLINE GROUP

For Shirley Hughes
and for
Jennifer and Katharine and their parents, my friends,
Sue and Les Manton
with much love

Long-renowned as the authoritative source for self-guided learning – with more than 30 million copies sold worldwide – the *Teach Yourself* series includes over 200 titles in the fields of languages, crafts, hobbies, sports, and other leisure activities.

Library of Congress Catalog Card Number: 95-71309

First published in UK 1997 by Hodder Headline Plc, 338 Euston Road, London NW1 3BH

A catalogue record for this title is available from the British Library

First published in US 1997 by NTC Publishing Group
An imprint of NTC/Contemporary Publishing Company
4255 West Touhy Avenue, Lincolnwood (Chicago), Illinois 60646 – 1975 U.S.A.

Typeset by Transet Limited, Coventry, England.
Printed in England by Cox & Wyman Ltd, Reading, Berkshire.

Impression number	10 9 8 7
Year	2000

CONTENTS

List of Illustrations and Figures

Page

ACKNOWLEDGEMENTS

I very much want to thank Shirley Hughes for all the practical research and loose ends she tidied up for me in London, especially at the Society of Genealogists, a task she undertook with much humour and promptness. Besides thanking her I also want to express appreciation to Bill Cubin of The Laurel and Hardy Museum, Ulverston, Cumbria, for generously lending me his copy of *Laurel before Hardy*, Joyce Brown, Area Librarian at Grantham Library for her help in locating the obituary of Arthur Jefferson and other local items about him, Rev G Shrimpton and parishioners of Barkston, in Lincolnshire, for searching out his gravestone, Malcolm Pinhorn for information about the licensee Chaplins, Neville Taylor for finding the biography of Fred Karno, Cecelia Doidge Ripper for helping with theatrical sources about him, the staff of the Office for National Statistics, the General Register Offices of Jersey, Scotland, Northern Ireland and the Republic of Ireland, Dorothy Hammond at the Office for National Statistics, staff of the London Metropolitan Archives, the Public Record Offices in London and Belfast, the Scottish Record Office, the National Archives of Ireland, and National Library in Dublin, the National Archives in Washington, DC, the British Library and the Priaulx Library, Guernsey for supplying me with up-to-date information.

I would like to thank Sue Gibbons, Else Churchill, Nicholas Fogg, Marie Hickey and Sue Spurgeon at the Society of Genealogists for help with specific queries, Eric Franckom and Jeremy Gibson for invaluable guidance on recent publications of the Federation of Family History Societies, Elizabeth Simpson for her generosity with *Genealogical Research Directory*, staff of the Guildhall Library for advice on their new books, staff of the National Register of Archives, Greater London Record Office, the Suffolk Record Offices, the Friends' Library in London and Colchester Library, for their assistance, staff in the library of the United States of America Embassy in London, for information from the Internet, local volunteers of the family history centre of the Church of Jesus Christ of Latter-day Saints at Chelmsford for their pack of information about FamilySearch and the International Genealogical Index, and the following friends and associates who kept me going through a particularly difficult time in a variety of ways: Sieglinde Alexander, Celia and Ted Auld, Michael Armstrong, Janice Bloomfield (for feeding my cats and keeping them happy), Pat and Douglas Brown, John Brooke-Little, Patrick Canavan, Bobby Collins, Sue and Tony Dawkins, Tony Heybourn, Jonathan Huggins, Peter Kennedy-Scott, Alyn Marriott, Mary Neads and the dog, Daisy, Stan Newens and his daughter Sarah, Vanessa Thompson-Royds, Margaret Thomson, Roy Varley, Stanley West, David Williamson, all my other friends who know who they are, and my special cousins John, Dorothy, Gary and Marie Thexton. Thanks to Polstead Community Shop for keeping me stocked up with the usual doughnuts, treacle and liquorice toffees. Last, but not least, grateful thanks to my erstwhile editor, Helen Coward, for her patience, which is definitely worth a medal, and especially to Sarah Mitchell and Rosie Clay for seeing the project through.

Stella Colwell, 1997

1

INTRODUCTION: IN PURSUIT OF YOUR FAMILY'S PAST

My enthusiasm as a family historian was first fired as a late teenager. Because I bore little physical resemblance to my parents I had long harboured a suspicion that I was not their child. In the summer of 1965, I persuaded a London friend to take me to the General Register Office to look for our indexed birth registrations. The resulting copy of my certificate reassured me of my parental origins, but my initial brush with these centralised records made such a deep impression that for the rest of my life genealogy has been my professional pursuit.

When I first became interested there was little choice of books to teach me; generally one learned the hard way, by experience, picking up practical tips from the very occasional willing professional searcher. Members of the Society of Genealogists in London numbered less than a thousand worldwide, the users of its library a small hushed coterie. It was difficult to determine what of the bewildering mass of national, local and private archives I should search, let alone where they were to be found; now there are so many more sources available I can sympathise with the beginner, for there is nothing more excruciating than not knowing what you are doing. As a genealogist at the College of Arms, dealing with many hundreds of histories of families of diverse social and geographic backgrounds, I was exposed to a plethora of records of different eras and localities, gradually building up my knowledge, in the same way as you, tracing your own forebears, will gain expertise and immense pleasure as you reconstruct your family's past.

What you can learn

Piecing together your own ancestry brings history alive in a special and personal way; each avenue you explore is full of surprises and some disappointments, but is always guaranteed to present new clues to follow, like a never-ending treasure-hunt. You may discover living relatives all over the world, with whom you can resume family contact. There is no substitute for doing it yourself. The skills are not difficult to master. All you need is a curiosity about the past, a logical line of thought, accuracy, patience, a little ingenuity, and persistence, and a resistance to accepting everything at face value because it conveniently fits a prior assumption. You also need to work methodically, or you will soon find your notes in a muddle, to the point where it is too off-putting to try and sort them all out. Family history is fun, but do not let it become an obsession, your papers taking pride of place over everything else.

As you progress, you come to appreciate your family's place in the community, and in the greater canvas of local and national history. You can compare the similarity or divergence of your own family's experience with that of other family historians' ancestors, and from your wider reading learn whether it typified national or geographic trends, how people's behaviour was affected by events, and find an explanation behind the shape of your forebears' lives.

My mother and her older brother George moved to the Lakeland village of Grasmere in their youth, where my parents eventually took over my maternal grandfather's sub-post office. They had met through my father's friendship with my merchant seaman uncle, who himself married the daughter of a hotelier and produced an only child, John Thexton. John left the parental nest to become an architect in Northumberland, before going to work in the Middle East, and we lost touch with each other after his father's death in 1981. He found my present whereabouts from the publisher of a book I had written, and we now regularly correspond. From things my mother told me and what we overheard or observed my cousin and I have been able to bridge some of the gaps in our knowledge about each other's parents, and because he is older he can remember things which happened before I was born.

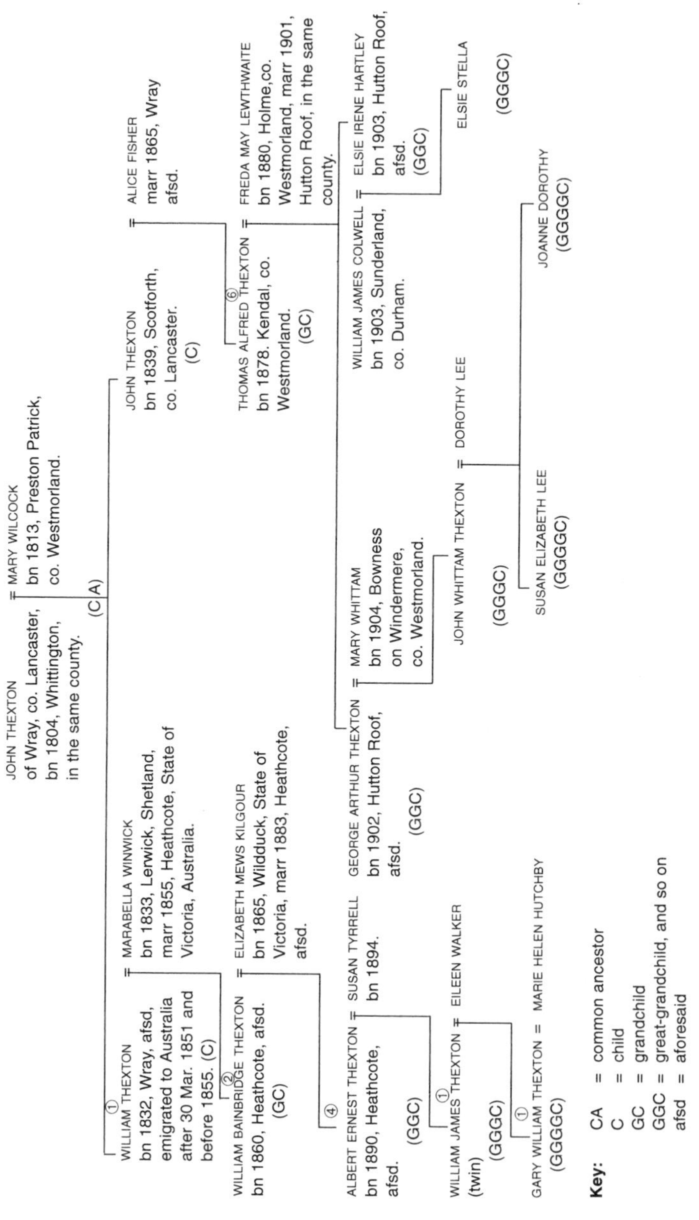

JOHN THEXTON
of Wray, co. Lancaster,
bn 1804, Whittington,
in the same county.
‖ MARY WILCOCK
bn 1813, Preston Patrick,
co. Westmorland.
(C A)

① WILLIAM THEXTON
bn 1832, Wray, afsd,
emigrated to Australia
after 30 Mar. 1851 and
before 1855. (C)
‖ MARABELLA WINWICK
bn 1833, Lerwick, Shetland,
marr 1855, Heathcote, State of
Victoria, Australia.

JOHN THEXTON
bn 1839, Scotforth,
co. Lancaster.
(C)
‖ ALICE FISHER
marr 1865, Wray
afsd.

② WILLIAM BAINBRIDGE THEXTON
bn 1860, Heathcote, afsd.
(GC)
‖ ELIZABETH MEWS KILGOUR
bn 1865, Wilduck, State of
Victoria, marr 1883, Heathcote,
afsd.

⑥ THOMAS ALFRED THEXTON
bn 1878, Kendal, co.
Westmorland.
(GC)
‖ FREDA MAY LEWTHWAITE
bn 1880, Holme, co.
Westmorland, marr 1901,
Hutton Roof, in the same
county.

ALBERT ERNEST THEXTON
bn 1890, Heathcote,
afsd.
(GGC)
‖ SUSAN TYRRELL
bn 1894.

GEORGE ARTHUR THEXTON
bn 1902, Hutton Roof,
afsd.
(GGC)
‖ MARY WHITTAM
bn 1904, Bowness
on Windermere,
co. Westmorland.

WILLIAM JAMES COLWELL
bn 1903, Sunderland,
co. Durham.
‖ ELSIE IRENE HARTLEY
bn 1903, Hutton Roof,
afsd.
(GGC)

ELSIE STELLA
(GGGC)

① WILLIAM JAMES THEXTON
(twin)
(GGGC)
‖ EILEEN WALKER

JOHN WHITTAM THEXTON
(GGGC)
‖ DOROTHY LEE

SUSAN ELIZABETH LEE
(GGGGC)

JOANNE DOROTHY
(GGGGC)

① GARY WILLIAM THEXTON = MARIE HELEN HUTCHBY
(GGGGC)

Key:
CA = common ancestor
C = child
GC = grandchild
GGC = great-grandchild, and so on
afsd = aforesaid

Figure 1 The Thexton Family Tree

Cousin Gary turns up

George Thexton sailed to Australia a good deal, taking messages and gifts from Grasmere people to emigrant relatives. He mentioned visiting Thextons, but not in any detail. Early in 1996 John's wife received a speculative letter from a Gary Thexton in Australia from which it was clear that we share a direct ancestor. A quick glance at the family tree showed him to be our third cousin, his forebear, William Thexton, having emigrated in the 1850s. One afternoon, Gary and his wife arrived on my front doorstep, like an echo from our family past and a reminder of how small the world really is.

I am sure my family is not unique, and by renewing our links and preserving our common heritage we can now ensure they are not so easily severed again.

Finding the time

You can undertake research as and when you have time. Indeed, returning to a seemingly intractable problem after a while brings a fresh eye to it, and you can always pursue another branch of the family's history before coming back, perhaps turning to fresh sources, a new personal name index, or acting on someone's suggestion of a possible solution.

What determines success

One of this country's foremost genealogical scholars commented in 1960 'The prospects of success in solving problems of genealogy depend on many factors, but chiefly, I think, on four; property, continuity, name and record. The possessors of property, other things being equal, are better recorded and more easily traced than those with none, and the more so the greater their possessions. Those who from generation to generation maintain a continuity, whether of dwelling place, of trade, or of anything else, are, other things being equal, more easily traced than those who break with family tradition. Some names are rare, some common and the genealogical advantage is all with rarity, whether the question be of surname or Christian name or the two combined or of a pattern of names of brothers and sisters recurring in a family. Finally there are areas, both geographical and social, where the records are good and full and others where they are poor...

Sometimes all four factors are favourable, sometimes one or two or three, sometimes none, but the presence of one may compensate for the lack of another.' (*English Genealogy*, AR Wagner, page 411).

These maxims are as true today as when they were first propounded. When Sir Anthony Wagner wrote, interest in the history of the common man had yet to receive impetus. Research was confined mainly to the scholarly and legal pursuit of proving claims to title or estate, to the study of influential and powerful landed dynasties and their scions to illustrate patterns of political and social networking, patronage and intermarriage between land and trade. In the nineteenth and early twentieth centuries enterprising clergy and local antiquarians researched and published limited editions of parish and family histories, abstracting and indexing a variety of national and regional sources which appeared in the printed journals of county historical and archaeological societies. The nineteenth century also saw a flowering of scholarly interest in the Medieval period, the products of which are the numerous printed calendars and translations of original Latin documents into English, putting them at the disposal of the modern student, who is perhaps less skilled in Classics, and lacking practice in deciphering and understanding old handwriting.

——— Family history societies ———

In the mid-1960s an interest in the history of ordinary people started to gain momentum, and local groups of enthusiasts began to band together as county family history societies, eleven of which formed a Federation of Family History Societies in 1974. This was soon followed by Welsh and Scottish Associations of Family History Societies, a trend copied widely overseas.

The British-based Federation now boasts a membership of almost two hundred societies worldwide, listed in its half-yearly *Family History News and Digest*. Almost all the counties have established sub-groups, actively engaged in indexing and transcription projects to help future searchers. Such work removes the risk of further wear and tear of original archives, and makes accessible for purchase copies of what has been done. Occasionally all the societies collaborate on a joint task, the 1881 Census Index of England, Wales, the Channel Islands, Isle of

Man, and Scotland being an example. Their members prepare copies of graveyard inscriptions which might otherwise be destroyed, compile marriage and other personal name indexes, and through their regular meetings, provision of a reference library, bookstall and magazine, do much to enhance the searcher's enjoyment of his or her hobby. They also exchange journals with other societies. Many offer a research service for members living further afield, and they possess a pool of knowledge about the area. For all these reasons it is a good idea to join your local society, to meet others with similar interests, and to enrol in the society serving the county where your antecedents lived so that you can learn of their activities and use their journal to advertise your research to other readers.

Society of Genealogists

The Society of Genealogists, founded in 1911, was the first British organisation solely devoted to encouraging the study of genealogy, and it has a library rich in copies in book- and microform of hosts of genealogical resources and nominal indexes throughout the world. Regular updates of its holdings are published so that you can plan a visit in advance. The library is open to non-members and details of its opening hours and charges can be obtained from the Society (see 'Useful Addresses,' page 281). The Society is associated to the Federation so its library is well stocked with local family history society periodicals and publications, and the bookshop sells many of the latter with its own and other genealogical guides and textbooks. It also operates a mail order service, like the Federation.

Church of Jesus Christ of Latter-day Saints

The other major institution to have revolutionised our approach to family history is the Church of Jesus Christ of Latter-day Saints (LDS), through the Genealogical Society of Utah. Since 1976 it has produced at frequent intervals updated microfiche and latterly CD-ROM editions of the International Genealogical Index. The latest version, part of a larger database, contains over two-hundred million names of deceased people born, baptised or married before 1885 throughout the world, in a regional arrangement, so they can be simultaneously scanned by any number of searchers. From this you can select information to print or to download on to disk for browsing over and analysis at home. The family history centres make available for hire on their premises microfilm copies of many other sources like the census, will indexes, parish registers, and indexes of civil registrations; for people with a strong desire to link up with families abroad this is a cost-efficient way of tracking them in international archives held outside their own country of residence.

One-name groups

Finally, for those dedicated to tracing the history and distribution of their family surname, there is a growing list of compilers registered with the Guild of One-Name Studies, founded in 1979, and based in London. A number of one-name societies hold reunions and circulate a newsletter to subscribers. Journals and newsletters of family associations are identified in *Surname Periodicals, a World-Wide Listing of One-Name Genealogical Publications*, edited by IJ Marker and KE Warth.

To belong to the Guild applicants are required to extract all entries of the surname and its variants from prescribed name lists and indexes. Whilst name-collecting does not necessarily yield filial links, nonetheless they can be a guide to geographic surname groupings, and you have someone willing to share the results of many hours' labour in records containing countless other surnames over a wide area and time-span. Such lists may give a pointer to where you should be looking. For Scotland, *Whitaker's Almanack* publishes an annual list of addresses of Chiefs of Clans and Names, and for Ireland the Clans of Ireland Office, in Dublin, has a list of associations of family surnames.

If you want to know more about the possible origin of your surname then there are several books which you can consult in your local library, and these are listed in the Bibliography.

Meeting new-found relatives and friends

What all of the above do is provide help, and as you work back from the known to the unknown they bring you into contact with others sharing a common interest, each of whose ancestry is a unique and special record of that family's heritage and achievements. You become aware that you are not working in isolation, for there are lots of people now and in the past who have beaten the same path seeking their ancestry, and from whom you can benefit.

How to begin

This book's purpose is to help you teach yourself, step by step, where to look for those records linking generations or pinpointing people in time and place. It will explain why these records were created, their genealogical uses and limitations, for none was ever intended for the future family historian. There is a bibliography and list of useful addresses, whilst the selected case studies illustrate some of the problems you may encounter. I have chosen Fred Karno and two of his Army, Charlie Chaplin and Stan Laurel, but they could have been examples from your own family. If any reader can positively identify Stan Laurel's paternal grandfather than I shall be forever indebted, for one lesson every genealogist learns is that family history is full of traps and loose ends. Someone, somewhere, knows the answer, but all too often it lies beyond our easy reach, or we have left it too late to ask.

It is never too soon to start, and the best place to begin is with living relatives, not forgetting yourself, for who is better qualified to write an authoritative account about you and your experiences than yourself?

2

YOU AND YOUR RELATIVES

Your family's history starts with you, the golden rule being to work back from the known to the unknown, looking for names, family relationships, dates, places and occupations. None is much use without the other, a name without a date or place is next to useless, and likewise the absence of any link connecting a name with a particular individual or as part of a family group. The first step is to write down all you can remember about your own life and that of each relation, not forgetting your children and any grandchildren. Allow a separate sheet of paper per person, whose name should be at the top. Use paper of a consistent size, an A4 pad with narrow feint and margin is ideal, and you may find it helpful to draw up a sketch family tree first to ensure no-one has been omitted. There will be some gaps, but you will be surprised at what you already know. Leave your notes for a while and come back to them, for you may be able to add more. Then you can decide which family you want to trace.

The paternal line is usually favoured by family historians because of the continuity of your surname at birth, but there is nothing to stop you embarking on that of your mother; if you do then I strongly recommend separate filing systems to avoid any later confusion.

Choosing your relatives

Identify your known living relatives, their connection to you, their present whereabouts, approximate ages and decide who to arrange to visit first. It is obviously advisable to choose older relations but do not ignore younger ones, who may have cared for elderly parents or have memories or recollections to share about their grandparents. Spoken history has the advantage of immediacy, a source which can be challenged or elaborated on by others.

Setting up a visit

In planning your interview, an advance letter explaining your interest and a short list of questions you would like to ask allows each person time to find the answers or to decline your request. Suggest a date for a visit and keep the appointment punctually. This approach is infinitely preferable to a surprise call which catches a person off-guard and unprepared. An atmosphere of panic then prevails and is not conducive to easy conversation. If you see a relative often then you can raise the topic informally; this has the advantage of being less stilted and the speaker may be more forthcoming if the atmosphere is already relaxed. As a place for conducting the interview, your relative's own home is best, surrounded by his or her own possessions. This ensures privacy and allows him or her to support stories by producing family archives. It is a good idea not to have anyone else present to interrupt or inhibit the disclosures, or to sidetrack you.

Questions to ask

A checklist of questions to guide you appears in Appendix 1, page 281.

The listed questions tell a person's life story chronologically, which is the easiest method of recall, rather than jumping from one era to another and risking the loss of some of it. The list can be used for reference to keep a conversation moving but need not rigidly be adhered to so that it degenerates into a kind of market research exercise.

Your main purpose is to draw out genealogical facts, so good listening skills and empathy are paramount, avoiding an imposition of your own life history. Peoples' relatives should be referred to in their way, their father (although perhaps also your grandfather) being consistently so described to prevent misinterpretation. The two grandfathers should be referred to as mother's father, or father's father, especially when it is unlikely that their forenames and surnames will be used more than once.

What to be wary of

Memories play tricks, as drastic pruning commences very soon after an experience, one person's selective processes operating differently from another's, offering several perceptions of even the most mundane of incidents. Memory is a mixture of fact and opinion, full of inconsistencies and excisions. Events may be re-interpreted over time, may relate to occurrences which had no great significance for or made a huge impression on a child, several may be telescoped together, or recalled out of order, whilst a person's role in them might be enlarged by wishful re-enactment. Some may remember events as participants, others re-tell a story based on hearsay which has been recounted many times over with embellishments at every telling.

Family souvenirs

Time spent chatting about family ephemera can trigger more anecdotes; documents such as old family photographs, franked letters and postcards, journals and diaries, medals, uniform buttons, samplers, rent books, ration books, title deeds, newspaper cuttings, certificates, school reports and other souvenirs may not have seen the light of day for many years, and act as a spur to the memory. Christmas cards may be misleading, for instance for years I received annual cards from 'aunts' and 'uncles', who were actually friends of my parents, some using pet names. Most do not give surnames, and as I never met them I have no clues as to where they fit into my parents' life.

A family Bible is a special treasure, frequently given as a wedding present, the first entry recording the recipients' marriage, followed by the names and birthdays of their children. Details might be entered of children dying in infancy, whose existence might otherwise go undetected, and of issue born before civil registration began. However, some entries were written up years after the event, perhaps incorrectly, so always look at the publication date of the volume to check it predates the earliest one. Birthplaces may be omitted, so you are left with a family chronicle whose location is unknown. I have inherited my maternal grandmother's Book of Common Prayer, and a hymn book inscribed 'To Freda May Bush' in 1897. My mother was always adamant that her surname was Lewthwaite, the name used when she married my grandfather. As an orphan she was brought up by a Mrs Bush, and was obviously known locally by her adopted family name, but to my mother her original identity mattered a great deal, as she died when my mother was a baby. Conversely, I also have the family Bible of the Wilsons, who are totally unrelated, but whose possessions my parents inherited when they bought their house in 1955.

Ask if you can list the various items and photocopy any documents and old photographs. Other relatives may be able to identify people unknown or forgotten by the present owner, so it is worthwhile taking unattributed photographs with you.

Dealing with different types of relative

Do not expect all your queries to be answered fully or unequivocally. By interviewing as many family members as possible you may be able to piece together the essential ingredients of its recent history. You may never have met some of the relatives before, so you will need to identify yourself by your place in their family, perhaps producing photographs of your branch through which it is established. This will bring them up to date about people with whom they might have lost touch. Other relatives will express no desire whatsoever to talk about the family, and this wish has to be respected, however much you long to quiz them; memories might be too painful to resurrect, or there might be an embargo on discussion of certain subjects, so you will need sensitivity and tact. Others will be only too happy to reveal everything they know and will become valued allies as you progress, but again, remember to be discreet about their revelations, as what they may divulge might be suppressed elsewhere in the family. You should resist a temptation to interrupt or disagree with anything you find distasteful or controversial, and not pass value judgements, which are likely to bring the visit to an abrupt end.

What to do if there is a language problem

If your informants are first-generation immigrants there may be a language barrier to overcome, what they actually tell you not always being always what was intended, or being ambiguous. Talking to others of the same ethnic origin, especially if they came from the same area, might help recreate a picture of their former life and family, and if they can converse in the native language with your relative they might act as interpreter, or know someone else who can. Be sure first that your relative consents to this.

Seeing it from your relatives' point of view

Be prepared to visit your relations at least twice, but not so often that it becomes a trial. It is vital that they do not feel 'used' by a single visit without any follow-up by way of thanks or a share in the results of their efforts. Your relatives will probably also much appreciate being kept in touch with your progress summarised clearly and simply, but avoid bombarding them with minutiae. Christmas is a good time to send an updated family tree which is easy to understand and pass round, and recent additions to the family can be included.

One person's fascination may be viewed by someone else as an obsession, so do not outstay your welcome. People's concentration wavers after about an hour, older people's perhaps in less time if they are unused to much conversation, especially when it is all focused on them and half-remembered people and events of long ago. The interview should therefore not be rushed, as this is a chance for quiet reminiscence, not an interrogation. Reliving the past leaves your informant vulnerable and exposed, so you should respect his or her trust and confidence, and once the chat is over, do not hurry away but make sure the revelations have not caused distress. Having your sole attention for however short a time may be enjoyable, allowing memories to be unlocked in which no-one else has ever expressed an interest, and he or she may have eagerly looked forward to your visit.

Ask for names, relationships and addresses of anyone else of the family in the area you might contact (especially married daughters), as you may be able to combine your second visit with an introduction to them.

The second interview allows you to fill in gaps or resolve conflicting assertions or misunderstandings. Your relative may appreciate having a short list of points to work on beforehand. An interval of a week or so between visits allows time to mull over the conversation and jog the memory, and your informant will know what to expect the next time. An older person living alone will also welcome a gift of favourite biscuits, home-made cake or chocolate, and certainly if it can be arranged, a trip to your informant's childhood haunts, as the spirit of place is an excellent memory prompt.

Write or record?

You will need to decide the method of recording your interviews. If you intend to keep written notes, an A4 pad with a narrow feint and margin is recommended, for easy filing, headed by the name of your relatives, the date and place of the interview. Do not attempt to write the conversation verbatim as you will slow the conversation, distracting the speaker; all you need jot down are dates, places and other key information, with headings for anecdotes which can be written up in full immediately you arrive home.

Tape-recorded interviews

If you elect to tape-record then you build up an oral archive, reflecting individual nuances of pronunciation, dialect and phrase. The speaker may be inhibited if he or she fears the permanence and future destination of the tape, or senses any nervousness in operating the recorder on your part, so always secure his or her consent first.

The tape-recorder you use may be determined by what you already own, can borrow, or how much you can afford. A recommended model is a portable cassette-player with two sockets for external microphones, one each for the speaker and the interviewer. A battery-operated type is more versatile than a plug-in recorder, as you can do the interviewing anywhere without the need of an adaptor, but always carry new or recharged spare batteries with you. The best microphones are tie-clip or lapel type, worn about nine inches away from the mouth, the lead tucked under the person's arm. This allows the speaker to concentrate on the interview without affecting the quality of recording by head movements. Ferric tape, running for thirty minutes each side (C60), and sold by a brand-leader, is the most reliable and stable medium.

The room selected for tape-recording should have no extraneous background noises such as a ticking clock, creaking chair, pets, children or boiling kettles, and if possible the telephone should be temporarily silenced. The microphone is very sensitive and will record everything; a bad recording will forever remain a bad and irritating reminder. Try and place the recorder out of the speaker's sight, and sit facing each other, at a slight angle. If you have to share a microphone, sit close together, and if it is free-standing, place the microphone at a different level to the recorder on a soft, absorbent surface. The tape should run for at least five seconds before you record your name, the date, place and name of the interviewee. Allow the person to develop responses to your questions at his or her own pace and do not be tempted to interrupt a train of thought. Silence can often be meaningful. A nod of the head as encouragement, and open questions which require more than a 'yes' or 'no' will produce a more flowing conversation, but expect the first few minutes to be slightly stilted until the speaker relaxes. Then let the interview run its course, but be prepared for it to go off at a tangent, requiring your intervention merely to gently steer it back to what you want to know, or to pursue a promising line of thought raised by any remarks. This is where your structured checklist can come in useful.

It is tiring listening closely and picking on extra topics, so practise with a friend beforehand, so that you are comfortable in charge of the recorder, and know what to do if anything mechanical goes wrong. Ask to be interviewed yourself, to become aware of how it feels. Training in oral history and interviewing skills under expert tuition will give more practice, and local libraries advertise adult education classes; the National Sound Archive, part of the British Library, in London, also runs excellent short courses.

Each recording is unique and irreplaceable so once it is completed you should break the safety lug at the top of the cassette (one for each side) to prevent erasure or over-recording, and label it with the date of the interview, the name of the speaker and his or her date of birth, plus your own name, and give each tape a sequential number for listing and simple retrieval once stored away. A copy should be made of each tape and kept apart from the original (marked 'Master'). They should be filed upright in their boxes, in a shady, cool, dry and dust-free place away from the television set or any other electrical equipment which might interfere with their magnetic fields.

Copyright

The copyright of the tape content belongs to the speaker. If you wish to use it for later publication or to lodge a copy in a local oral history collection you must ask for copyright to be assigned to you. A pro forma which can be signed by each recorded relative is best, and this provides a safeguard in the event of your informant's death.

Next, write a summary of the taped conversation. A complete transcript is not necessary, just a short account of the salient points, as you listen to the replay, and then organise it under headings.

Use a camera

Do not forget to take a photograph of your relative, identify and date it on the back in pencil to build up a family album of living members as a memento of your visits, to pass around the family.

Writing to relations

Sometimes your relatives may live too far away for you to visit them so you may have to rely on correspondence. People are less likely to commit themselves to paper so a good deal of intimate information may be withheld. Always send a short list of questions to be answered and if the relative is not personally acquainted with you, a stamped self-addressed envelope (or international reply coupon if writing over-seas). This will give any reply some kind of structure and the writer guidance on what you want. Some people are so busy that they may intend to reply but simply have not found the time to do so. A second, friendly, letter, with your address written outside on the envelope will lend another opportunity and if the person has moved away then the letter can be returned to you. Do not write a third time, as this can be construed as a nuisance. Remember that you are asking a favour and a reply is not obligatory, however much it is wanted.

The dead and those moved away

Occasionally the person you want to interview died recently. Nursing home staff, neighbours and visitors may know more about that person than their own family, for people often confide more in friends and those in close proximity than they do in their relations, fearing disap-proval of their actions or want of discretion. A trip to the nursing home or street where the person last lived, chatting to such people can produce a wealth of information. If they know the name of the person's solicitor he or she may be able to advise where all the family papers went and the names and addresses of the next of kin, but this requires tact. A local newspaper may contain an obituary, the parish magazine a short biographical profile, the undertaker have details of the chief mourners, the officiating clergyman the name of the person supplying information for the funeral oration, and the names of close friends and associates with whom you can make contact.

If a relative was last known to be at a specific address in the recent past, the local post office or neighbours may have a forwarding address or provide some indication of where he or she went. Find out the names and whereabouts of friends who may still be in touch or who can tell you more.

Electoral registers

The current yearly revised electoral register of each polling district parish is open to inspection at the local post office, the district council office and reference library holding copies for the entire Parliamentary ward (the electoral division of one or several polling districts). It lists alphabetically by street every house title or number, plus the full names of all occupants entitled to vote in Parliamentary or local elections, or who will reach the qualifying age of eighteen during the ensuing year. Some lists are arranged alphabetically by surname, the address coming after the forenames. A set of the previous year's registers for the British Isles will be availble in the public search room of The Family Records Centre in London, from 1st April 1997. Current overseas electoral rolls may also be held by institutions representing governments abroad.

Advertising in the press

A letter to the editor of the local newspaper, setting out briefly your interest in the family and its history and asking for information about surviving relatives and their whereabouts will often result in its publication and wide circulation. A local magazine, published less often, but subscribed to by people further afield with local connections, can also yield response via its correspondence columns. The annual *Willing's Press Guide*, found in your local reference library, contains a place-name index and alphabetical listing of all national and provincial newspapers and periodicals published in Great Britain, Ireland and overseas, specifying editorial addresses and frequency of issue. Local family history society journals are another good publicity outlet as overseas readers may be able to help.

Telephone directories

Another effective resource is to look at telephone directories of the reputed areas of residence of your family to extract the names and addresses of current subscribers of your surname. Write a short letter to each of them, enclosing a stamped self-addressed envelope, explaining your interest and what you already know and asking whether there is a family link. It can be a costly exercise; if you have to widen the ambit beyond one regional directory, to several contiguous areas, to the country itself or the entire British Isles, you could be involved in a lot of expense with little response, so you need to be selective and methodical. Complete sets of current directories are to be found in your local reference library, on line in the United States of America, and if your name is common then it is best to start by writing only to those people living nearest to where the family was last known to be. The directories are not fully comprehensive, for they do not include ex-directory subscribers, and not everyone has a telephone, but it is likely that at least one of any family group will be listed, through whom links can be made to others and with married female members. If the surname is uncommon you can plot its geographic distribution and relative density of concentration.

Other resorts

Other desperate searchers have followed up news items in the press or radio and television programmes in which the surname has been mentioned, often with surprising results, so be alert to the media too. Another possibility is to advertise your interest on the Internet, whose subscribers may come up with instant communication.

— How to start, relative-unassisted —

If you have no known living relatives you may recall your parents referring to scenes from their childhood, trips to places of their youth, or elderly relatives' homes. A visit to the graveyard where your father or other members of the family were interred should enable you to collect dates of birth and death from the headstones; in the absence of these the burial registers belonging to the local authority or private company owning the cemetery will record death date, age, interment and plot number, and if several of the family lie in the same grave then you may be able to collect sufficient information to construct a simple family tree, and to start looking for their birth certificates and for their wills. Some beneficiaries might still be alive, or the executors might know more about the family's recent history.

Summing up

Time and effort expended locating and listening to relatives establish the best possible foundation for your family history, and you may recruit a willing team of searchers to share the cost.

3

COMPILING YOUR
FAMILY TREE

Once you have gathered all the information from your family, arrange it in a ring binder with the sheet of paper about yourself on the top, followed by those on your father and mother, then your brothers and sisters with the oldest filed before the younger ones in descending order, followed by your grandparents, their children, the oldest first and if any were married, the sheet about their spouse next, followed by their children, and so on, going back a generation each time. Do not forget to file separately any papers relating to your mother's family. You can now use these sheets of paper to extract details for the pictorial summary of your family history. The sooner you begin the less formidable the task and you will always be able to see at a glance the point you have reached in your research if you keep it updated with your latest discoveries.

Your family tree should clearly and tidily show every generation link, and should be capable of being understood without any need of further explanation.

Some simple guidelines

There are several ways of recording your family tree, but the one you will find easiest to follow is the drop-line pedigree chart, which begins with yourself at the bottom (leaving enough space underneath for succeeding generations), and shows each previous generation in a series of steps up the page, with your earliest known forebear at the top. There are no hard rules for setting out a pedigree chart, but you may find the following advice helpful. A large sheet of ruled paper (or several sheets of ruled A4 glued together with Prittstick), a sharpened HB pencil, rubber and ruler are all that are required.

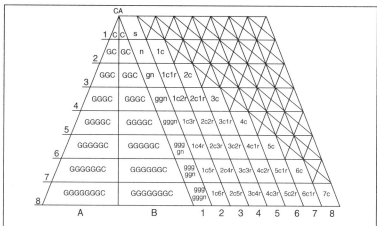

- Find the common ancestor of the two relatives.
- To work out a family relationship, identify the person of the earlier generation in column A. Note the number to the left.
- Then find the relative you want to link with the person in column B. Note the number to the left.

Look at the THEXTON pedigree on page 3; for example, JOHN WHITTAM THEXTON is the great-great-grandson of JOHN THEXTON and MARY WILCOCK. The number next to this is 4.

GARY WILLIAM THEXTON is the great-great-great-grandson of this couple, the common ancestors. The number next to this is 5.

- With your finger on the line at the higher diagonal number (5) move it across to find the box over the lower horizontal number (4). This shows that they are 3rd cousins once removed. JOHN THEXTON is the 3rd cousin of GARY's father, one generation earlier.

In canon law they are related in the 5th degree, the maximum number of steps away from their common ancestor; in civil law it is the 9th degree, the total number of steps back and forwards separating them both.

Key:

CA	= common ancestor	s	= sibling (brother/sister)
C	= child	n	= nephew or niece
GC	= grandchild	gn	= great or grand nephew (or niece)
GGC	= great-grandchild	ggn	= great-great nephew (or niece) and so on
GGGC	= great-great-grandchild and so on	1c	= 1st cousin
		1c1r	= 1st cousin once removed and so on

Figure 2 Working out family relationships

ELEANOR GWYNN actress, bn 1650, died 14 and bur 17 Nov 1687, St. Martin's in the Fields, co. Middx.

X CHARLES II King of England, crowned 23 Apr 1661, at Westminster, bn 29 May 1630, K.G. 1638, died s.p. legit., 6 Feb 1684/5 bur Westminster Abbey.

= CATHERINE of Braganza, Infanta of Portugal, only dau of John IV, and sister of Alphonso VI, Kings of Portugal, marr 22 May 1662, Portsmouth, co. Southampton, d.s.p. 31 Dec 1705, Lisbon.

CHARLES (BEAUCLERK) Baron of Hedington and Earl of Burford, both in co. Oxford, so created 27 Dec 1676, Duke of St. Albans, co. Hertford, so created 10 Jan 1683/4, bn 10 May 1670, Lincoln's Inn Fields, co. Middx, K.G. 1718, died 10 May 1726, Bath, co. Somerset, bur 20 May, Westminster Abbey.

DIANA 1st dau and eventual sole heiress of AUBREY (DE VERE), Earl of Oxford, marr 17 Apr 1694, died 15, bur 20 Jan 1741/2, St. George's Chapel, Windsor, co. Berks.

JAMES BEAUCLERK (commonly called Lord JAMES BEAUCLERK), bn 25 Dec 1671, Pall Mall, co. Middx, died ... Sept 1680, Paris.

MARY dau and coheiress of THOMAS CHAMBERS, of Hanworth, afsd., marr 13 Apr 1796, died 21 Jan 1783.

LUCY eldest dau and co-heiress of Sir JOHN WERDEN, Bart., of Leyland and Cholmeaton, co. Lancaster and Holly-port, co. Berks, by his 1st wife, marr 13 Dec 1722, by special licence, died 2 Nov 1752, bur Westminster Abbey.

WILLIAM BEAUCLERK (commonly called Lord WILLIAM BEAUCLERK), bn 22 May 1698, died 23 Feb 1732/3, bur Westminster Abbey.

CHARLOTTE 2nd dau and co-heiress of Sir JOHN WERDEN, Bart., afsd., by his 2nd wife, marr 13 Dec 1722, by special licence, died 17 June 1745.

VERE (BEAUCLERK) Baron Vere of Hanworth, co. Middx, so created 28 March 1750, bn 14 July 1699, died 1 Oct 1781, St. James's Square, bur 6 Oct, St. James's, both in co. Middx.

CATHERINE dau of WILLIAM (PONSONBY), Earl of Bessborough, marr 4 May 1763, St. George Hanover Square, co. Middx, died 4, and bur 14 Sept 1789, Hanworth, afsd.

CHARLES (BEAUCLERK) 2nd Duke of St. Albans, succeeded 1726, bn 6 Apr 1696, K.B., 1725, K.G., 1740/1, died 27 July 1751, St. James's Place, co. Middx, bur 3 Aug, Westminster Abbey.

GEORGE (BEAUCLERK) 3rd Duke of St. Albans, succeeded 1751, only son, bn 25 June 1730, died s.p. legit., 1 Feb 1786, Brussels, bur 11 March, Westminster Abbey.

JANE dau and coheiress of Sir WALTER ROBERTS, Bart., of Glassenbury, in Cranbrook, co. Kent, marr 23 Oct or Dec 1752, died 16 Dec 1778, bur Cranbrook.

AUBREY (BEAUCLERK) 2nd Baron Vere, succeeded 1781, and 5th Duke of St. Albans, succeeded 1787, 4th and only surviving son, bn 3 June 1740, died 9 Feb 1802, bur Hanworth, afsd.

ELIZABETH dau of ... JONES, died 5 Dec 1768.

CHARLES BEAUCLERK Col. the 107th Foot, 2nd and only surviving son, died 30 Aug 1775.

WILLIAM (BEAUCLERK) 8th Duke of St. Albans, succeeded 1816, bn 18 Dec 1766, St. Marylebone, afsd.

GEORGE (BEAUCLERK) 4th Duke of St. Albans, succeeded 1786, bn 5 Dec 1758, and bap 2 Jan following, at Berwick-on-Tweed, co. Northumberland, died unm. 15 Feb 1787, Grosvenor Square, co. Middx.

MARY dau of JOHN MOSES of Hull, co. York, marr 9 July 1788, Mayfair Chapel, co. Middx, died s.p.m. 18 Aug 1800, St. Paul's Walden, co. Hertford

AUBREY (BEAUCLERK) 6th Duke of St. Albans, succeeded 1802, bn 21 Aug 1765, died 12 Aug 1815, Stratford Place, Marylebone, co. Middx.

LOUISA GRACE 3rd dau of JOHN MANNERS, of Grantham, co. Lincoln, marr 15 Aug 1802, by special licence, died 19 Feb 1816, Great George Street, Hanover Square, afsd., bur 11 March, Hanworth, afsd.

Daughter stillborn, 4 May 1813.

AUBREY (BEAUCLERK) 7th Duke of St. Albans, succeeded 1815, bn 7 Apr, bap 22 May 1815, St. Marylebone, afsd., died 19 Feb 1816, Great George Street, afsd., bur 11 March, Hanworth, afsd.

Figure 3a Finding the 8th Duke: St Albans Family Tree. This illustrates most of the guidelines in drafting a pedigree, and the often tortuous route taken to find the next heir to a title.

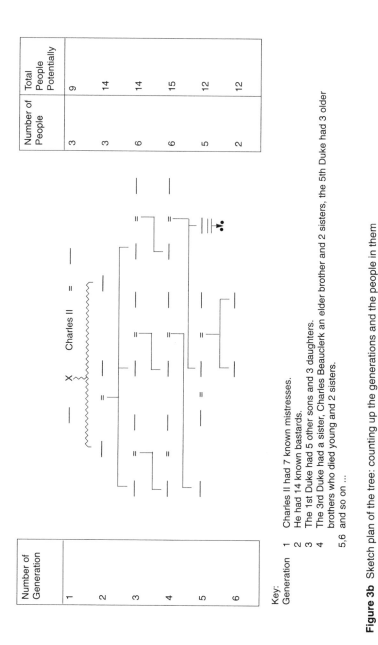

Number of Generation		Number of People	Total People Potentially
1		3	9
2		3	14
3		6	14
4		6	15
5		5	12
6		2	12

Key:
Generation 1   Charles II had 7 known mistresses.
2   He had 14 known bastards.
3   The 1st Duke had 5 other sons and 3 daughters.
4   The 3rd Duke had a sister, Charles Beauclerk an elder brother and 2 sisters, the 5th Duke had 3 older brothers who died young and 2 sisters.
5,6   and so on …

Figure 3b Sketch plan of the tree: counting up the generations and the people in them

- Everyone of the same generation is recorded on the same line, so that their exact relationship to each other and to anyone else in the family can be determined at a glance.
- Children of the same parents are placed in birth order, the eldest on the left and the youngest on the right. Sometimes you may have to alter the order to slot in inter-family marriages, so indicate seniority by numbers above each name.
- All names are written in capitals; males always have their forenames and surnames entered on the pedigree, whereas females' surnames are omitted.
- A wife's name is placed to the right of her husband, but where he has married more than once then the first wife is placed to the left and the second to the right.
- A vertical descent line from the marriage symbol (=) connects parents' and children's names and a horizontal line connects brothers and sisters.
- Illegitimate children are indicated by a wavy descent line.
- Where it is uncertain but likely that there is a parental or sibling connection, a dotted line is used.
- Adopted children are recorded on the same line but after the names of true children of the adoptive parents, and no descent line is used, because there is no blood relationship.

Drawing up a drop-line chart takes a little time and patience, so a rough pencil sketch first is a good idea to plot the number of generations and count the people you wish to include in each, so that you can be sure they will all fit in. In doing this you can plan the pedigree layout so that it is balanced, spreading out the differing numbers per generation over the paper. Many beginners make the mistake of writing the names so small that they are lost in acres of blank space: allow about two inches depth for each generation and about one and a half inches width for the biographical detail you are going to write about each person, none impinging on the paragraph space allotted to adjacent names. You will discover that some names appear to belong nowhere; you can go back to your informants for advice on their place in the family. A clear and attractively presented chart can jolt your relatives' memories and elicit even more information, as well as sum up what you have learned from them so far. A photocopy, perhaps reduced in size, is also a kind gift in reward for their efforts.

The pedigree chart should be a constant source of reference.

What to include

Here is a checklist of items you should aim to include, although you will not manage all of them, and the further back you go in time the more scanty the information will be; you will see that it closely resembles your interview checklist. All dates should give the day first then the month in writing rather than numbered, preferably with Jan for January and Jne for June, as handwriting legibility varies. Remember to record places by county, to avoid ambiguity.

1 Full name.
2 Residence now, and previous ones, with dates if possible (earliest first), including county.
3 Occupation now and previously, with dates if possible (earliest first), or rank or title, any awards and decorations, degree and university.
4 Date of birth, and place, and date of adoption if appropriate.
5 Date and place of baptism, with the county, and religious denomination if not Anglican.
6 Where educated, starting with the first school, plus dates, date of apprenticeship, public appointments such as justice of the peace, and details of any wartime service.
7 Females only: date and place of marriage, and the county. Religious denomination if not Anglican.
8 Ownership of land, and where it was.
9 Named in the census, giving the year and age then.
10 Whether named in someone's will, giving the date, and probate date if he or she was the executor.
11 Date and place of death, and the county.
12 Date and place of burial with the county, and whether there is a headstone.
13 If a will was made, its date plus the date it was proved, or when letters of administration were granted.
14 The full name, address, occupation, rank, title and degree of the father are given immediately after the name of a man or woman marrying into the family, and whether deceased at the time of the wedding.

A list of abbreviations frequently used in compiling pedigrees is given in Appendix 2, page 000.

Uncertainties can be question-marked or square-bracketed for further checking.

What to do if you have lots of relatives

You may find that you have so many relatives that they cannot all be accommodated on the paper without the pedigree becoming unwieldy. When this happens have a master chart showing your own direct descent; where aunts and uncles or others in the family marry indicate the marriage, and draw a descent line from it cross-referenced to another numbered chart. The second chart can then concentrate on this marriage and its descendants, each generation being spaced out in the same way as the master, so that you can still distinguish the exact relationship of everyone to each other when the pedigrees are placed alongside.

Alternative types of family tree

Another pedigree layout is the printed birth brief, recording horizontally from left to right the names, births, baptisms, marriages, deaths and burials of parents, grandparents, great-grandparents and great-great-grandparents, but rarely having room for siblings. The space for personal details decreases as the number of names grows, but it shows the different families from which you are directly descended.

You may prefer to use a computer package, which can easily be updated and printed out, giving a tidy overall appearance. Some offer a choice of the drop-line or birth brief chart.

A family tree written as an indented narrative, moving in a space for each generation, every person allotted a number according to his place in his parent's family, can sometimes be difficult to visualise, whereas a pictorial display can be interpreted at a glance. You can however include much more information in this type of pedigree.

Is anyone else researching your family?

Having set out what you know on your family tree your next step is to find out if someone else is already making investigations.

- *National Genealogical Directory* (edited by MJ Burchall and IL Caley, and *Genealogical Research Directory* (edited by

KA Johnson and MR Sainty), are both annuals listing alphabetically family names currently being researched, the period, and places, and the name and address of the contributor. Each directory is different, the latter incorporating families in many countries. All the surname, subject and one-name sections published in the *GRD* between 1990 and 1996 are now amalgamated on CD-ROM, with updated addresses of contributors. Thus advertisements placed by thousands of people have been circulated throughout the world establishing crucial contacts between readers with mutual research interests. Many local reference libraries, regional record offices, and most family history societies will have copies for consultation.

- The *British Isles Genealogical Register (BIG–R)*, first produced by the Federation of Family History Societies in 1994, records on microfiche those surnames, periods and places in the British Isles the family histories of which are presently being explored, arranged in pre-1974 county microfiche for England, thus allowing concentration on one area. Ireland, Scotland and Wales are listed by country, then alphabetically by historic county within each. Surnames are included as supplied rather than grouped under variants. A further set of microfiche lists the names and addresses of contributors, arranged sequentially by number, corresponding to each numbered research entry. A union register is planned, and a completely new edition will appear in 1997.

- FamilySearch is a series of five computer programs and files, including the current 1993 edition of the International Genealogical Index of births, baptisms and marriages, of millions of deceased people worldwide, to which there are 1994 and 1996 addenda. Whereas this merely identifies each person with spouse, parents or relatives, the Ancestral File contains names, family relationships, births, baptisms, marriages and deaths of deceased individuals drawn from pedigrees and family group sheets submitted to the Church of Jesus Christ of Latter-day Saints (LDS) after 1978. Names and addresses of the contributors are supplied and the records can be printed or copied on to disk. The Church is not responsible for the quality and reliability of the pedigrees, which may be corrected and updated at any time. Earlier family group records are divided into two main sections, 'Archive Records' and 'Patron Section', microfilm copies of which can be borrowed at a family history centre, quoting the call number on the Family

History Library Catalog of records in Salt Lake City, Utah, which is included in FamilySearch. Besides family history centres, you may find the FamilySearch program in larger local history libraries. The Family Registry, now superseded by Ancestral File, is a microfiche index of names, and addresses of over 300,000 people willing to share their family history researches. One problem of using this may be that contributors have moved on, without there being any forwarding address.

- The *Register of One-Name Studies*, published by the Guild of One-Name Studies, London, lists the surnames and all variants extracted by members from the indexes of civil registration of birth, marriage and death in England, Wales and Scotland, current telephone directories, all printed will indexes up to the present day, the International Genealogical Index, relevant parish registers, county histories, and publications of local historical and antiquarian societies.

In writing to any of the above state briefly what you already know and ask if there might be any link with their research, enclosing a stamped, self-addressed envelope or International Reply Coupon. If you are a contributor yourself always acknowledge an enquiry, even if it is in the negative. The purpose behind advertising any interest is to share it, co-ordinate research and make the task easier. However, never accept exchanged information at face value, and be prepared to double-check any asserted connection, using it for guidance only.

- Many family history societies publish directories of members' interests. *Family Tree Magazine*, published monthly, also features readers' research interests.
- The Society of Genealogists, in London, has a card index of surname interests and indexed 'birth briefs' deposited by members showing descent from sixteen great-great-grandparents, and it also has sets of most of the sources cited in this section.

Published pedigrees

For printed pedigrees and their whereabouts, *The Genealogist's Guide*, by GW Marshall lists alphabetically those of three generations or more and the books or periodicals in which they appear. This was updated and amended in *A Genealogical Guide*, by JB Whitmore in 1953, up to 1975 by *The Genealogist's Guide*, by GB Barrow.

If the family history has been written up and published then it should be listed in *Catalogue of British Family Histories*, by TR Thomson. Look also at the growing series of county genealogical bibliographies compiled by SA Raymond. For printed Scottish pedigrees you need to consult M Stuart and J Balfour Paul's *Scottish Family History*, published and updated by JPS Ferguson in *Scottish Family Histories;* printed Irish pedigrees may be listed in B de Breffny's *Bibliography of Irish Family History and Genealogy*, and E MacLysaght's *Bibliography of Irish Family History*. Many of the works referred to in these guides are in the library of the Society of Genealogists.

The *American Genealogical Biographical Index*, Series 1 and 2, edited by F Rider (known as Rider's Index), aims at listing alphabetically all printed family histories in books, articles and brief biographies before 1950. Each entry sets out the name, birth year and state of the person, abbreviated biography and book and page reference.

The reliability of printed pedigrees should not be taken for granted, especially when source references are sparse or lacking, dates are missing or look suspicious, generation spans seem dubiously long or short. Collateral branches and defunct lines may be omitted altogether, so they are incomplete. The sources used may no longer exist but where they do, or where others equally good if not better are now accessible, they should be examined, the content of the printed pedigrees being taken only as a rough guide. The best printed pedigrees appear in the *Victoria County History* series, richly annotated with source references which can be easily checked, but they principally deal with major landowning families. Other printed county histories are variable in quality, so use them with caution, for even where sources are cited they may have been mistranslated, misinterpreted, misunderstood and relationships misplaced. High standards of evaluation of evidence have never been universally adopted and just because it appears in print does not mean that a pedigree is correct, but that is not to decry the numerous published scholarly pedigrees.

Manuscript pedigrees

The College of Arms has a huge number of officially registered and unauthenticated pedigrees of families spanning the Medieval period to the present day and this is a growing archive, albeit not open to the public, though specific searches of the official records can be undertaken by an officer of arms for a fee. Many, but by no means all, are linked to the right to use a coat of arms, and they can be helpful in proving connections with early settlers in the American Colonies and West Indies plantations, as well as families of all social backgrounds.

The Court of the Lord Lyon, Edinburgh, preserves Scottish heraldic and genealogical archives, and The Genealogical Office, Dublin, Irish records. Like the College of Arms, neither is open to the public, though both offer a research service to enquirers. The Genealogical Office has separate indexes to the manuscript authenticated and unregistered genealogies of Irish families, including those drafted by Sir William Betham in the mid-nineteenth century from abstracts of wills which no longer survive, and other genealogists' compilations. There is also a computer-index of research undertaken by the Office, especially for Australians and North American descendants of emigrants, and a further series of files devoted to Anglo-Irish ancestry. Some files are available to the public at the National Library in Dublin, at the discretion of the Chief Herald, and a number are on microfilm.

Collections of manuscript pedigrees and notes, many prepared by antiquarians, heralds, herald painters or their assistants in the sixteenth and seventeenth centuries and extending back well into the Middle Ages, may be inspected at the Department of Manuscripts in the British Library, London, and at the Bodleian Library in Oxford. You will need a reader's ticket to use these. Each series of manuscripts has its own catalogue, and some of the pedigrees have been published.

The National Library of Wales, at Aberystwyth, the British Library, and the College of Arms, in London, hold the principal volumes and rolls of manuscript Welsh genealogies, many of them written in the native language, including fifteenth- and sixteenth-century copies of ninth- and tenth-century originals which were once transmitted orally. The National Library of Wales has microfilm copies of many elsewhere. You need a reader's ticket to look at the records. There are published catalogues and a number of the pedigrees have been published, especially for the Medieval period.

Welsh pedigrees are marked by the common ancestry claimed by many families from a small number of 'patriarchs', and by the substitution of patronymics for surnames, using a genealogical string of names as personal identification, so place-names form a vital component. From these pedigrees it is apparent that parents drew on a small range of Biblical and saints' names for their offspring.

The Library of Congress, in Washington, DC, has in its care thousands of manuscript pedigrees, listed alphabetically in *National Union Catalog of Manuscript Collections*, to which there is a consolidated *Index*, and you should also scan *Genealogies in the Library of Congress: A Bibliography*, edited by MJ Kaminkow and the *Supplement*, which record the Family Name Index entries of printed and manuscript genealogies, with their call numbers. *A Complement to Genealogies in the Library of Congress*, covers other library holdings in the United States, including foreign and unpublished family trees. The New York Genealogical and Biographical Society, New England Historic and Genealogical Society, Boston, and the Newberry Library, Chicago, all boast notable collections of pedigrees.

The Society of Genealogists, in London, possesses a vast document collection of manuscript pedigrees and notes taken from disparate sources by researchers and passed there for safekeeping and the benefit of others, organised alphabetically by more than 14,000 surnames.

The Public Record Office, Kew, the Scottish Record Office, Edinburgh, and the National Archives of Ireland in Dublin, house a host of pedigrees and supporting evidence used as exhibits in legal proceedings. Pedigrees filed in the English Court of Chancery are accessed via a nominal index giving the name and date of death of the earliest progenitor and the title of the relevant case, be it a claim to a title, to land or a dispute over a will, a trust, settlement or intestacy. Others were produced in the Medieval courts of law to prove a person's free status granting entitlement to be heard.

County record offices too are increasingly expanding their holdings to embrace family histories and pedigrees of local families, and likewise family history societies, to each of which there will be a card index or reference list. However they will not generally have been exposed to independent examination to test their accuracy.

Printed books can often be located in various places, whereas manuscript collections are generally only accessible where preserved, unless on microfilm, but it is often worth the effort finding out if any exist for your name.

Some words of warning

Where your family's history has been previously researched, you may not always find it ties in with what you know already, or stops too soon for any immediate link. You can still use it for occasional reference, as sooner or later it might be eliminated or be found to complement your own work.

4

HUNTING FOR YOUR ANCESTORS' BIRTHS, MARRIAGES AND DEATHS: ENGLAND AND WALES

Look at the family tree showing your direct ancestry, and find the earliest date on it. Most probably it will fall in the mid- or late nineteenth century. Where did the event occur, in England, Wales, Scotland, Ireland or elsewhere? What does the date relate to? If it was a birth do you know who the parents were, including the mother's former name before marriage? Do you know the person's place in his family, as the eldest or a younger child? If it was a marriage, where was this information taken from? Was the ceremony in a church, chapel or register office? If a chapel, do you know its denomination? Do you know the full names, ages and paternity of the couple? If it was a death, do you know the person's purported age, and where he died? If the event happened in Scotland, Ireland or elsewhere, look at the next two chapters.

In England and Wales centralised registration of birth, marriage and death commenced on 1 July 1837.

For registration purposes the country was divided up into superintendent registration districts, based on the newly created civil Poor Law Union boundaries of 1834, and then into smaller registration districts, each containing about seven civil parishes. The district registrars recorded births and deaths in special books. Ministers of the Established Anglican Church kept two sets of marriage registers in their churches, the superintendent registrar performing civil ceremonies in his office, and recording these and weddings supervised by him at dissenters' chapels until 1898, after which some other authorised person could preside. Quakers and Jews maintained their own registrations of marriages. Since 1970 civil marriages have been permitted in exceptional circumstances by Registrar General's licence in other premises, such as hospitals, where people are house-bound or detained, and from April 1995 in hotels, country clubs and other licensed venues outside the residential area of both parties.

Once a quarter the superintendents sent to the Registrar General in London certified copies of the district registrars' returns of births and deaths notified during the three months up to the end of March, June, September and December. Copies of marriage registers were furnished by the clergy, the superintendent, chapels, and officers of the Quakers and Jews. When the original register books were full they were passed by district registrars to the superintendent for safekeeping, and from these district indexes were compiled. Marriage registers were also deposited with the superintendent when completed, but it might be many years before this happened if the parish was thinly populated.

———— Scanning the indexes ————

Members of the public can freely inspect the union quarterly indexes of births, marriages and deaths throughout England and Wales to 1983, and the subsequent yearly indexes, in the public search room of The Office for National Statistics (ONS) at the Family Records Centre in London. If you arrive early you will avoid the crush during the lunch hour, when the search rooms tend to be congested and tempers short.

There are separate indexes for births, marriages and deaths, each organised alphabetically by surname, then forename, and giving the registration district, volume and page number of each entry in the register, and from 1984 the month and year of registration. Microfilm and microfiche copies of the indexes can be seen at the National Library of Wales, in family history centres, a number of local libraries, county record offices and family history societies, obviating the need to go to London, but always check that they cover the period you want. The Society of Genealogists also has a set of microfiche indexes up to 1920. Local family history societies, family history centres, and advertisers in the monthly *Family Tree Magazine*, offer a courier service to apply for certificates on your behalf, using the given index reference.

If you know where your antecedent was born or died, it may be easier and cheaper to make an appointment to have the superintendent registrar's indexes searched. A five-year search of the indexes can be conducted for a fee, and you may undertake a general search yourself, paying for up to six consecutive hours' work, and this includes a maximum of eight entry checks if you are uncertain which is correct. For further checks or certificates, additional fees are charged. This is done whilst you are there, whereas there is a delay of four working days including the application date before you can collect certificates from London, or have them posted to you. There is no consolidated index to marriages in a particular superintendent registrar's district. Non-civil marriage registers are more easily examined if deposited in county record offices, as there is no fee for access, but more recent records may still be at the church or chapel. Maps of registration districts in England and Wales between 1837 and 1851, and the adjusted boundaries between 1852 and 1946, can be purchased from the Institute of Heraldic and Genealogical Studies, Canterbury. Current ones are listed in the *Municipal Year Book and Public Services Directory,* published annually, and *Register Offices of Births, Deaths and Marriages in Great Britain and Northern Ireland,* by VJ Price. You can also locate them in a telephone directory.

If you are doubtful as to which district a place belonged, consult the decennial census place-name indexes, 1851–1981, an open access in The Family Records Centre, or try a contemporary county trade or commercial directory at the Society of Genealogists, or Guildhall Library, London, your local history library or record office, for the name of the Poor Law Union. They are also listed in *Poor Law Union Records, Part 4: Gazetteer of England and Wales,* by J Gibson and FA Youngs, jr.

- When scanning the indexes, be careful to look under all likely surname variants, for example Aughton and Haughton, Bermingham, Birmingham, Burmingham, or Burningham; check misread or interchangeable letters, especially vowels, and surnames starting with T or D, G or K, P and R, L and S, T or F.
- Because of the Welsh patronymic naming scheme and relatively few surnames and forenames in circulation you may find it difficult to identify a specific event from the indexes unless you know the place or district where it took place, and even then children of the same father might be registered under different surnames. In some cases hyphenated surnames developed, perhaps a clue to the mother's maiden name.

- Search indexes consecutively, as it is easy to miss one, and note down every likely entry found, which saves having to repeat your efforts.
- Names might be misspelled, because they were misread or written phonetically, or might even be omitted altogether, combine two entries into one in the central union indexes yet can be found in the local indexes of the superintendent registrar.

The cost

You cannot see the registers themselves; a certified copy of an entry is issued for a fee on completion of an application form giving details from the index. You can collect or have the certificate posted to you, and a priority twenty-four hour service is available. Prepaid postal five-year searches of the indexes can be made for a fee of which part is refunded if the result is negative. Alternatively, a certificate can be sent to you if you can provide the index reference yourself. Cheques, payable to The Office for National Statistics (ONS), or credit/debit cards are accepted. Postal enquiries are dealt with at Southport, and replies sent out within twenty-eight days, or within ten working days if a precise index reference is given. Priority telephone requests can also be made to Southport, the certificate being posted to you the next day. You should quote your credit/debit card details for this, and the fee is reduced if you are able to quote the exact index entry. Full addresses and telephone numbers are given at the end of the book.

Looking for a birth

Until 1874, district registrars were responsible for collecting information about births in their area, thereafter registration was up to the parents themselves. They were to be registered within forty-two days, extended with a penalty, to six months. You should thus always examine at least the two subsequent indexes after the quarter of the year in which a birth was thought to have occurred, as not everyone registered their children's birth's promptly, if at all. Indeed, there is evidence that in the early years some parents opted either to have their children baptised or to register the birth, but not both, in the mistaken belief that choice was possible. So if you cannot find a birth, always look at the baptism registers of the parish where your family lived.

Illegitimacy

Late registration of a birth to parents who married afterwards may give a false date to conceal illegitimacy. The index may list a child under its mother's surname. Before 1875 there was nothing to prevent an informant naming or inventing a putative father of an illegitimate child. Later, only if the father agreed and was either present in person to register the birth, of his written or sworn acknowledgement of paternity was produced could his name be inserted. After the Legitimacy Act of 1926 once the parents of such a child were married, the child became legitimate, and the birth was frequently registered a second time under the married name.

Some reasons why you may not find a birth registration

Parents sometimes totally altered children's names at baptism, which the officiating minister was bound to notify to the Registrar General and the register was amended, but unfortunately not the index. First names might later be dropped or reversed, names shortened into nicknames, or further names adopted, so always ask your relatives about this. Where parents had not decided on a name for their offspring at the time of registration, the birth was recorded as 'male' or 'female'.

Births were registered where they happened, which might not be local to the parents' usual address, so faced with several entries of the same surname, forename and quarter of the year, the given registration district may be wrongly discounted. If you do find several possibilities take the most probable one first, list them in order of likelihood and request a verification check to be made of the registers against known details, such as exact date and month of birth, or the parents' names. If you are in the slightest doubt about any details do not insert them on the reference checking sheet, as you will not be issued with a certificate of an entry which does not correspond exactly and this could prove costly, as it might be the very one you want. There is a prepayable fee for the first entry and an additional one for each successive check, so ask for the search to stop at the first one which tallies. You will be given a refund for each unchecked reference. If no certificate is produced you will also receive a similar refund. You can fill in separate application forms rather than the reference checking sheet, but whilst the latter will merely state 'yes' or 'no', the reverse of each application form ticks or rings every matching or unmatched checking point. A refund is made for a negative search.

Have a look at the International Genealogical Index of the county where the family lived in case you can pick up the child's baptism date and place, or at least eliminate some of the other candidates in the birth indexes.

If you fail to locate any likely entry, you may be looking for an event in the wrong year, so examine the indexes for those preceding and succeeding it, widening this if necessary to two years on either side and so on, for anything up to fifteen years. You may pick up other siblings' births, or children of the same surname in that district or region; note these, because if you fail to find your direct ancestor, and you know the identity of a brother, sister or parent, an appropriate birth certificate can be an invaluable substitute.

The birth certificate

A full birth certificate reveals the date and place of birth, registered forenames, surname and sex of the infant, the parents' names including the mother's former or maiden name, the father's occupation, name, address and relationship to the child of the birth's informant, whether he or she signed or marked the register, and the date of registration. From 1 April 1969, the parents' birthplaces are recorded too. Details about the informant may show that it was some relative other than the parents, especially if the child was illegitimate, and if a parent, the address may be different from the birthplace. A final column records any name given after registration. The short (abbreviated) certificate is of minimal use to the family historian as it only contains the child's name, sex, date and place, registration district or sub-district of birth.

Adoption

Indexes of adoptions by court order in England and Wales since I January 1927 are openly accessible in the The Family Records Centre search rooms in London. To 31 March 1959, a full adoption certificate contains date of birth, the child's adoptive name, the name and address of the adopting parents, the adoptive father's occupation, date and court making the adoption order, and the date of entry in the Adopted Children Register. Between 1950 and 31 March 1959 the country of birth is included too, whereas later certificates disclose the English or Welsh registration district or sub-district. A short certificate identifies merely the adoptive name and date of birth, registration or sub-registration district (before 1 April 1959 the country of birth) if recorded in the adoption order.

Since November 1975 an adopted person can discover his or her name at birth on reaching eighteen, and is offered counselling in case he or she wants to try and trace the true parents, once a copy of the birth certificate has been obtained. People adopted before 12 November 1975 are obliged to attend an interview with an adoption counsellor.

An Adoption Contact Register is held at the Office for National Statistics in London, starting on 1 May 1991. Part 1 contains names of adopted persons of eighteen and over, and part 2 the names of relatives (the true parents, or other adults related by blood, half-blood or marriage, but not adoptive relatives). The address of a consenting third-party, given by either the adopted person or his or her relatives, can be released as a go-between when a link is made. The relative is also informed when a contact is established. The National Organisation for the Counselling of Adoptees and Parents (NORCAP), based at Wheatley, Oxfordshire, has a similar computerised contact register, and it offers an intermediary service.

Earlier adoptions than 1927 were effected privately via the Poor Law Union or through charities, to which there are no central indexes accessible to the public. *Poor Law Union Records*, by J Gibson, C Rogers and C Webb, contains references to the known whereabouts of Union adoptions and boardings out. Names and addresses of charities may appear in the annual editions of *Charities Digest*. If you know the original name of the child and the date of birth you may have sufficient information to find the birth certificate.

Abandoned children

A register of births since 1 January 1977, giving the date and place of birth, name, surname and sex of the child, is held by The Family Records Centre, London, though parentage is unrecorded.

Stillbirths

Certified copies of stillbirth registrations from 1 July 1927 can be issued only with the Registrar General's permission, applied for in writing to the Office for National Statistics at Southport.

Looking for a marriage

Drawing on the information about parentage on the birth certificate you can now look for their marriage, or this may be your starting point if you already know when it occurred. If you know the place of marriage, it may be quicker and cheaper to search the original register, which contains actual signatures of bridal couples and their witnesses. You can inspect it in the local county record office, church or chapel. A duplicate is deposited in the superintendent district registrar's office on completion, where a search fee is payable.

Some registers are available on microfilm, have been copied or indexed, and entries from many are included up to about 1885 in the county International Genealogical Index.

Like the centralised birth indexes, those relating to marriages record alphabetically for each partner the surname, forename, registration district, volume and page number of the entry in the register. From the March quarter of 1912 the spouse's surname is also included, so that entries can be more easily matched.

Start searching in the same quarter of the year as the eldest child's birth registration and work backwards (you may also have to go forward a few years as well!). If you do not know who was the eldest child the search may be protracted. It is advisable to skim the indexes for the more unusual surname or forename, as there are likely to be fewer entries to cross-check for the match. Beware of nicknames and alternative spellings, such as Hannah and Anna, Margaret, Peggy, and Nancy, Mary and Molly, reversed or dropped forenames. You may not find the bride's name in the index because the former name given on her child's birth certificate was that of a previous marriage, whilst she reverted to her maiden name on remarriage, or vice versa. If you do find an entry that otherwise looks correct have it checked to see what emerges. Occasionally the parents were not married at all, but cohabited in a common law arrangement, perhaps because one partner was already married, thus explaining the absence of the name you expected. It is also possible that the couple married out of the country in which they later resided, so you may need to consult indexes of Scottish, Irish or overseas marriages, particularly if the husband was in the Armed Services, or travelled abroad.

The marriage certificate

Having found two entries which tally exactly for the same quarter and year, you can then apply for a certificate. This records the date and place of the religious or civil ceremony, denomination of the church or chapel, and whether it was after banns, by licence or registrar's certificate. The venue's affiliation is an indicator of the religious creed of bride or groom. The full name, age, current marital status, rank, profession or occupation, and residence of each party at the time of marriage, is followed by the father's name and occupation, together with the names of at least two witnesses and the officiating minister, all of whom signed the register.

Asserted ages can prove misleading. Until raised to sixteen in 1929, twelve was the minimum age at which a girl could marry, fourteen for a boy. Up to 1969, when it was lowered to eighteen, parental consent was necessary until twenty-one, and a certificate may thus only record a party was 'of full age' or a 'minor'. An under-age couple marrying against parents' wishes might add on a few years, conversely where there was a significant disparity in age, one might be increased or the other reduced to bring them closer together.

Given occupations were frequently exaggerated to suggest a higher social or employment status, whilst others are obscure or now obsolete, so you may need to find out what was meant from a work such as *Occupations of the People of Great Britain 1801–1981*, by G Routh, or *An Introduction to Occupations, A Preliminary List*, by J Culling. Given addresses were frequently ones of temporary convenience to comply with the minimum legal residential requirement (three weeks for banns, fifteen days for a licence to marry in the chosen parish).

The father's name might be incorrect, perhaps to conceal illegitimacy, given in good faith when the person had been brought up by grandparents or as part of a family which was not that of the true parents. If the father had died some years before his name might be forgotten or never known by his offspring, who used his initials as a guide. A certificate does not automatically indicate a deceased father's status. When the father's surname is different it may be because he was an adoptive or foster parent, or the true father, whose name was missing from the birth registration, and whose consent was not required for inclusion.

Such factors can obviously blunt your chances of success when you come to look for birth certificates, more so when the age on the certificate is also inaccurate. Witnesses and officiating clergy should always be noted as they were often other relations, whose own immediate ancestry might yield important clues if you get stuck.

A partner might be described as widowed, pointing to an earlier marriage, and where it was the bride her father's name on the certificate will identify her maiden name.

In 1907 it became possible for a man legally to marry his deceased wife's sister, and in 1960 the sister of his divorced wife. From 1986 a step-parent has been able to marry a step-child of eighteen or over, provided that person has not been treated as a child of the other's family while under age.

Divorces

Divorced partners are usually described as such, but may occasionally be recorded as single. Since 1858 divorces by decree absolute have been granted in civil courts. Copies of the indexes to divorces, 1858–1958, are in the Public Record Office at Kew, with various matrimonial cause petitions up to 1937. The indexes contain titles of cases, and a prepaid copy of the decree nisi (intermediate stage), or decree absolute (final termination of the marriage coming at least six weeks later) can be obtained from the Principal Registry, Family Division, London. Searches of the indexes there can be undertaken by staff, charged for each ten-year period. The information given includes the names of both partners, date and place of marriage, the date and court granting the decree, to whom it was issued and on what grounds, citing the name of any co-respondent.

Before 1858, marriages ended in a variety of ways other than death, but divorce permitting remarriage could only be effected by private Act of Parliament. This was expensive and involved two preliminary stages: judicial separation granted in a church court was the precursor to a common law writ of trespass filed by the husband in the Court of King's Bench alleging criminal conversation (crim. con.) by the wife's lover, and seeking damages. Armed with a favourable judgement he could then promote a private bill of divorce.

Annulment of a marriage by a church court rendered it void only on limited grounds. The practical effect of this was as if the marriage had never taken place, whereas divorce '*a mensa et thoro*' (from bed and board) merely led to a lifetime suspension of the marriage. Some marital disputes went straight to the Court of Arches of the Archbishop of Canterbury rather than local church courts, and there is a published index of cases in the Court between 1660 and 1913.

Private separation deeds were mutual agreements to maintain the status quo, the husband promising to pay the wife alimony and the wife indemnifying him against any future liability for her debts in cases brought by her creditors. They were not enforceable in a court of law. Desertion was a more popular resort, the absconder sometimes assuming a new identity, contracting a bigamous marriage or entering a common law union and founding a new dynasty. Wife-selling involved her being led by a halter to a public place and exchanged for a nominal sum as a chattel. None of these private solutions legally freed either for remarriage, so any issue by later partners was illegitimate.

Looking for a death

Many family historians disregard death certificates as evidence of generation links, yet they supply addresses for the deceased and the informant at a specific date as well as their names and any relationship between them. This can be invaluable if the death was close to a census year, as you can then search the address for its other occupants, as well as the named person. A death certificate marks a date beyond which you are unlikely to find out anything more about that individual, except from his or her will, or gravestone inscription. An in-memoriam card, newspaper cutting among family archives or grave headstone may reveal the date of death, which was registered within eight days (reduced to five in 1953) by a witness, someone in attendance during the last illness, the occupier of the premises, or by the person causing disposal of the body (such as a coroner). Since 1874 a doctor's medical certificate has been mandatory, setting out the time and cause of demise, supplemented after 1 January 1927 by any secondary causes, and this is presented by the informant to the registrar. The death certificate authorised the undertaker to arrange burial. Since 1902, two doctors' signatures have been necessary for cremation.

From the first quarter of 1866 the indexes give age at death in addition to the surname, forename, registration district, volume and page number of the entry, superseded since the June quarter of 1969 by date or birth, if known.

Coroners' inquests

If registration was by coroner's order, look for a local newspaper account of the inquest. Coroners are obliged to retain their records for fifteen years, after which they can exercise discretion about their preservation or destruction. Generally, coroners' records are closed for seventy-five years, and not all have been transferred to county record offices; access is granted on their written prior consent. All those before 1875 are extant, and *Coroners' Records in England and Wales*, edited by J Gibson and C Rogers, contains a handlist of most known local holdings. In the case of post mortems, the examination reports are kept by coroners, but there should be a local press item.

Hospital records

Where death occurred in a hospital or infirmary, surviving admission and discharge registers may be helpful. You will not be able to search hospital records yourself, unless they have been deposited in a record office.

Why you may be unsuccessful

A person may have died under a different identity from his or her original one, making the search for a birth certificate almost impossible without other information, which may have been carefully suppressed; conversely, the task of finding the death certificate of an individual who had changed his or her name informally may also prove intractable. People disappear relatively easily, only to resurface in a new life, frustrating the family historian's efforts. A person may have died outside his or her usual environs, so positive identification is difficult if there were several of the same name registered at the same time, unless ages appear in the indexes, and even then there may be a discrepancy with what you expected. The person might have died abroad, although not a long-term resident, and the death registered there.

As ages at death were provided by someone else they are rarely entirely reliable. Until 1866, always indicate the minimum age you expect to avoid buying the death certificate of a child, as ages were not included in the indexes.

Possible substitutes for finding out about deaths

Details of date and place of death in England and Wales from 1858 onwards can be culled from the annual printed calendars of wills and administrations in the search room of the Principal Probate Registry in London, indexed alphabetically by surname. Copies may also be seen locally in probate district registries, county record offices and family history centres, but few run up to the present day. *Probate Jurisdictions: Where to Look for Wills*, edited by J Gibson, lists cut-off dates of many local holdings. Death duty registers, 1796–1903, in the Public Record Office, also set out dates of death of people whose estates attracted tax.

Churchyard, cemetery and cremation registers, and memorials, also reveal death date and age, the burial registers and headstone inscriptions referring to others in the same plot. There is usually a cemetery plan to help you find each grave, and these can be inspected by appointment in the county record office, or at the local authority or private cemetery company office. A number of older burial grounds have been cleared, and copies of gravestone inscriptions deposited with the Registrar General are now in the Public Record Office, Kew, to which there is a handlist, organised alphabetically by county. Copies of gravestone inscriptions may also be found in county record offices, local history libraries, the Society of Genealogists, and for Wales, in the National Library of Wales, at Aberystwyth.

The death certificate

English and Welsh certificates give date and place of death, the person's name, sex and age, occupation (or in the case of a married woman, the name and occupation of her husband and whether she was widowed), the cause of demise and duration of last illness (extracted from the medical certificate), the signature, description and residence of the informant (specifying any relationship to the deceased), and the date of registration. From 1 April 1969 you will find date and place of birth if known, usual address and the maiden name of a married woman. You can thus look for her wedding entry, and if she was a widow, her husband's death certificate. The informant may have organised the funeral, the local newspaper or parish magazine contain an obituary or funeral report, sometimes giving the name of the undertaker, whose records may be worth tapping. The cause of death may indicate family susceptibility to particular ailments, genetic disorder or to an occupational disease. Ages at death will reveal family longevity.

— Coming up against a brick wall —

If you have scanned centralised indexes of births, marriages and deaths to no avail, you may wonder what you can do next to find a particular ancestor. If you have some idea of the year and area, then the following might be of help, assuming you have already perused the relevant International Genealogical Index:

- Newspaper announcements of births, marriages and deaths may be a substitute for civil registration, assuming you already know the approximate date and place, otherwise you could be faced with a protracted and fruitless search, as local papers were published as often as once a week.
- Baptism registers are also recommended as alternatives, but are unreliable, chiefly because fewer children seem to have been taken for baptism from the mid-nineteenth century and you will also have to take into account the large number of new churches and dissenting chapels which sprang up, many of which still have custody of their records.
- Often unknown and untouched by family historians are the compulsory smallpox vaccination registers, dating from a series of enactments after 1853, and recording up to 1948 under sub-district the date and place of each registered birth in England and Wales, the child's name, sex, father's name (or that of the mother if illegitimate), his occupation, date when notice of the birth was given by the district registrar and to whom (usually a special vaccination officer), the date of the medical certificate of successful vaccination, of 'insusceptibility' (after a maximum three failed attempts at vaccination), or of having had smallpox, and the date of death if before vaccination.
- Copies of the appropriate certificate were sent by the vaccinator to the parents and to the registrar who submitted to the Poor Law Union Board of Guardians, vestry meeting or council of the parish of residence six-monthly lists of children lacking certificates so that further enquiries could be made. The district registrar kept the registers, surviving ones and their whereabouts being listed in

Poor Law Union Records cited earlier. Most are in county record offices, and a few are in the Public Record Office at Kew.

A major drawback is that notice was given using the district registrar's records, so where a birth went unregistered obviously the child remained unrecorded. The parents were put on notice to take their baby for vaccination within three months by the public vaccinator or a medical practitioner where they lived. Since parents may not have registered the birth in his district, were newcomers or temporarily absent, they might be overlooked. Conversely, as parents were to take their infants for vaccination in the district of domicile, it might not coincide with the registration district, and the child's name will not appear in the vaccination registers serving the birthplace. If the vaccinator considered the child not to be in a fit or proper state to undergo successful vaccination, it could be delayed for renewable periods of two months. Under an Act of 1867 justices of the peace could order all unsuccessfully vaccinated children under fourteen to undergo a further attempt, so you may need to look for vaccinations of older children missed out earlier.

The vaccination registers are augmented by weekly vaccination returns made by vaccinators to the registrars, and these give place of residence of the parents at the time of vaccination, though not their names, nor the child's date or place of birth. From these you should be able to gather enough information to track the original birth registration, parentage, or address to search in the census. As deaths are also annotated against the entries this source can be very helpful too in establishing infant mortality.

Monthly returns of registered deaths of infants under a year old, as well as births, were furnished by district registrars to the vaccination officers, recording date and place, name, age, father's name and occupation, cross-referenced if it was in the same district. The father's home address was given in cases where death happened elsewhere, such as in a hospital.

- Registers of the British Lying-in Hospital, Holborn, London, record admissions by personal recommendation of wives of servicemen and poor married women between 1749 and 1868. The records, on microfilm in the Public Record Office at Kew, give the husband's occupation, current whereabouts or last place of legal settlement, the wife's name and date of admission, discharge or death, plus the child's date of birth, and from 1849, the parents' place of marriage. Accompanying birth and baptism registers for the period 1749–1830 include after 1814 the mother's address, and these entries have been extracted for inclusion in the International Genealogical Index for London and Middlesex.

- From 1862, statutory school registers began to be kept of admissions and attendances of new pupils to be educated in places receiving government grants. You will find that many only start in 1880, because education was not universally mandatory for children aged between five and ten until then, though districts could make it so from 1870. Surviving volumes may remain on the school premises, or have been deposited in county record offices or with local education authorities. They give the child's name, date of birth, father's name, address and occupation, date of admission, progression from the infants' class, via the various standards of the junior and elementary school until the date of departure. Sometimes a previous school or tutor's name will be recorded, and the reason for leaving, perhaps to attend another school, start work, or move to a different town. The books are often indexed, the pages tracing several generations of a local family, brothers and sisters and other relations who passed through the school. Even if you are not sure when or where a birth occurred but you know where the family lived, you may pick them up in school registers.

- School attendance registers, kept by local education authorities from 1875, and now largely in county record offices, may also survive yielding similar information, as well as placements of local children in schools throughout the county. The 'particulars registered... concerning the deaths and births of children' submitted to them by district registrars ensured that the registers were an up to date summary of local youngsters for whom educational provision had to be made and proof obtained of its satisfactory completion. These record the date and place, name and sex of each child, the father's name, and the description and residence of the event's informant. Like the school attendance registers, existing files are held mainly in local record offices.

- Notices of intended marriages after 1 July 1837 made to the superintendent district registrars and minuted by Poor Law Union Boards of Guardians indicate where they were to be solemnised, under the superintendent's supervision. They were often signed by the informant. However notification of intention does not necessarily mean that the wedding actually took place. Surviving records, usually in county record offices, are listed in *Poor Law Union Records*.

● Records of Burial Boards, established after 1850 in London and from 1852 in the provinces to administer public cemeteries, are held at the cemetery offices or in county record offices, and contain the deceased's name, residence, occupation, age, date and place of death, date of interment and plot number in consecrated ground (or unconsecrated if the person was not an Anglican). You may find stillbirths, and some entries show the relationship of the defunct to the head of the family or to the person paying for the burial, the cost of the plot and who underwrote it. The main difficulty in using these sources is that not everyone was buried where he or she died, nor could everyone afford to purchase grave space, while some people continued to be interred in the churchyard or were cremated.

Summing up

All the above demonstrate what you can turn up with a little ingenuity if you cannot find a birth, marriage or death registration, although each series suffers from not being centrally housed, incompleteness, and lack of thorough indexes. You will need to have an idea of at least the county, if not the place of each event in order to examine such material, but the rewards may well be worth it.

5

HUNTING FOR YOUR ANCESTORS' BIRTHS, MARRIAGES AND DEATHS: THE CHANNEL ISLANDS, ISLE OF MAN, SCOTLAND AND IRELAND

Records of births and deaths, and marriages registered from August 1842 onwards on Jersey are kept by the Superintendent Registrar, St Helier. A five-year prepaid search can be undertaken only by staff, for a fee. The certificates are similar to those of England and Wales, though marriages record the couple's birthplaces. There is also an Adoption Register, commencing in 1948.

Statutory registers of births, marriages and deaths on Guernsey date from 1840, and are held with similar records for Alderney and Sark from 1925 by the Registrar General at St Peter Port. These indexes are open to the public by appointment, on payment of an admission fee. There is a postal specific search service for a five-year period including a certificate. Deaths prior to 1963 are indexed under parish, and those of married women before 1949 by their maiden names. Anglican marriages earlier than 1919 are registered by parish. Microfilm copies of the birth and marriage indexes to 1963, birth and death registers, 1840–1907, and marriages 1840–1901 are at the Society of Genealogists in London, and can also be seen in family history centres.

Unfortunately no other index copies are held outside the Channel Islands, though the local family history society is actively engaged in compiling personal name indexes for publication. Some indexed births, marriages and deaths may be found in the Miscellaneous Returns of the Registrar General, 1831–1958, on microfilm at the Public Record Office, Kew and the International Genealogical Index is worth consulting.

Isle of Man

Registers of births and deaths after 1878, marriages since 1884, and an Adopted Children Register from 1928, are in the custody of the General Registry, Douglas, where an appointment is not necessary, but recommended. You can look at the indexes, certificates being available for an additional fee, and you can apply in person or by post. The staff undertake index searches based on a fee per year searched, plus that for any certificate. Also at the Registry are records of people married outside the Established Church from 1849, with a few birth registrations after 1821. Microfilm copies of the indexes to dissenters' marriages, 1849–1964, and of those in the Church of England, 1884–1964, are at the Society of Genealogists, and should be available in family history centres too.

Scotland

Civil registration of births, marriages and deaths dates from 1 January 1855, the indexed registers being at the General Register Office (GRO), Edinburgh, which is open to searchers aged sixteen and over. A search pass is issued before or on the day by postal or personal application, based on a daily or weekly fee. There are also monthly, quarterly and yearly rates. Prior, cheaper, 'Apex' bookings must be paid for between two to six weeks in advance and can be done by telephone. Both schemes guarantee a seat in the search room up to a 10 a.m., unless you advise the GRO otherwise. All other seats are offered on a first-come first-served basis. A part-day search fee is applicable after 1 p.m.

Looking at the indexes

It may be more convenient to scan the indexes elsewhere and to order a certificate by post. The indexes have been computerised at the GRO, but there are microfilm copies of the original volume indexes at family history centres, and up to 1920 at the Society of Genealogists in London, which also has film copies of the 1855 registers. A copy of the computerised indices will be available, for a fee, at the Family Records Centre, London, from 1st April 1997. A 'particular search' of five years in and around a specific year can be undertaken by staff for personal callers or in response to postal or faxed enquiries for a fee, plus the cost of a certified extract. There is also an inclusive priority twenty-four hour service. Certificates are available for collection or posting within five working days, postal applications taking twice as long. Cheaper, uncertified photocopies of the registered entries over a hundred years ago are available which are generally sufficient for most researchers, although you can extract the information yourself from the registers.

The yearly indexes list males and females separately under surname, forename, parish or district, and entry number in the original register. When searching be careful to look under Mc— and Mac—; you will find that married women may well be registered twice or more under maiden and married names. The birth indexes from 1929 reveal the mother's maiden name. From 1966 the registration number of the district or parish also appears. Look at the decennial census place-name indexes, 1851–1981, at the GRO to find the district to which any place belonged.

Having located an entry you can help yourself to the microfiched registers.

Scottish birth registration

As well as recording details found on English and Welsh birth certificates, the 1855 registrations give time of birth, ages and birthplaces of both parents, their date and place of marriage, the number and sex (though not the names) of older children, whether still alive or dead, and the parents' usual address. Thus you are told the parents' places of origin, approximate years of birth, their parish of marriage and progeny born before civil registration whose details you can pursue in Old Parochial Registers. That one certificate may lead you to the parental household enumerated in the 1851 census, and extend the family's history back to the early part of the century. Between 1856 and 1860 the entries were modified to follow the English model, except that hour of birth was retained. Later registrations record the date and place of the parents' marriage.

Adoptions and stillbirths

An Adopted Children Register was started in 1930, and information about birth parents can be released to adopted persons at seventeen.

There is a similar Adoption Contact Register scheme to England's for births and adoptions in Scotland. If birth or adoption occurred there a voluntary contact service, Birth Link, operates from the Adoption Counselling Centre in Edinburgh.

The Registrar General's permission is necessary for details about stillbirths in Scotland from 1939.

Looking for a marriage in Scotland

From their inception, Scottish marriage indexes show the married name of the wife in brackets next to her maiden name, but only from 1929 is there a cross-reference to her surname against that of the husband. In 1855, the marriage registers contain the following additional particulars to English certificates: dates and places of birth registration of the couple (and before 1922 specifying any blood relationship between them), whether this was a second, third or later marriage, the number of living and deceased issue by each previous union, and the names and maiden names of their mothers and if now dead. Thus places of origin are given, the names of both parents, and whether still living. Between 1856 and 1921 birthplaces and previous marriage details were dropped, the former being restored in 1922.

Up to 1939, if the marriage was by consent, or without banns (irregular), the entry recorded the date of conviction, decree of declaration or sheriff's warrant granted by the local sheriff's court.

Divorces

From 1922 the registers note a person's divorced marital status. A central register of divorces in Scotland has been kept since May 1984, containing names of both parties, the date and place of their marriage, and its dissolution, with details of any court order relating to children. This information does not appear in the marriage entry itself. A microfiche index is available on request in the GRO. From 1855 until April 1984 divorces in and outside Scotland notified to the Registrar General were annotated as 'divorce RCE' (Register of Corrected Entries) against the original marriage entry, but not in the indexes.

28938

1861–1965

Extract of an entry in a REGISTER of DEATHS

Registration of Births, Deaths and Marriages (Scotland) Act 1965

No.	1 Name and surname Rank or profession and whether single, married or widowed	2 When and where died	3 Sex	4 Age	5 Name, surname and rank or profession of father Name and maiden surname of mother	6 Cause of death, duration of disease and medical attendant by whom certified	7 Signature and qualification of informant and residence, if out of the house in which the death occurred	8 When and where registered and signature of registrar
636	Margaret Jefferson Married to Arthur Jefferson Theatrical Manager	190 8. December First 8h. 30m. a.m. 14 Craigmillar Road Lanoride	F	50 years	George Metcalfe Bootmaker (Retired) Sarah Metcalfe M.S. Bushby	General Debility as cert. by Robert MacLeod Watson L.R.C.P.W.	William Jefferson Widower (Present)	190 8. December 2nd A: Mount Florida Leonard Gunnell Asstst: Registrar

The above particulars are extracted from a Register of Deaths for the ..... District of ..... Cathcart

in the ..... County of ..... Renfrew

Figure 4 Margaret Jefferson's 1908 death certificate. She was the mother of Stan Laurel. The design of the Death Certificate is Crown copyright and is reproduced with the permission of the Controller of HMSO.

Looking for a death in Scotland

Indexes of deaths in Scotland include age at death from 1866, and from 1974 the maiden surname of the deceased's mother. The 1855 index gives a married woman's maiden name in brackets, and from 1859 there are two index entries, one for each surname. The death registrations add to English certificate details the time of demise and deceased's usual address if not the place of death, his or her birthplace, and how long a resident in the district where he or she died, the duration of the last illness, name of the medical attendant certifying death and when he last saw the deceased, the name of any spouse and offspring, father's name and occupation, mother's name and maiden name and whether the parents were dead, and (up to 1860) the place of burial and name of the undertaker.

The 1855 certificate spans three generations, discloses the deceased's parish of origin, and approximate year of birth, and identifies the spouse, children and parents. From 1856, however, birthplace was excluded, though date of birth has been recorded since 1967. From 1856 until 1860, a person's marital status was substituted for the names of spouse and children, but you may be able to identify one of them as the informant. From 1861 the spouse's name was restored.

Ireland

Irish civil registration of births, marriages and deaths began on 1 January 1864, although marriages between non-Catholics were recorded from 1 April 1845.

Indexes and microfilm copies of original registers sent by superintendent registrars for all Ireland up to 31 December 1921, and those in the Republic after 1 January 1922 are held at the General Register Office, Dublin. You can either just turn up or book an appointment, and searches are charged on the basis of period covered or time spent. Photocopies of registered entries and certificates are obtainable on payment of a fee. Prepaid postal applications are for a five-year search plus either a photocopied register entry or a certificate. There are yearly indexes of births, marriages and deaths to 1877, and of births from 1903; otherwise the indexes are quarterly between 1878 and 1973, thereafter on microfiche or computer. From 1903 the birth indexes record the mother's maiden name, enabling easy identification of her children. Each index contains the surname, forename, registration district, volume and page number of every registration. Microfilm copies of the indexes may also be inspected at family history centres.

Certificates of births, deaths and Roman Catholic marriages in the city and county of Dublin are issued by the Superintendent Registrar's Office, Dublin, on the same premises as the GRO, provided that you can supply full details.

Searching the indexes in Northern Ireland

Microfilmed and duplicate indexes and registers of births and registers of deaths for the whole of Ireland up to 31 December 1921 are in the General Register Office in Belfast. Thereafter, the indexes at the GRO are for births, marriages and deaths in the six northern counties (Antrim, Armagh, Derry, Down, Fermanagh and Tyrone).

A prepaid 'particular search' of the indexes for five years can be conducted for postal applicants and postal enquiries are processed within eight working days. If a particular search is likely to be protracted, or you want to conduct a prepaid general search of the indexes, you can do this yourself for a period not exceeding six hours, any requests for certificates being dealt with within three working days. The Office is open by prior appointment to people over sixteen and you need to book at least four months in advance.

Whilst there is no difficulty obtaining details of births registered from 1864, pre-1922 marriage registers, including those between non-Catholics, are kept in district register offices (whose addresses may be culled from the *Municipal Year Book*), and in the GRO, Dublin. The indexes to them there and in Belfast are organised under district and religious denomination.

The death registers before 1922 are also arranged by district, and include purported age at death from the outset. Date and place of death may however be gleaned from the post-1858 annual printed calendars of wills and administrations in the care of the National Archives of Ireland in Dublin, and for the six northern counties in the Public Record Office of Northern Ireland in Belfast.

The contents of an Irish certificate

Details in the birth, marriage and death registers follow the English and Welsh examples, and like them, are withheld from the public. From 1 January 1956 marriage entries record 'intended future permanent residence' which is helpful if you are trying to trace emigrant relations.

Adoptions and stillbirths

Adoptions by court order in Northern Ireland commenced on 1 January 1931, the papers being filed at the GRO, Belfast; any enquiry should be addressed to the Registrar General if both birth and adoption took place there. The indexed Adopted Children Register for the Republic is at the GRO, Dublin, and relates to court orders made from 10 July 1953.

Information about stillbirths in the Northern counties since 1 January 1961 is not accessible to the public.

Divorces and deaths

Records of divorces in Northern Ireland are held by the Probate and Matrimonial Office, Royal Courts of Justice, Belfast.

Points to note

When examining the indexes, look under surnames with and without the prefix O'—, Mc— and Mac—. Where surname ranges were relatively few, positive identification of one of many people registered with the same names can present a problem, so if you know the district or townland of birth this can prove invaluable.

Births in Ireland were supposed to be registered within twenty-one days, extended up to three months, with penalty, half the delay permitted in England and Wales. Late birth and death registrations are listed at the end of the yearly index when the events occurred, late marriage registrations alphabetically by place amongst other marriages.

6

HUNTING FOR YOUR ANCESTORS' BIRTHS, MARRIAGES AND DEATHS: FINDING PEOPLE OVERSEAS

The Office for National Statistics, relocated to The Family Records Centre in London, holds a wide range of indexed registers relating to British subjects born, married or dying overseas. Having found a likely reference in the index you then apply for a certificate in the usual way. The information given is similar in content to English and Welsh registrations, though for the Armed Services, rank, regiment, ship or squadron are identified. Copies of these indexes are on microfilm at the Society of Genealogists.

—— Britons at sea and on land ——

English and Welsh births and deaths at sea on United Kingdom registered vessels between I July 1837 and 1965 are in the Marine Register Book, and from 1875 foreign registered ships carrying passengers to and from the Kingdom are included. Births and deaths on board British-registered hovercraft from 1 November 1972, and deaths on off-shore installations since 30 November 1972 are also indexed. Births and deaths of Britons in United Kingdom registered civilian aircraft from 1949 until 1965 are to be found in the indexes to the Air Register Book.

The following have indexes relating to British people abroad:

- Consular Returns of births, marriages and deaths in most foreign countries from 1 July 1849 to 1965.
- Births, marriages and deaths in Commonwealth countries, 1951–81, with a few earlier births from 1940, are indexed in United Kingdom High Commissioners' Returns.

- Indexes to births in the African and Asian Protectorates, 1941–65, can be linked to the original registers, 1895–1957, and further indexes from 1904–40, in the Public Record Office at Kew.
- Other Miscellaneous overseas births, marriages and deaths are indexed at the GRO for the years 1956–65.
- From 1966 there are consolidated indexes for all births, marriages and deaths of British subjects abroad, into which were merged marriages and deaths in Commonwealth countries, and births from 1982.

Service families

There are a variety of indexes for Armed personnel and their families:

- Regimental Registers of births and baptisms, 1761–1924 (including returns sent by overseas stations from about 1790), and an unindexed list of regiments making similar returns of marriages is preserved at the Overseas Section of the GRO, Southport.
- Army chaplains' returns of births, baptisms, marriages and deaths in the United Kingdom and overseas stations, 1796–1880, may contain people not found in the former indexes, as neither is complete. After 1881 these relate only to Army personnel and their families overseas, augmented by returns for the Royal Air Force from 1920.
- Indexes to Combined Service Department Returns of births and marriages abroad, 1956–65, contain entries for the Royal Navy from 1959.
- An index of military, civilian and chaplains' registers of births, marriages and deaths in the Ionian Islands, 1818–64.

Men at war

You can scour indexes for names of war casualties in the Natal and South African Forces, 1899–1902, war deaths of Army officers, and of soldiers, 1914–21, with companion indexes for Royal Naval officers, and for ratings, and Indian Service personnel; similarly organised discrete indexes for the Army and Navy extend between 3 September 1939 and 30 June 1948, and for all Royal Air Force personnel in the same period.

Scottish travellers

Scots born, marrying or dying at sea or abroad can be tracked via the following indexes and registers at the General Register Office, in Edinburgh:

- The Marine Register includes births and deaths on board British-registered merchant ships from 1855 where at least one of the child's parents or the deceased was usually resident in Scotland.
- The Air Register extends to births and deaths on UK registered aircraft from 1948.
- Separate indexes are available for births of children of Scottish parentage, marriages and deaths of Scots in foreign countries notified by the parties between 1860 and 1965, marriages performed according to local law (*lex loci*) after 1947 without a British consular official being present.
- Consular Returns of births and deaths of people of Scottish birth or descent from 1914, and marriages from 1917.
- High Commissioners' Returns of births and deaths of persons of Scottish descent or birth in Commonwealth countries from 1964 (though there are some earlier entries for India, Pakistan, Bangladesh, Sri Lanka and Ghana). There are some returns of marriages too.

Scottish servicemen and their families abroad

Army Returns of births, marriages and deaths of Scots at overseas military stations, 1881–1959, marriages performed by Army chaplains abroad since 1892 where one party was Scottish and at least one serving in the Armed Forces, and Service Department Registers from 1 April 1959 of births, marriages and deaths of Scots and their families serving overseas or employed by the Armed Forces should enable you to plot a soldier's, naval man's or airman's movements throughout the world as well as identifying his rank, regiment, ship or squadron. There are also indexes of Army fatalities of Scots during the war in South Africa, 1899–1902, war deaths of soldiers (excluding commissioned officers), petty officers and men of the Royal Navy, 1914–18, and incomplete returns of Scots killed whilst serving in World War II, 1939–45.

Irish migrants

Irish people who were born, married or died outside Ireland may be found in the following indexed records at the General Register Office, in Dublin:

- Births of children with at least one parent who was Irish, and deaths of Irish-born people at sea, 1864–85 (indexes available on request), and 1886 onwards (listed at the back of each yearly index of births and deaths in Ireland) relate exclusively to subjects of the Republic after 1 January 1922.

- Unindexed British Consular Returns of births abroad to Irish parents and deaths of Irish-born people from 1864 to 1921.
- Registers of births, marriages and deaths of Irish subjects outside the State since 1972, and a register of Lourdes marriages from the same year.

Irish servicemen and their families

Births, marriages and deaths of Irish servicemen and their families in the British Army overseas, are indexed at the back of the yearly Irish birth indexes from 1879 until 1930, 1888–1930 for marriages, and deaths, 1888–1931. Deaths of Irish soldiers in the South African War, 1899–1902 appear in the 1902 index.

Northern Irish records since 1922

If you are tracing people travelling outside Northern Ireland since 1 January 1922 you will find the following indexed registers at the General Register Office, in Belfast useful:

- Births at sea of children of at least one native parent, and deaths of Northern Irish-born persons;
- Consular Returns of births and deaths abroad on similar conditions; the returns of marriages starting a year later, in 1923; of marriages in foreign countries since 1947 according to local law (*lex loci*) without a British consular official being present;
- High Commissioners' Returns relating to births, marriages and deaths in Commonwealth countries since 1950.

Northern Irish servicemen

Service Department Registers of births, marriages and deaths in the British Army from 1927, and indexes to war deaths of Northern Irish servicemen, 1939–48, may help you to track a family's movements and to locate other records relating to casualties.

The Commonwealth War Graves Commission

The Commonwealth War Graves Commission, at Maidenhead in

Berkshire, holds computerised indexes containing the names of one and three-quarter million servicemen and women killed or reported missing during both World Wars and commemorated by headstones or memorials near where they fell, or on the Naval Memorials erected at Chatham, Plymouth and Portsmouth for those who died at sea. There are cemeteries and memorials in a hundred and forty countries, two-thirds of which relate to unknown persons. The headstones do not distinguish between ranks, and each has a published alphabetical register of war dead, and for World War II there is also a war dead roll of honour for Commonwealth civilians. Searches of the records can be undertaken by staff for a particular grave or memorial inscription and a fee may be charged.

Other places where you can find Britons abroad

Unfortunately all the ONS overseas returns are incomplete, and the same is true of material held elsewhere in the British Isles, some of which duplicates the above. You can, however, freely consult both the indexes and registers deposited at the Public Record Office at Kew and at the Guildhall Library in London.

The Public Record Office at Kew has by far the largest and most diverse collection mainly filed among the records of the Board of Trade for events at sea, 1854–1913, of the Register General for maritime, Colonial and Commonwealth Returns, 1874–91, and events at sea or in other countries may be traced in the Registrar General's Miscellaneous Returns, 1627–1960, or those of the Foreign Office. A number of the returns have personal name indexes, those for the Registrar General being on microfilm in the public search room at The Family Records Centre at ONS, London.

If your family was nonconformist then births overseas might have been registered between 1742 and 1837 at Dr Williams's Registry, London, or between 1818 and 1837 at the Wesleyan Methodist Metropolitan Registry, London, both of whose indexed records are on microfilm at The Family Records Centre.

Tracing servicemen and their families

Army personnel and their families can be traced not only in the Registrar General's Miscellaneous Returns, but also in service returns of officers after 1828, attestation and discharge papers, pensions, and regimental musters of non-commissioned officers and men from the mid-eighteenth century to about 1913. Only a small fraction of personal records survive about soldiers in the Great War. Birthplaces of officers may be gleaned from printed *Army Lists*, 1879–1900 and from their applications for commissions from 1793. You can scan the lists of campaign casualties in the Boer War, 1899–1902, and in World War I. For World War II there is a key-coded series of registers relating to the Army Roll of Honour, 1939–45.

Ships' musters, passing certificates, and service returns of Royal Naval officers, and continuous engagement books of seamen reveal when and where they were born. Reports of naval deaths between July 1900 and October 1941 are closed for seventy-five years, though you can inspect the indexed registers of killed or wounded, 1854–1911, and 1914–29, and alphabetical reports of deaths of ratings, September 1939 to June 1948. There is a card index of names of commissioned officers killed in action between 1914 and 1920, and an alphabetical War Graves Roll, 1914–19. Examining these will be cheaper than looking for indexed entries of casualties at The Family Records Centre.

Besides crew lists, nineteenth-century registration, ticketing and certification of service or competency of merchant seamen should reveal birth details. Returns of deaths running from 1852–90 are filed in the records of the Board or Trade. Petitions to Trinity House by injured merchant seamen or their dependants between 1787 and 1854 also contain personal information. There is a published list of names of applicants.

What else to try

There are other less extensive series of documents at the Public Record Office in which you can trace individual people abroad, most of which are arranged under the country concerned. You can find out about many of these in my *Genealogical Dictionary of Genealogical Sources in the Public Record Office*.

The Guildhall Library holds indexed ecclesiastical 'International Memoranda' of baptisms, marriages and burials of Britons at sea or abroad notified between 1816 and 1924 to the Bishop of London. To 1865 the returns contain entries retrospectively up to thirty years before, later ones including events happening up to five years prior to notification. For more information on which countries are covered here and elsewhere look at *The British Overseas*, produced by Guildhall Library.

The British in India and Asia

The Oriental and India Office Collections of the British Library, London, house ecclesiastical returns of baptisms, marriages and burials (excluding Roman Catholics before 1836), and civil registrations of birth, marriage and death of Britons in India up to 1968, though these are complete only as far as 1948. Former parts of India (Burma, Pakistan and Bangladesh) are included. The indexed records relate to the Presidency of Madras from 1698, Bengal from 1709, and Bombay from 1713.

The British Association for Cemeteries in South Asia has been responsible for the compilation of notes, information and photographs relating to graves and epitaphs of European residents, especially in territories once administered by the Honourable East India Company, taking on the restoration, repair and upkeep of the cemeteries themselves. The resulting material has been handed over to the Oriental and India Office Collections for safekeeping, but is not open to the public. The Association publishes monograph booklets listing in full gravestone inscriptions in various cemeteries, with potted biographies and articles about the social life of residents, drawing on this research.

Other parts of the world

It is worth trawling the International Genealogical Index (IGI) for births, baptisms and marriages of Britons in countries overseas, many entries predating civil registration, although it is not fully comprehensive, and you should check the accompanying *Vital and Parish Records Listing* to see which places and periods are included. It includes few deaths or burials.

Births, marriages and deaths of Britons, nationals, and foreign residents overseas will otherwise be located in registration records of that state or country. Addresses of registration offices, or bureaux of vital statistics, start date of registration, the cost, and percentage of completeness of the records can be elicited from *International Vital Records Handbook*, compiled by TJ Kemp, a copy of which is at the The Family Records Centre, and at the Society of Genealogists. The General Register Offices also keep lists of overseas offices. Many of the indexes and registers are available at family history centres worldwide.

Civil registration did not begin uniformly in every state, perhaps not until as recently as the twentieth century; in places where people were itinerant and not permanently settled, they may have to be tracked down in records of a number of states, where early registration was haphazard.

Certificate content varies between the Scottish and English examples. The death certificates are frequently immensely useful, as they can yield vital clues about length of stay in the country, parentage and birthplace. In non-English speaking countries the records will be in the vernacular, so you may need help translating them.

If you fail to find an event when and where expected try a few years on either side, and widen your scope to neighbouring districts or places; indeed you may find no records exist for an actual place of residence, so you will be forced to look at those of the nearest towns and settlements. Some events were never registered at all, or the records have long since disappeared, but occasionally such frustrations can be overcome by finding birth, marriage or death announcements in local newspapers, baptisms, marriages and burials in church registers, and personal and family details from gravestone inscriptions.

United States of America

As well as Kemp's *Handbook* cited above, you can find information about civil registration in the United States of America in *Where to Write for Vital Records of Births, Deaths, Marriages, and Divorces*, by RL Berko and S Sadler.

Certificates may be ordered by post from the bureau of vital statistics in the state capital, citing date and place. Microform indexes may be consulted in county courthouses as well as at family history centres throughout the world.

Most states have late birth registrations, mainly of applicants for Social Security benefits after 1937. Unfortunately they are usually filed in the county in which the applicant then resided which may not be where he was born, but the information submitted had to be supported by documentary evidence such as affidavits, school records, a baptism certificate or family Bible, so they are worth seeking out.

There is no inter-state standardisation of entries beyond date, place and name of the subject, but twentieth-century death certificates can prove invaluable as parents' names and birthplaces are frequently recorded, as well as the date and place of birth of the deceased, and place of burial or cremation. If the person was a first generation settler, you can immediately forge a link with the country or origin. Because they are so full, death certificates also establish generational relationships. You can follow them up in newspaper obituaries and gravestone inscriptions. Conversely, a tombstone may be the only evidence you have for birth and death dates.

Other ways of finding recent deaths and military killed in action

FamilySearch on computer disk, includes the Social Security Death Index, listing deaths between 1962 and 1988, from which you can glean birth and death dates, the person's last place of residence, Social Security number, and the state he or she lived in when it was issued, plus the address to which death benefit was sent. Another file contains a Military Index of names of American servicemen who perished in Korea, 1950–57, and in Vietnam, 1957–75, and from this you can glean birth and death dates, marital status, religious affiliation, the address at enlistment, country of death, rank, serial number and service branch, and date of last tour of duty.

The National Archives, in Washington, DC, has records of births, marriages and deaths at American Army facilities spanning 1884–1912 (although some run up to 1928), and searches can be undertaken by staff for births, provided you can supply the child's name and those of his parents, place, month and year of birth, names of the contracting parties if you want details of a marriage, or the name, date, place and rank for deaths.

Americans abroad

Births and marriages of American citizens overseas, registered at Foreign Service Posts up to 1941 and reports of deaths up to 1949, are also filed in the National Archives. Details about registrations over seventy-five years ago can be obtained from Civil Reference Branch (NNRC) of the National Archives, Washington, DC and about those since then from the Department of State in Washington.

7

SEARCHING
THE CENSUS

A sequence of birth, marriage and death certificates forges a chain between one generation and another, but each of these only relates to an individual, his parents, spouse and any relative who was the informant. However they lead directly to another rich nineteenth-century source, in which you will find a person as part of a household. The ten-yearly census is a complete population count of a given place at a given date, enumerating everyone sleeping overnight at a specific address, so by using the place of residence given on a certificate close to a census year you can see who was present when it was taken. Conversely, details of approximate date and place of birth and marital status gleaned from the census enable you to delve for certificates which might otherwise have eluded you.

The first decennial census in the United Kingdom was in 1801, but names were not systematically recorded until the census night in 1841. No enumeration was undertaken in 1941, and returns for 1931 were destroyed. You can inspect returns only after a hundred years, with the exception of Ireland, for which 1901 and 1911 records are available to make up for the scarcity of earlier material.

England, Wales, Channel Islands and the Isle of Man

The English, Welsh, Channel Islands and Isle of Man returns are in The Family Records Centre, London. On payment of a fee, the Office for National Statistics (ONS) may release details of age and birthplace of a named person at a particular address in England and Wales on 31 March 1901, but prior written consent of the person concerned, his or her direct descendant or next of kin where the individual died childless, is required. Application forms may be obtained from the Census Division at Titchfield in Hampshire, (see page 281 for addresses) and are dealt with in four to six weeks.

How the census was organised

The birth and death registration districts served as census districts under the supervision of superintendent district registrars. They were carved up into smaller enumeration or sub-districts of about two-hundred households within every city, borough, parish, hamlet or township, for which locally appointed enumerators were responsible. Each person was listed in the dwelling in which he or she remained overnight on Sunday 6 June 1841, 30 March 1851, 7 April 1861, 2 April 1871, 3 April 1881 and 5 April 1891. During the preceding week the enumerators delivered a numbered schedule to every household, defined as people sharing the same roof, boarding and eating together. The schedules were completed by heads of households and collected up afterwards, the enumerators copying up the details into special books for checking by the district and superintendent district registrar before transmission to the Registrar General in London.

From 1871 the returns indicate by the initial 'W' where they were originally completed in Welsh by the householder and subsequently translated into English. You can also find out from the 1891 census if a person was bi-lingual or spoke only Welsh or English.

In The Family Records Centre the decennial census returns may be freely seen on microfilm, for which you will be allocated a seat number. The 1891 census is also on microfiche. Many local record offices, libraries and family history societies have purchased copies relating to their area, and they can also be hired at family history centres run by the Church of Jesus Christ of Latter-day Saints if they are not already on the premises. A complete set of Welsh census microfilms is at the National Library of Wales, Aberystwyth, for Jersey at the States Library, and Société Jersiaise, both in St Helier, for Guernsey, Alderney and Sark at the Royal Court House, St Peter Port, and for the Isle of Man at the Manx Museum Library in Douglas. *Census*

Returns 1841–1891 in Microform, by J Gibson and E Hampson, is a complete directory of local holdings.

Indexes and transcripts

The main finding aids at The Family Records Centre are the decennial place-name indexes, those for 1841 recording a page number and for later years a registration district number against each entry, which is then matched up with the microfilm number in the reference books. There are street indexes for most large towns and cities with a population in excess of 40,000 which identify their folio, page and district numbers; where streets were divided by enumeration district boundaries this can save you valuable time. A list of these and of personal name indexes appears in *Marriage, Census and Other Indexes for Family Historians,* by J Gibson and E Hampson. Copies of the indexes are available on the open shelves, accessed via handlists.

The major personal name index is for 1881, masterminded by the Genealogical Society of Utah in conjunction with the PRO and the Federation of Family History Societies. It is composed of county microfiche for England and Wales, and a separate set each for the Channel Islands and Isle of Man. Each is divided into four sections: as enumerated, a surname index, birthplace index, and a place-name index. There are also indexes for enumerated institutions and ships. For Welsh counties there is also a forename index. There are complete sets of these at The Family Records Centre. Family history centres and the Society of Genealogists in London also have complete collections and family history societies each have a microfiche for their own county.

Look at the surname index first to find the forename, age, relationship to named head of household, occupation, birthplace and abode of a specific person, and using the microfilm, folio and page references you can either examine the 'as enumerated' microfiche, or go straight to the microfilmed returns from which the entries were extracted.

The birthplace index is attractive because it lists all people of the same surname who were born at the same place, whilst the place-name index records inhabitants alphabetically.

However, transcripts and indexes are only as good as their compilers, so always check the original in case of misreading or omissions. What personal name indexes do is bring together everyone of the same surname in a county, district or place, including itinerants, and temporary visitors, on a particular night. What they do not do is show related people with different surnames lodged together, nor any indication of household size and age structure.

Maps

There is a complete set of microfilmed 1891 Ordnance Survey maps, marking out English and Welsh registration districts and sub-districts, and London boundaries, with an incomplete series for England and Wales in 1870 and 1921, and for London in 1851–61, and 1921. There is a map index. The original, coloured, maps are at Kew. Where hamlets and other thinly-populated areas cannot be identified in the place-name indexes, a gazetteer, or the provided list of parishes in England and Wales and hamlet index, might help. Individual townships and parishes in Wales may be traced in *Welsh Administrative and Territorial Units*, by M Richards.

What the censuses reveal

Every enumerator's book was numbered and began with a short description of the hamlets, townships, roads and streets it covered. The pages in the 1841 books are headed by the title of each place, with columns recording personal details about household members. Only occasionally are names of roads, streets or buildings given and each dwelling is marked by two diagonal lines drawn through the left margin, each household demarcated by a single diagonal line. Starting with the head of household the first forename and initials of each person were recorded, followed by the surname, age (by sex), profession, trade, employment or if of independent means, whether or not born in the same county in which enumerated (Y or N), and if in Scotland (S), Ireland (I) or in Foreign Parts (F), and relating to anyone who was not a British-born subject). Unfortunately family relationships and marital status were not stated, and the head of household was not invariably the oldest person there. Ages were supposedly rounded down to the nearest five, so a person of fifty-nine would be fifty-five, though anyone younger than fifteen was ascribed correctly, down to infants of a few days, weeks or months. Where it is unclear from the spelling whether a person was male or female the attribution of age by sex is helpful.

The 1851 census returns assigned a sequential number to every household, and generally you will find roads and streets named, if not individually numbered or named houses. In 1891 you can even discover how many rooms were occupied if it was less than five, as central government used the returns to find out the extent of overcrowded housing. If there is a collection of local photographs of the period you can form a graphic impression of what each property looked like.

From 1851 the decennial census records under headings the occupants' names, beginning with the head, their relationship to him or her, marital status, age by sex, rank, profession or occupation, and the place and county of birth. A final column notes if a person was blind, or deaf and dumb, and, from 1871 whether they suffered from certain mental disabilities.

Because relationships to the head of household were given, wives, children and other kinsfolk, servants, lodgers and apprentices can be easily picked out. This does not mean that the head of household's children were always by his present wife. A change in marital status by the time of the next census gives you a decade in which to search for a marriage or death. Ages were allegedly at the last birthday but may not be consistently ten years more or less in each census, and given birthplaces may also vary, especially where the person was not himself the informant head of household. You can approximate year of birth, and because counties are specified for birthplaces, this resolves any uncertainty about duplicated place-names.

Common occupations were often abbreviated throughout the period, for example 'Ag Lab' for agricultural labourer. 'Living on their own means' usually indicated a shareholder, or someone living off rents or an annuity. The occupations of wives and children at home, employed in the family's business but not drawing wages, went unrecorded until 1891, whereas retired and temporarily unemployed persons were described with their last or usual employment before 1871, making it impossible to know who was and who was not in work. Thenceforward they were designated as 'retired' or 'unemployed'. In 1891 the returns note whether a person was an employer, employee or neither. When a person pursued several occupations only one might be listed, whichever earned most income at that season of the year. Nightworkers were enumerated in the homes to which they returned on the day following census night.

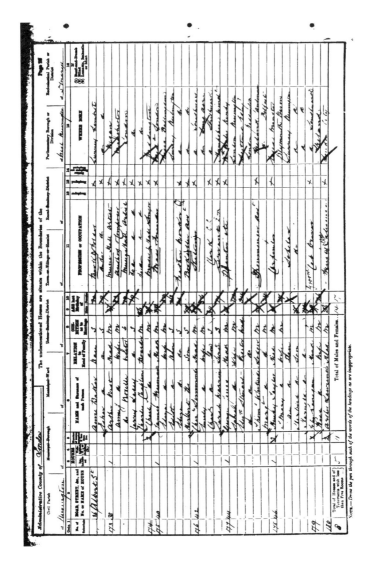

Figure 5 Newington Census return 1891, Charles Chaplin (Charlie's father) was enumerated twice, by his landlord and on his own schedule. Note the variation of information given. He occupied two rooms of the house. (I am grateful to Dan Harris and Family Tree Magazine for this information. (Reproduced by permission of the Greater London Record Office).

From 1851 until 1881, farm acreages, numbers of labouring men and boys, employees and apprentices were noted. The size of the business undertaking may have fluctuated during that period, and you can compare the farmholding with those of neighbours. Concentrations of people following similar occupations and from the same area of origin may suggest a mass recruitment of labour and chain migration using family networks.

Children were frequently described as scholars, regardless of how many hours' formal weekly education were being received in relation to the number of hours in gainful employment. It was only in 1891 that occupations were recorded for children aged ten and over who were legally allowed to leave school to take up work.

People in institutions, not in a dwelling, or mobile

There were separate rosters for Army barracks and military quarters, Royal Naval and merchant ships, public and endowed schools, colleges, certified reformatories and industrial schools, workhouses (including pauper schools), hospitals for the sick, convalescent or incurable, public and private lunatic asylums, prisons and houses of correction where the number of people in them exceeded a hundred. The returns will be located at the end of the town, port, hundred or registration district to which they belonged, as indicated in the reference books. Staff, their families and servants were enumerated first, and in gaols, houses of correction and asylums normally only initials of inmates were recorded.

Total numbers sleeping in barns, sheds or tents, or in the open air, were only counted in 1841 and 1851, and as the former census was taken in June during the height of summer when seasonal labour was at its most mobile, there must have been many folk whose names do not feature at all. In 1861 they appear in a 'list of persons not in houses' and from 1871 in whichever named road or street they slept.

Travellers by coach or train were rostered at whatever house or hotel they lodged in overnight, or took up residence the morning after census night. As they might arrive late and leave early some are sparsely enumerated as 'NK' where name, age and other particulars were unknown.

People at sea or on inland waterways

The first surviving Royal Navy ships' enumerations date from 1861, and there is a complete microfiche index to the returns of 1881. Special schedules were completed by the commanding officers of all men and passengers on board in home waters and abroad, setting out name, rank or rating, marital status, age and birthplace. The 1861 returns are filed at the end of the record class, but later ones, of vessels in British ports, are to be found at the end of the registration district concerned, and rosters of ships at sea or in foreign waters at the end of the class.

Returns of passengers and crewmen of merchant vessels are located with Royal Naval ships in 1861, later ones under the port of closest proximity on census night, or to which the completed schedules were delivered on eventual arrival within a prescribed period. Enumeration was extended over several weeks, but the periods covered and the categories of vessel recorded vary from census to census. A few returns are extant for 1851 relating to British ships in port and at sea in the home trade around the United Kingdom, Channel Islands, Isle of Man and Europe from the Elbe to Brest.

If you are trying to track ships' passengers to and from the Continent or emigrants in port or en route to their ultimate destination, then these merchant shipping schedules are worth culling to pick up people travelling as part of a family unit or wider social group, and they give ages and birthplaces, albeit usually just the country for foreign passengers. The schedules are also effectively crew lists and include details about foreign recruits to the merchant service, as well as ages, ranks and birthplaces of Royal Naval personnel and men in the merchant service.

The earliest apparent returns for fishing boats in port relate to vessels arriving in harbour during April 1861 and these are filed with the enumerations for the Royal Navy and merchant ships. The 1871 and 1881 schedules are for a slightly shorter period than for merchant vessels, but in 1891 they are the same, and include returns for foreign fishing boats landing their catches at United Kingdom ports.

People on canals and inland navigable waterways were listed too under the enumeration or sub-district where they were moored on census night, using similar schedules as for ships.

Scotland

The 1841-91 censuses can not only be seen on microfilm at the General Register Office in Edinburgh, and hired at family history centres of the Church of Jesus Christ of Latter-day Saints, but local area holdings are in many regional libraries throughout Scotland, and for the Orkneys and Shetlands in their respective Archives. The Gibson guide cited above (*Census Returns 1841–1891 in Microform*) provides a location list, and *Genealogical Microform Holdings in Scottish Libraries*, by M Nikolic, provides a fully comprehensive local directory.

A search pass is required to use the microfilms in Edinburgh for which a fee is payable, but as they are stored with the indexes and registers of births, marriages and deaths from 1855, and earlier Old Parochial Registers of baptisms, marriages and burials, you can achieve a good deal in a day if you are successful.

Census arrangement and indexes

The returns are organised by district or parish, to which there are street indexes for larger burghs and cities, the volume number being indicated against the appropriate entry in the census index reference books. Microfiche county indexes are available for 1881, arranged in a number of ways: by surname, by birthplace, by place-name and finally as an 'as enumerated' transcript, from which you can glean sufficient information to check the original microfilm, and trace surname distribution and family groupings. The surname index gives forenames, age, birthplace, relationship to named head of household, occupation and abode of each person on census night. The birthplace index shows everyone of the same surname who was born there. The place-name index gives an alphabetical list of residents on census night, each entry being cross-referenced to the 'as enumerated' index and to the original returns. Complete sets are at the General Register Office and at some family history centres of the Church of Jesus Christ of Latter-day Saints. A computerised personal name index is in progress for 1891. As widows sometimes reverted to their maiden names look under both surnames.

The census index reference books embody two consecutive enumerations, so be careful to select the correct microfilm. If you cannot find a particular place, *Gazetteer of Scotland*, edited by F Groome, in the search room, will identify the parish to which it belonged.

The returns correspond with those for England and Wales, except that in 1841 England is substituted as country of birth in place of Scotland, and in 1891 Gaelic replaces Welsh as the spoken language. There are a few extra facts about schooling and housing conditions which can be obtained from the Scottish entries.

Passengers and crews at sea

Returns of Royal Naval and merchant shipping from 1881–91 and 1861–91 respectively are unlisted in the indexes, but are available on request. The rosters, like their English and Welsh counterparts, give name and type of vessel, port to which it belonged, name, age, marital status, and birthplace of all aboard.

Ireland

A few returns are known to exist for 1841–71, but no census was undertaken in either 1881 or 1891. Returns for 1901 and 1911 are held by the National Archives of Ireland in Dublin, where they may be inspected free of charge. Microfilm copies of the former can be hired at family history centres of the Church of Jesus Christ of Latter-day Saints.

The way the census was planned and indexed

Ireland was organised for census purposes under county district electoral divisions, then by townland. The relevant return can be found from the *1901 Townland Index*, which notes each division name and number. There is no townland index for 1911. County books list sequentially the numbered district divisions and townlands from which you can requisition the volumes for Sunday 31 March 1901, or boxes of loose paper schedules for Sunday 2 April 1911. There are street indexes for Belfast, Cork, Dublin and Limerick. County by county personal name indexes are under preparation for 1901.

Census content

The household returns for 1901 contain forename and surname of all occupants, relationship of each to the head, religious affiliation, level of education, age, sex, rank, profession or occupation, marital status, Irish county or city, or country of birth, whether bilingual or Irish- or English-speaking only, and if deaf and dumb, dumb only, blind, imbecile, idiot or lunatic. The number of rooms and windows in the main dwelling and in any outhouses was also specified, and the roof fabric. Because the returns are at the turn of the twentieth century photographic evidence may exist to show what the houses actually looked like.

The 1911 census adds the number of years' marriage of each wife unless she was widowed, her total live-born children, and how many were still living, so from this you can calculate when she married, the approximate number in her family, and learn about their size of accommodation.

Copies and extracts from previous censuses

Unlike returns for other parts of the United Kingdom, the Irish 1841 census gave by household the name, age, occupation, relationship to the head of each person sleeping there on census night, date of marriage where appropriate, level of literacy, and names of absent family members and of those who had died since 1831. You can see who in the family was then still alive although not part of the household on census night. There are a number of extant transcripts from which you can reconstruct the family's recent history, tied to key-dates of marriage and mortality within a decade of enumeration. In 1851, details of religious denomination were added, with names of people in the family dying since 1841; from this you can identify which church or chapel they are likely to have attended, taken their children for baptism, relatives for burial and their spouses for marriage, and of course you know approximately when they were born, which may long predate civil registration in 1864. Transcripts of 1841 and 1851 entries produced as proof of age in individual applications for old age pensions are held by the National Archives of Ireland and in the Public Record Office of Northern Ireland, Belfast, to which there are personal name indexes, by county. Other copies, including some for 1861 and 1871, are catalogued under pre-1901 census items in the National Archives. Surviving material is listed by county in *Local*

Census Listings, 1522–1930: Holdings in the British Isles, by J Gibson and M Medlycott.

Because access is granted in Ireland to records about people living less than a hundred years ago, a number of them are likely to be still around, perhaps residing in the same neighbourhood or area; their memories of former friends and neighbours, even if your own family is no longer represented, can often help fill in vital gaps, especially about when and why people emigrated or moved away.

Earlier censuses

A number of incidental parochial lists of householders have come down to us from the four previous censuses on Mondays 10 March 1801, 27 May 1811, 28 May 1821 and 30 May 1831. Surviving fragments of such schedules and their whereabouts are arranged by county in *Local Census Listings, 1522–1930*. The majority of these incidental lists are deposited in county record offices.

England and Wales

Mostly prepared by clergymen, schoolmasters or overseers of the poor, who were then the enumerators, the scraps of paper containing English and Welsh returns were stored in the parish chest for safe-keeping. Sometimes other family members were named and their kin-ship, ages and occupations given. More usually though they delineate merely the householders, and the numbers and ages of other occupants, but nevertheless they show household size and names of people born in the late- or mid-eighteenth century.

Scotland

For Scotland, there are some earlier lists for 1821 and 1831 among Old Parochial Registers of baptism, marriage and burial held at the General Register Office, Edinburgh, kirk session records in the Scottish Record Office, Edinburgh, and in local archive collections.

Ireland

A few returns remain for the first two Irish censuses, in 1821 and 1831, arranged under county, barony, civil parish and townland, giving, as instructed, all inhabitants' names, relationship to the householder, ages and occupations, and the acreage of each landholding. The number of storeys of each house was originally noted, but excluded from the 1831 lists. They can be searched mainly at the National Archives of Ireland in Dublin, or the Public Record Office of Northern Ireland, Belfast.

Additional listings to try

Other sporadic nominal lists of inhabitants were drafted from time to time to meet various civil or ecclesiastical purposes like taxation, rent collection, assessment and payment of the poor rate, distribution of poor relief, fixing a rota of parochial offices, noting communicants and recusants.

Some lists, by their nature, were limited to people above a certain age, social or economic status, householders, or defined groups, but nonetheless they are a guide to who was where at a particular date, and the entries can be checked against contemporary church registers of baptism, marriage and burial, wills and other relevant material.

Census surveys overseas

Census counts have been taken at regular or infrequent intervals in almost all countries of the world; some, for the first time only in the twentieth century, but not all are thorough surveys, have been pre-served, or are open to public inspection. When civil registration began later than the census, and church records are unreliable or absent, such lists assume great importance for the family historian, providing evidence of year and place of birth, and family relationships.

United States of America

In the United States of America the first decennial federal census occurred on 1 June 1790, but many of the 1890 returns were destroyed. The available 1790 schedules have been printed and where places are deficient inhabitants' names have been added from other contemporary sources. Microfilm copies of returns up to 1920 can be seen in the National Archives, Washington, DC, its branch Regional Archives, in state archives, family history centres and branch libraries of the Church of Jesus Christ of Latter-day Saints. The National Archives has produced printed catalogues listing microfilm copies of each federal census.

Indexes to the census

There are personal name indexes for each census to 1850, arranged under state, and thereafter they are by county, many of which are printed or in microform and widely accessible in state archives, public and research libraries, but to use them you need to know your ancestor's full name, or the head of household and the state or county where he lived. The best indexes are the microfilm copies relating to the 1880 state schedules, embracing households with children aged ten or less, and giving name, age and birthplace of each member. It is not a complete index, so you cannot rely solely on it for all that was included in the census, but it gives a clue to the distribution of a particular surname at a given date. This and later indexes adopt the Soundex system, running alphabetically by first letter of the surname, then phonetically by sound using a number code, followed alphabetically by every householder's forename. Each householder's card includes other family members listed with him or her in the census. Miracode index cards are used for some states for 1910, enumerators' household numbers rather than the Soundex system of page and line references linking them to the original census entries.

All the indexes are subject to errors and omissions, so consult every compilation for a given census year to pick up references missing elsewhere, and check every likely surname variant for others grouped with it, especially when the Soundex system is used. Whilst the 1890 index is complete, just over six thousand original schedules survive, so there is not much left to inspect.

You may be able to locate city and town addresses of people in census years from directories of the period. The Library of Congress in Washington, DC, and many public libraries and historical societies have extensive runs.

How the census was organised and what it contains

The early returns are arranged by county and town of domicile, and until 1840 identify merely the head of household and number of other occupants by age and sex. Only from 1880 are individual streets and houses numbered or indentified. Starting in 1850 the returns are far more expansive, as every free person was named, specifying age, sex and colour, the profession, occupation or trade of males over fifteen, to 1870 the value of any real estate (and personalty from 1860), the state, territory or country of birth, whether attending school or married within the previous year (the latter up to 1890 only, in 1870 giving the actual month), educational level of each person over twenty, and if deaf and dumb, blind, insane, idiot, pauper or convict. Given natal months of infants born during the year prior to the 1870, 1880 and 1900 censuses simplify searches for registrations or baptisms.

The 1880 and later census schedules give marital status, the relationship between everyone in the household to its head, and number of months of unemployment during the past year. From 1890 onwards you can also discover a mother's total surviving children, the 1900 and subsequent censuses revealing duration of the wife's present marriage, the number of children within it. You can find out as well if the house or farm was owned, rented or mortgaged at the time of the 1890 and later enumerations. The 1880 and 1890 censures recorded any current illness or disability.

In 1870 you can learn for the first time whether each named person's parents were foreign-born, about naturalised immigrants qualified to vote, and then track them down in naturalisation records. The parents' state or country of birth was invariably included from 1880. For newcomers, the number of years' residence in the United States was specified from 1890, and whether already naturalised or applying for naturalisation. Year of immigration, and current nationality of first-generation settlers over twenty-one can be traced in returns from 1900. The 1890 census onwards also indicate ability to speak English, from 1910 citing native language. The one crucial missing feature is the exact birthplace of immigrants, but family tradition or other clues may hold the key.

Special uses of the census

The federal census returns are particularly helpful in identifying people and parents of overseas origin, pinpointing their year of arrival and application for naturalisation as American citizens; they also help plot migration of individuals and family groups from state to state, and by providing approximate years of marriage, birth years and states the returns can lead you on to church or civil records from the eighteenth to the present century. You can also find out more about men fighting in the Revolutionary and Civil Wars from their service papers and pension claims.

Ancillary surveys

In 1885 a census was taken in some of the frontier states (Arizona, Colorado, New Mexico, Nebraska, Florida, North and South Dakota) partially compensating for the lost 1890 returns. In a period of rapid migration and population growth these form an important directory of immigrants and their families, plotting their ages and origins.

Mortality schedules of returns of deaths during the year before each census, starting on 1 June and ending on 31 May 1849–50, 1859–60, 1869–70, 1879–80 and 1884–85, supply by state and county each person's age, sex, colour, marital status, birthplace, month of death, occupation, cause and duration of last illness, and because they predate civil registration, and supplement under-registration in church records, they are a vital genealogical resource, tying in with the decadal census household enumerations. In 1869 parental birthplaces began to be added, and in 1879 how long the deceased had been resident in the area of demise. The original documents are dispersed among individual state archives, the National Archives, and the library of the National Society of Daughters of the American Revolution, both in Washington, DC, though copies and indexes are also available in many libraries. The National Archives probably possesses the best collection of microfilm copies, and you can also hire them at family history centres and branch libraries.

State and local censuses were also taken periodically from 1623–1918, usually as a pretext for taxation or military purposes. They have been listed, with their whereabouts, in *The Source: A Guidebook of American Genealogy*, by A Eakle and J Cerny, and a number have been printed.

Veterans

Veterans' schedules listing names and ages of Revolutionary War pensioners (including women) alive in 1840 were filed by county and place of residence on the back of the main returns, under the name of the householder with whom they lived. These have been published in *A General Index to Census of Pensioners for Revolutionary or Military Service*.

Another incomplete series of Veterans' schedules dates from 1890, and concentrates on Union veterans and their widows, arranged by state or territory of abode and then by county or sub-division. Current postal address, rank, company, regiment or ship, date of enlistment and discharge, length of service and medical disabilities are recorded. Widows have the names of their deceased husbands written alongside. You can link the numbered schedules to those in the federal census, where they might be listed as living with married daughters or other relations.

The Veterans' schedules are in the National Archives, those for 1890 relating only to states running alphabetically from Louisiana to Wyoming, about half of Kentucky, and Washington, DC.

Slaves

Details about slaves are recorded on the back of the main returns under the name of the householder with whom they lived. Special schedules of slave owners were also filed in 1850 and 1860, listing age, sex and colour, and these can be linked to wills and probate inventories of the period in which slaves' names were mentioned. Like the Veterans' schedules, these can be found in the National Archives.

General advice on tackling the census

The census is a rich source of information, presenting a ten-yearly snapshot of several generations of a family spanning at least half a century, from which you can discover the changing size and age structure of a household, track its members from infancy and childhood until they took up work, married and set up households of their own, into which their parents might move as elderly dependants. You can determine the relative proximity of family units dotted down a street, or their dispersal about the town or wider area, the social neighbourhoods in which they moved and the variety of employments they followed. You can calculate approximately when people married, gave birth and died. Census personal and place-name indexes have removed a lot of the speculation from searches, making some years and places relatively easy to examine.

Present-day inhabitants' recollections of former residents may provide vital clues about why and when they left and their destinations, particularly if overseas, so do not forget to go forwards as well as backwards making full use of what you have found.

- Always search every household in an enumeration district for others of the same surname, and where they are found with people of a different surname there might still be a family connection by marriage. Servants and employees might also be kinsmen, so always note down their names too.
- The census does not tell you how long a person had been in the household, nor about multiple or seasonal occupations at other times of the year, or between censuses. The household might therefore have been atypically swollen or shrunken on census night by visitors or absentees.
- You may find your forebear listed by an unfamiliar forename, rather than that by which he or she was known, enumerators being instructed to record only the first name and then initials.
- When family relationships and marital status are given you can discover those of particular people at a given date, eliminating the need for any further research if circumstantial identification of an ancestor can be discarded, or there are several likely candidates to be sorted out.
- If you are unsure about a birth registration, especially where the name was a common one, the census provides a clue to the approximate year and birthplace, and to parents' names. As other children might be listed the birth certificate of a sibling will give the mother's maiden name which you can then use as a checking point against possible indexed birth entries of your direct ancestor.
- Children dying before adulthood may also be tracked via the census, though it will not include births and deaths during inter-censal periods. Large gaps between children's ages may indicate movement away or mortality.
- Birthplaces also reveal the distances and surprising frequency with which families travelled; always have a look at the appropriate returns of a given birthplace not only for your direct ancestor and the work he or she undertook, but for other relatives, who remained there.

- A wife may have moved to a new neighbourhood before marriage, often accompanying her parents and siblings, so whilst her birthplace tells you where she originally came from, it is worth looking for the rest of her family near her married home once you know her maiden name from her marriage certificate or child's birth certificate. The birthplace of her eldest child is also a good indicator of where her parents might be living as daughters often went to the mother's home for their first confinement.

- Ages, based on the householder's information, may be inconsistently given each decade. The same is true of birthplaces, especially when the head changed, elderly kinfolk were involved, or there was a big difference between a married couple's ages. But if you examine contemporary and earlier returns of those places you may well pick up other branches and generations of the family, including your ancestor in his or her pre-marital parental home. Given birthplaces of aunts and uncles may have been applicable to the parents too.

- Sometimes a person was enumerated a long way from his or her place of origin, and the nearest town rather than the actual birthplace was recorded, because the head of household or enumerator could not spell it.

- Sometimes birthplaces were written phonetically or in dialect form, making them difficult to decipher, apart from knowing the county, so a gazetteer or map can often help, or pronouncing the word as seen.

- As birthplaces are recorded by county a gazetteer should help identify specific places, a contemporary directory or map the correct names for streets and houses.

- If you cannot find your ancestor but there are others of the same surname and generation in the area, look for him or her in the census of their birthplaces in the same year. They might be enumerated together in the same parental household a decade earlier.

- It is a good idea to explore surrounding enumeration districts, as people did not move far; besides, urban enumeration boundaries were frequently drawn down the middle of a street, opposite neighbours being listed under different districts. In rural areas you can quickly skim several districts, taking care always to note down each community, and marking them out on a local map to show the radius you have covered around your main focus of interest.

- Birthplaces of local people following the same trade or employment as your ancestor may be a clue to his, as group migration or recruitment might have occurred.

- If the address you have selected is not sufficiently close to a census year you may have to obtain a birth certificate of a younger or older sibling, a death certificate, consult other contemporary listings, or try an earlier or later census. This is where county or district census indexes come into their own as they pick up itinerants and temporary residents as well as pinpointing surname clusters, and if you are lucky at least one of the census years you need will have been indexed.

- The handwriting of census returns often leaves a lot to be desired. Spelling of surnames and forenames may be idiosyncratic, phonetic or indecipherable. In Welsh returns they may be a poor translation of the vernacular. Microfilm copies take no account of nuances of handwriting pressure and overwriting in the original script, those for 1841 and 1861 being notably poor. The film itself might be a strain to read especially if the handwriting was faint or indistinct to begin with. By enlarging or decreasing magnification you can render a particular word legible; look for its clearer occurrence elsewhere, write it down exactly as you see it, or take a photocopy for analysis at home.

- Sometimes pages were filmed twice or missed, and if you are in any doubt ask to search the original enumerators' books.

- There are numerous people whose names do not feature at all in the census, and the accuracy and reliability of given details depended entirely on the honesty and knowledge of the informants, which may explain why some appear so contradictory and misleading.

- In Wales, you may come across people who are obviously identical but recorded under different surnames in a sequence of returns. This may be explained by the patronymic custom, still to be found in remoter communities in the late nineteenth century. As the population was relatively small people should be easily identified from the names of their habitations, which like their personal names, may be left in the Welsh original, and from the details about other members of the family sharing the household.

8

LOCATING INDIVIDUALS IN TIME AND PLACE WITHIN THE BRITISH ISLES

If you fail to find people in the census at an expected address there may be other sources to help locate them, then or in inter-censal years.

———— Registers of voters ————

The publication theoretically recording the name and address of every adult male after about 1884 is the annual electoral register, but alas the series is not fully continuous nor complete, as many were destroyed. Annual registers of voters in Parliamentary elections have been published since 1832, except in 1916, 1917, and 1940–44. In 1832 the franchise was widened from forty-shilling freeholders to include copyholders and leaseholders of property worth £10 a year, tenants at will (i.e. dependent on the goodwill of the landlord) paying £50 a year in rent in the shires and £10 householders in boroughs, with the result that the electorate now embraced tenant farmers and shopkeepers. Later statutes of 1867 and 1884 extended it even further until virtually all males over twenty-one could vote. Similar acts were passed for Scotland and Ireland. By their nature the earlier registers are selective, and not until 1918 were women over thirty able to vote, the age limit being lowered to twenty-one in 1928; in 1918 too the property qualification was abolished, the right to vote being based on six months' residence or occupation of business premises worth £10 a year.

The Family Records Centre in London has an incomplete set of electoral registers for English and Welsh counties and boroughs between 1872 and for the whole of the British Isles for the past year, 1995–6 in the public search room of the ONS, at The Centre. British Library holdings are patchy from 1832, though complete for 1937 and 1938 and from 1947 onwards. Many are on mircofilm. *Electoral Registers since 1832; and Burgess Rolls*, by J Gibson and C Rogers, is a handlist to known English, Welsh and Scottish lists and their disposition, including rosters relating to local government elections from 1888, and to borough electors from 1835 onwards (in which qualified married women occupiers were named after 1869). There are electoral lists for Ireland in the Irish National Archives, in Dublin.

To 1915 the electoral registers are arranged by constituency, ward and polling district, then township, listing alphabetically by qualification the allotted number, surname, forename, actual and qualifying address of every voter; from 1918 they are organised alphabetically by street or road, and then by voter, making them less easily handled. Voters absent in the armed forces were separately listed in their home Parliamentary divisions after 1918. You need to know the town or parish where a person lived or was qualified to vote in order to locate his address, which may be incompletely recorded, whilst lodgers and other short-term residents may not appear at all.

The qualifying inclusion date was October, for publication the following February and entries remained valid until the next edition. During the intervening period voters might die or move away, so you would be better advised to consult a register for the year after a census for a specific address.

Another problem is that constituency boundaries changed from time to time so you may not always find an address in the same electoral division. Changes up to 1971 can be located, with maps, in *Boundaries of Parliamentary Constituencies, 1885–1972*, by FWS Craig.

Nonetheless the registers do reflect the nature of voting qualification, identify resident and non-resident voters, change of property ownership and occupancy, the first and last date of a person's appearance at a given address, newly qualified occupiers, and from 1951 people reaching the minimum age during the year (including birthdate from 1971, when the threshold was lowered to eighteen). You can also plot surname distribution and family groups.

Landowners

Another useful directory of addresses around a census year is *Return of Owners of Land of One Acre and Upwards*, published in 1875 for England and Wales, in 1874 for Scotland, and in 1876 for Ireland. Copies can be found in many libraries of the county listings of owners' names, addresses, extent and nature of the land, and gross estimated rental.

— Trade and commercial directories —

Trade and commercial directories are also useful in that they were devised to help traders and merchants advertise and meet their markets by circulating a list of potential suppliers, distributors and customers, and to promote local industry and commerce. The earliest directories, mainly confined to naming private residents and merchants, were printed in the late seventeenth century, and by the end of the next century competing publishers had covered almost every county and large town. Prominent among these was the annual *Post Office London Directory*, dating from 1800. The first telephone directory was issued in 1880.

Good runs of London and provincial directories are held by the Guildhall Library, and Society of Genealogists, both in London, whilst local record offices and libraries generally have copies for their own areas. Scottish directories were compiled less often, but may be seen in the Scottish Record Office in Edinburgh and in regional offices, those for Ireland in the Irish National Archives, and National Library, both in Dublin. A number of facsimiles and microfiche copies of early directories are widely available for purchase or use.

You can discover the background history, purpose, dates of publication and scope of known directories from *Guide to National and Provincial Directories of England and Wales, excluding London, published before 1856*, by JE Norton, *British Directories: A Bibliography and Guide to Directories published in England and Wales (1850–1950) and Scotland (1773–1950)*, by G Shaw and A Tipper, and *The Directories of London, 1677–1977*, by PJ Atkins.

How they were compiled

Some publications had a short life, as they were costly to produce and market, ruining their promoters before their expenses could be recouped. Publication costs were partly borne by local advertisers and subscribers. The publishers generally relied on local agents to collect their information, and no payment was asked for a single entry, though further ones might attract a charge.

Each edition was about a year out of date and, although regularly revised and updated, a number were often little more than reprints. Although rival publishers lifted from each other's work, you can still find diverse entries in those years when several publishers produced volumes for the same places. Some of the stolen names and addresses were themselves out of date. Thus the reliability of addresses may be questionable, range and quality of content depending on the purpose of the compiler, the integrity of his agents, and the response of the public.

Listing only householders, the directories are not a complete population listing, especially in urban centres of high shift and properties of multi-occupancy, nor will agricultural labourers, domestic servants, other employees and lodgers be mentioned. Some addresses are omitted altogether, by choice, error or for other reasons. The absence of or alterations to street naming and numbering may also present problems, even in late nineteenth-century editions.

Provincial directories

Each county volume was divided alphabetically into hundreds and then parishes, or by town, village and hamlet. Other directories were devoted to a single city and its hinterland, and still others combined several contiguous counties in one book. Every place was prefaced by a short topographical description, describing the type of farming or industry carried on there, and population total. Names of major landowners, descent of relevant manors, church history, patron and present incumbent of the living, tithe and glebe income, foundation dates of denominational chapels, local charities and trust funds, and endowed schools, were all chronicled. Names of local public and parochial officers, details of postal, transport and carrier services, market days or date of any annual fair were followed by a list of names and addresses of private residents, giving rank and profession if applicable, plus the names and addresses of professional and trades-people, farmers and innkeepers. Later directories also provided a throwaway map of the district, which has seldom survived. The map or preface will indicate the distance from the nearest market town, and main thoroughfares, thus giving clues to likely migration direction.

As might be expected, directories of larger towns and cities are much more detailed. The first, for the City of London in 1677, was followed by regular editions from 1734, the earliest provincial town to be covered being Birmingham in 1763. The volumes often take in the countryside around them, so you need to check the table of contents for places out-side the town boundaries. Some contained a town plan, often predating the large-scale Ordnance Survey maps of the mid-nineteenth century.

London directories

The bulky *Post Office London Directories* were divided into sections; the *commercial directory* listed alphabetically the names, addresses and employment of people engaged in the professions or in trade, giving the name of the company or firm to which they were attached; the *court directory* listed town and country addresses of private residents; the *official directory* set out alphabetically people in government or legal offices; the *street directory* gave the principal London streets in alphabetical order, with the names and occupations of householders ranged sequentially by house number, indicating where the street intersected with others, sites of public buildings and churches or chapels; the *trade and professional directory* was organised alphabeti-cally, related occupations being cross-referenced under each heading (where two trades were carried on by the same person only one entry usually appeared, an asterisked note explaining dual employment); the *law directory* contained names and business addresses of judges and official staff in London and the provinces, including the police, barristers, solicitors and attorneys, proctors, notaries public, patent agents, district registrars, sheriffs and their officers, shorthand writ-ers, law booksellers and stationers; the *Parliamentary directory* listed peers and members, their country and town residences, constituencies and clubs, with a corresponding index of constituencies; the *city, clerical and parochial directory* recorded the names of civic officials, parish churches and other denominational places of worship, names of incumbents, officiating ministers and parish clerks, the titles of Poor Law Unions and their officers; finally, a *banking directory* outlined titles and registered offices of banks in London and throughout the United Kingdom. A map, on the scale of four inches to the mile, was usually attached for use with the street directory. There was also a section devoted to 'too late names' for people returning completed forms after the deadline.

What you can learn

Such directories provide a fascinating time capsule of a community, tracing its changing social and commercial structure, growth and development, as well as enabling you to track continuity of residence, local and regional surname distribution over time. You can plot a person's movements, diversity or continuity of employment, and hopefully an address to follow up in the census, bearing in mind that not everyone lived where they worked. Occasionally traders were listed twice under their various occupations, especially if they were connected with the sale of food, but sometimes a person carried out several quite distinct occupations. Given occupations may also vary from what was listed in the census or on a birth or death certificate. Street listings reveal the personality of adjoining streets or places. You can find more about ownership and property values in parish rate books.

People in public life

Annual court directories, like *Kelly's Handbook to the Titled, Landed and Official Classes*, published annually since 1874, *Who's Who*, from 1849 and *Who was Who*, from 1897, contain potted biographies, current addresses, clubs and hobbies submitted by people prominent in social, academic and political life. A cumulative index to the last two up to 1996, is available on CD ROM.

Occupational directories

Another type of directory began to appear in the mid-nineteenth century, specialising in certain occupations, sometimes covering a single town or city, or particular nationality. You can find out about published directories from *British Genealogical Bibliographies: Occupational Sources for Genealogists*, by SA Raymond. Annual professional directories listing practitioners in the law (from 1775), church (from 1836), and medicine (from 1847) were imitated during the course of the nineteenth century by similar volumes for newer professions such as dentistry and civil engineering. The founding dates and registered offices of their societies and associations can be traced in *Directory of British Associations and Associations in Ireland*, edited by SPA and AJW Henderson, or in *Associations and Professional Bodies of the United Kingdom*, edited by J Ramscar. Each association or society will have good runs of directories of past and present members, but their libraries are not always open to the public, although the staff may be willing to undertake short searches for you among these and other records in their custody. Limited collections are held in Guildhall Library and the Society of Genealogists.

Each profession or trade, on forming its regulatory body, determined a code of conduct and qualification for membership and fellowship; candidates might be admitted on passing professional examinations, be nominated or elected, or pay an annual subscription to join. The preface will normally give an outline of terms and conditions of membership. The entries are usually arranged alphabetically and summarise each member's education or relevant training, career, and current address, based on his own submission. When a name disappears look at the endmatter for a list of deceased members, which may reveal date of death. However, parentage is not given, nor date of birth, information which may be forthcoming from the records of the professional organisation itself, the place of education or formal training.

Newspapers

By scanning a sequence of directories you can track a person's entire career, checking a local newspaper for an obituary or funeral notice once the date of death is established. You can consult *Willing's Press Guide* or *The Times Tercentenary Handlist of English and Welsh Newspapers* for details of publications of the period. Microfilm copies may be found in the local library or record office, often accessed via a personal name index. There is an almost complete set of newspapers and periodicals for the United Kingdom and Ireland from 1700 in the British Library Newspaper Library, at Colindale, London. Newspapers will also tell you what people were reading about at the time, report local events, publish notices and trade advertisements.

Rate books

The name and address of every householder has been listed in parish rate books from the mid-eighteenth century. Rates were levied for a mixture of purposes at a fixed amount in the pound, based on the yearly value of occupied property. Surviving books should be deposited in county record offices, but rarely are they street-indexed or complete.

The books are arranged by road and street, and include under column headings each assessed property number, the names of the occupier and owner, a property description, its name or site, estimated extent, gross estimated rental, rateable value of the occupied land and buildings, the rate payable in the pound and the date of annual or half-yearly collection, citing any accrued arrears. Because occupiers are identified with their properties, they may give street addresses not specified or unclear in the census. Deaths and changes of occupancy or ownership since the last collection are indicated by marginal notes against the entries. Fluctuating values suggest property alterations, demolitions and enlargements, houses divided into apartments or consolidated under single occupancy. The books can also be used to date newly erected houses, street developments and name changes.

Although street numbering was started in the City of London in 1767, it was not generally introduced in provincial towns and cities until about 1847. Where a street name was changed or the numbering scheme altered it may be unclear whether a person continued to occupy the same premises over a number of years; by noting down the names of his immediate neighbours a fairly reliable impression of continuity may be gained, as it was extremely unlikely that they would all have moved away. Houses on street corners may also prove difficult to identify, listed inconsistently under one street or the other.

Rate collectors sometimes altered their routes, so the order in which streets appear may not be consistent from one year to the next, and because they lack street indexes you may have to search books covering several districts when boundaries were adjusted.

Maps and photographs

Electoral registers, directories and parish rate books can be used in conjunction with maps and town plans to plot exactly where your forebears lived. It is fun, too, to look at contemporary photographs to see what the property looked like, and compare it with how it is today. Most local libraries and record offices have substantial collections.

Maps worth looking for

There are three main series of maps of especial use to the family historian: tithe maps, Ordnance Survey maps and Valuation Office record sheet plans. Until the second quarter of the nineteenth century most parishioners in England and Wales contributed a tenth (tithe) of the annual produce of their land or stock nourished by it to the tithe owner (usually the parish priest). On agreement between owners of most of the land or by resolution of the largest landowner, a number of parishes had already commuted payment in kind to money when common land was enclosed. A list of Parliamentary enclosure awards and maps is in *A Domesday of English Enclosure Acts and Awards*, by

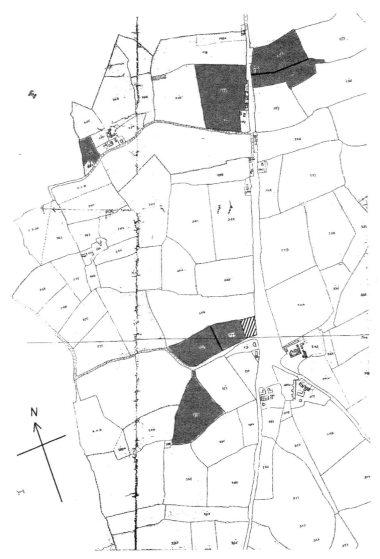

Figure 6 Tithe map of Great Finborough 1841, Suffolk, Meshech Chaplin farmed here until his death in 1849, aged 61. Reproduced by permission of Suffolk Record Office.

   properties occupied by Meshech Chaplin

    Meshech Chaplin's house

WE Tate. The remaining parishes (about seventy-nine per cent, or over 12,000) converted the tithe to a rent charge after the Tithe Commutation Act of 1836.

Between 1836 and 1852 professional tithe commissioners and their assistants visited each parish, hamlet and township to confirm the voluntary agreements reached by local landowners, or to draft a compulsory award. They drew up triplicate maps and plans of each place so that the rent charges could be fixed, based on land valuations and a seven-year average of the price of wheat, barley and oats. A list of surveyed districts can be found in *The Tithe Maps of England and Wales, A cartographic analysis and county-by-county catalogue*, by RJP Kain and RR Oliver. One map and written apportionment was lodged with the Tithe Office, later transferred to the Public Record Office, Kew, another with the diocesan registrar in case of future dispute, and the third was kept in the parish church. These last two copies are now usually in county record offices, to which were appended later revisions and revaluations perhaps not found in the Public Record Office version. A complete set of Welsh tithe maps and apportionments is kept at the National Library of Wales in Aberystwyth. It may be more convenient to look at local copies, and where one is in poor condition another might be better.

The maps were not all delineated to the same scale, but most were twenty-six-and-a-half, twenty, or thirteen inches to the mile, on which were marked out within the district boundaries the allotted number, size and shape of each affected plot, any waterways and roads. It is best to look first at the accompanying schedule or apportionment, summarising the date of agreement or award, and listing alphabetically under landowners the names of occupiers, map plot number, title and description of the land or premises, its state of cultivation, extent in acres, roods and perches, and amount of annual rent charge, and then find the number on the map. From the apportionment and map you can find the concentration, dispersal, central or marginal location of a person's property, its fertility, use and value, and proximity to water and land routes, whether the person was an owner/occupier or tenant, and who were the major landowners.

The entries are annotated with references to subsequent annexed amendments of altered apportionments when land was taken to construct railways or make way for suburban expansion.

In 1936 the rent charge was converted into a sixty-year annuity, paid by the landowner, and further maps were commissioned, but the charge was abolished in 1977. These maps and papers are also at the Public Record Office, Kew.

As the tithe commissioners' survey was undertaken close to the census years of 1841 or 1851 the maps and plans can be utilised to track down precisely where your antecedants lived, the latter census revealing current farm acreages and total workforce. Unfortunately not every occupier's name appears in the apportionment, especially if he or she was a sub-tenant or shared it with several other tenants. Secondly, property boundaries are not always accurately marked out, but 'first class' maps certified and sealed by the commissioners will be of higher quality than their working record sheets.

The map and apportionment complement extant county record office runs of parish lists of householders assessed to pay the Land Tax, which are particularly good from 1780 until 1832. They can also be used with parish rate books, and manorial rentals of tenants, whose dates and whereabouts can be gleaned from the Manorial Documents Register at the Royal Commission on Historical Manuscripts, in London.

Scotland

The survey of 1836 did not extend to Scotland, where teinds (a form of tithe) were levied in kind or money on proprietors of heritable property until abolished in 1925. Records of teinds may be found among family and estate papers, disputes and adjusted payments settled by the Teind Court and Commissioners in the Scottish Record Office, Edinburgh.

Ireland

As in England and Wales, a tithe was payable in Ireland until the second quarter of the nineteenth century. Tithe applotment books dating from about 1823–38 cover every barony, civil parish and its townlands, recording commutation based on the average price of wheat and oats over the seven years before 1823. The original books are in the National Archives of Ireland, in Dublin, those for the six northern counties being at the Public Record Office of Northern Ireland, Belfast, and on microfilm at the National Archives of Ireland. Microfilm copies are also held by the National Library, in Dublin.

The tithe books are incomplete surveys because certain types of land were exempt, but they yield the names of tenants in each townland, and in many cases those of immediate landlords. There is a surname index in the National Library giving by county the barony where a name was located, but you will then need to find the civil parish yourself. Because they long predate surviving census returns, central registration of births, marriages and deaths, and in some instances parish registers of baptism, marriage and burial, the tithe books are an important directory of individual people in time and place, and a guide to surname distribution and density.

Ordnance Survey maps and town plans

The tithe was the first large-scale survey of landownership and occupancy. The Ordnance Survey, set up in 1791, began to issue a series of official maps for England and Wales based on a standard scale of one inch to the mile, starting with Kent in 1801 and ending with the Isle of Man in 1873, when a thorough revision was commenced. Facsimiles of the first edition have been published by one or two commercial firms, and original maps are held in county record offices, local libaries, and in special cartography collections at the Public Record Office, Kew, the British Library in London, and at the Bodleian Library in Oxford, though a reader's ticket is required for the last three. The maps are immensely useful in showing place-names of villages, hamlets and towns, the geographic contours, topographical features, water and road networks of an area with which you might be unfamiliar, or which has since been drastically changed by urban encroachment, but they are not sufficiently detailed to permit identification of individual field-names and boundaries.

The survey was extended in 1840 and 1853 to furnish maps and town plans using scales of six inches and twenty-five inches to the mile respectively so that particular properties and field-names can be easily picked out. They were adopted by the Registrar General to demarcate census registration and sub-districts, but the other main purpose to which they were put was to assign hereditament (plot) numbers to every property during the general land valuation of England and Wales between 1910 and 1915, in preparation for a proposed (abortive) increment value duty. The resulting field books and record sheet plans of income tax districts are at the Public Record Office, Kew, to which there are index sheets on open access.

Because the plans and books relate to the years immediately before the First World War, and to every piece of private property, you have a unique insight into town and village layout, urban and rural housing conditions. The precise location of a place on the plan helps resolve problems of property name-changes. The plans and books form a bridge between the tithe maps produced less than three-quarters of a century earlier, and the communities we know today. You can look at contemporary photographs, track down estate agents' particulars of sale, sale catalogues and sale notices in county record offices or local newspapers from information given in the field books. Used in combination with the 1891 and previous censuses you can determine length and continuity of occupancy, the nature of any businesses run from the premises, and the size of household it accommodated, changes in size and land use since the tithe survey. You can also see how much property in a parish was concentrated in the hands of one or more families, and to whom it was let, kinsfolk or otherwise, how much they received by way of rents, and infer their influence over local affairs.

The scale of the record sheet plans, dating from 1880 to 1915, depended on population density, larger scale ones specifying street and road names as well as identifying larger buildings, and many were new revisions of urban and industrial centres. Occasionally you will find even bigger maps, up to a hundred-and-twenty-seven inches to the mile for some city centres, whilst others are enlarged for certain parts only. Each valuation unit (hereditament) was demarcated, shaded in and allocated a number in red ink, except for exempt Crown property and land owned by statutory and public utility companies (such as railways and canals).

The parish field books are organised sequentially by hereditament number, cited at the top of the page with its map reference, and any associated plot numbers. The valuation officers used parish rate books to extract names and addresses of owners and occupiers, the extent and rateable value of the properties, to which were added any unrated sites. There is a street index to the London books, but otherwise you need to find the appropriate record sheet plan first, locate the property number and then consult the field book.

Besides recording information taken from the rate books, the type of tenure was given (freehold, leasehold, yearly tenancy), annual rental, liability and amounts due for the land tax and tithe, liability for rates, insurance and repairs, and purchase price of the property if sold within twenty years up to 30 April 1909. There was a floor by floor description of the layout and function of each room, and a list of outbuildings, sometimes sketched on a plan before 1912; construction materials, type of roof, approximate age and present condition of the premises were also recorded, as well as recent expenditure on improvements or extensions. The property's gross market value, that of the site less buildings and timber, and total worth less fixed charges and any encumbrances were enumerated from which the assessable site value was calculated (site value less the cost of work undertaken to improve it by the owner).

The valuation (Domesday) books, prepared before the field books, are held in county record offices, with many of the initial working papers and draft record plans, except for volumes covering the City of London and Paddington (Westminster), which you can see at the PRO. They duplicate the field books, though building descriptions are excluded, and may give more specific addresses of non-occupying landowners.

National Farm Surveys

If the land was a farm you can also have a look in the county record office for land minute books kept by surveyors on behalf of the government between 1916 and 1918. Executive committees appointed by county War Agricultural Committees throughout England and Wales reported on land cultivation and efficiency of local farms and small-holdings. Correspondence, petitions and soldier labour books mention names of people who were tenant farmers, labourers or in 1918 deemed suitable for Army recruitment or listed for exemption because they were needed for essential work. Tenants threatened with eviction, fine or imprisonment for failing to raise their standards of husbandry or to convert grassland to arable are also identified, as well as women, aliens, soldiers and prisoners of war taken on to help.

In the PRO at Kew, is corresponding National Farm Survey material for England and Wales between 1940 and 1943, similarly collected with the intention of increasing wartime food production. The maps are of six inches or twelve-and-a-half inches to the mile, onto which the numbered plots of farms and farmland over five acres were marked. The returns, arranged by county and then alphabetically by parish, identify each farm, its owner's name and address and length of occupancy, with details of fruit, vegetables, hay and straw stocks, crops and grass, livestock and employed labour. A representative from the Ministry of Agriculture than made an inspection. His report commented on the condition and management of the farm, before grading it. Personal remarks on the farmer's age, health and ability might also be included. There are also parish lists drawn up in June 1941 giving the farm's full postal address, its acreage and owner's name. You can compare the two sets of wartime records for information on acreage, type of cultivation and manning levels a quarter of a century apart.

– Scottish Valuation Office records –

Scotland was divided up into twelve valuation districts by the Valuation Office in 1910 and the resulting record maps and field books have been deposited in the Scottish Record Office in Edinburgh, where you can also inspect the yearly Scottish valuation rolls beginning in 1855. These are organised under county or burgh, and list the landlord, tenant and occupier, name and value of every property, and some have been indexed. You can trace changes of occupancy and ownership by studying a sequence of rolls.

— The Primary Valuation of Ireland —

In Ireland, the Tenement Act of 1842 led to a countrywide valuation of every property as a prelude to assessment of tenants' contributions towards relief of paupers in Poor Law Unions. The printed county volumes and microfiche copies of *Primary Valuation of Ireland, 1848–64* (also known as Griffith's Valuation) can be seen in many larger libraries, and at the Society of Genealogists in London. The surname or householders' index, in the National Library, Dublin, notes by county the number of times a particular surname occurs in each barony, but not in individual townlands, though a comprehensive surname index is in preparation.

The county books, organised by barony, Poor Law Union and civil parish, give under headed columns a map reference number, name of each townland and its householders, their immediate lessors (landlords), a tenement description, including its extent, the rateable and annual value of the land and buildings, and their total annual value. Thus every landlord and householder is listed, but not every inhabitant. Householders of the same name residing in the same townland are distinguished by the father's name written alongside in brackets.

Because there are so few extant 1851 and 1861 Irish census returns, this valuation is invaluable as a guide to surname distribution and location of particular people, supplementing the tithe applotment books a quarter of a century earlier. As neither the 1901 nor 1911 census reveals exact birthplaces, the books can be utilised to show where a name was found within the county of birth fifty years before. Conversely, surname distribution in these two sets of books may enable you to find later family tenants of the same properties in 1901 and 1911. As they predate civil registration, the townlands and civil parishes indicate which churches and chapels might be appropriate places to look for baptisms, marriages and burials. You can also seek out title deeds for more information about sales and leases.

The National Archives of Ireland in Dublin, has an incomplete set of the valuation surveyors' original notebooks, house books, field books and tenure books, for southern Ireland, whilst those of the six northern counties are at the Public Record Office of Northern Ireland, Belfast.

They all give map references, the house books recording occupiers' names, the field books the size of each holding, and the tenure books the yearly rent and nature of occupancy (dated lease, or tenancy at will), which help anyone investigating estate papers or records at the Registry of Deeds in Dublin. They also note residential changes between valuation and final publication.

Other Valuation Office records

Subsequent cancelled land books and current land books, at the Land Valuation Office in Dublin or in the Public Record Office of Northern Ireland, also cite changes or ownership and occupancy from the Primary Valuation to the present day. Variations in the size and nature of the premises affecting valuation are outlined in the regular revisions. The books can help establish approximate year of death, movement out of area, or emigration. During the last decade of the nineteenth century a series of Land Acts allowed tenant-farmers to apply for subsidies to buy their land, so it could be passed on to the next generation, and you may therefore still be able to discover descendants living there today.

9

KNOWING YOUR SOURCES: WHERE AND WHAT THEY ARE AND HOW TO USE THEM

The major problem besetting all researchers at one time or another is knowing what source to look for, how to find it, and whether it will be of much use when they do. The family historian's focus is always on names, relationships, dates and places. Depending on the problem and period, and what is available, the sources you select will be those considered most likely to reveal vital events in a person's life, his relationship to others in his family, or where he and others of his surname lived at a specific date. Next, you have to discover the whereabouts of such records, if transcripts, microform copies or indexes exist, and what regulations are imposed for access to them.

So far most of your searches will have been in nineteenth- and twentieth-century centralised records, but as you progress you will need to search a variety of dispersed and locally kept archives for which there are no consolidated or comprehensive personal name indexes, nor any uniform or consistent scheme of classification.

What archives are

Archives are documentary or other material recordings of the decisions and activities of an individual or organisation. Initially kept where they were created, through time many were brought together under their original arrangement from a variety of places for preservation and future reference. Almost all run chronologically by date, by subject or area. Some which were in constant use have contemporary indexes, others were bundled up and rarely if ever opened again.

Searching these records may take time, but a disciplined approach to your research will save wasted hours later. Before you begin, therefore, you need to do some groundwork. A little preparatory reading and a well-thought-out search plan should ensure you find yourself in the right place.

What you have learned so far

Firstly, look at your family tree and assess what you already know. Are there any doubts about generation links? Why? Perhaps you failed to find a birth or baptism in the precise year, or at the predicted place, so you had to widen your search and have discovered several possible candidates. Did you try and track their later whereabouts, to see what became of them, to be sure that the one you think is correct actually survived to adulthood and did not marry another partner, alive when your own forebear married somewhere else? Did you examine wills of other family members for clues? Have you spotted information which you previously missed? What about forename, occupational and residential patterns in succeeding generations? If it is an elusive marriage, have you searched available indexes of the area and period? Have you scanned lists and indexes for people on the move? Sometimes you will have to rely on abstracts of documents which no longer exist, face conflicting or ambiguous statements about people bearing the same name at the same place and date, and have to exercise your own judgement about the connection between them if any. This is what makes the family jigsaw so challenging.

Drawing up a checklist

Think about the particular line you want to pursue, and list (in no special order) sources you think might help. Then find out what they actually contain, for what period and places, by reading up about them in textbooks or articles. These can be located via a library subject index, bibliography, source references and footnotes, indexes to relevant periodicals like *The Local Historian, Local History Magazine, Local Population Studies, Genealogists' Magazine, Family Tree*

Magazine, Family History News and Digest, and family history society journals. Current issues of periodicals are displayed in county record offices and local libraries. Have a look also at SA Raymond's series of county *British Genealogical Bibliographies, British Genealogical Periodicals: a Bibliography of their contents,* and *British Genealogy in Miscellaneous Journals: Supplement 1.* Although some articles and books may now be out of print, the background, content and utility of the records described will remain unchanged, if not further enhanced by personal name indexes or other records which were not then available.

Prioritise on your checklist the sources and venues most likely to contain what you are looking for, and restrict yourself to a generation at a time. A telephone call to each repository will quickly establish if the records are where you think for the years in question, and if not staff should be able to tell you their present whereabouts.

—— How archives are grouped ——

Records fall into three main groups: state, church and private. State archives divide into those of central and local government and courts of law, those of the church into those of the two Provinces (of Canterbury and York), dioceses, archdeaconaries, rural deaneries and parishes, and finally there are private archives, including those of semi-official public bodies, family and estate papers of major landowners and records of businesses.

National archives of the United Kingdom

The archives of United Kingdom government departments and agencies, and of the central courts of law of England and Wales, are in the Public Record Office at Kew. Access is by renewable reader's ticket. Self-service microfilms of the census, authenticated nonconformist registers, registered copy wills and administrations, some death duty registers and complete indexes to them and to the Registrar General's Miscellaneous Foreign Returns, are at The Family Records Centre, in London, with indexes of The Office for National Statistics.

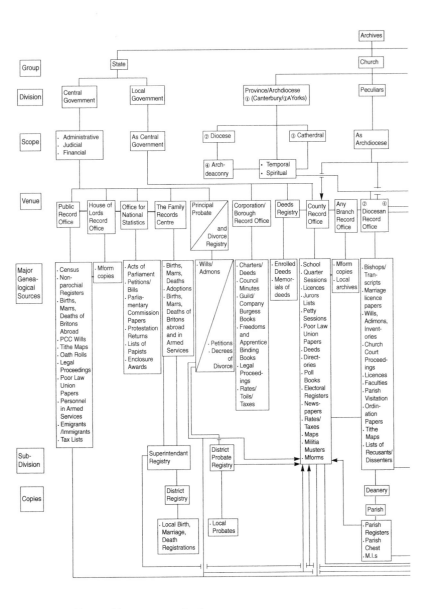

Figure 8 How archives are organised

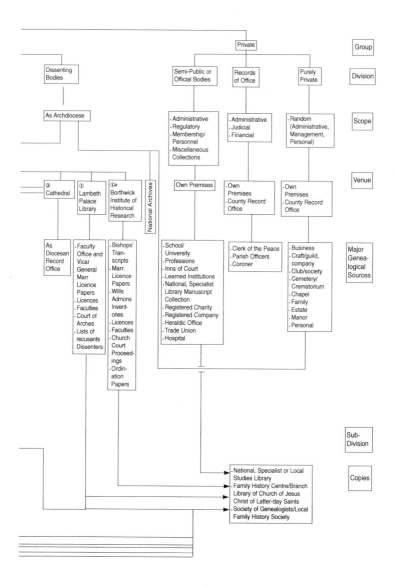

How to find what you want

There is no union personal name index to the public records, none of which were created or intended for the genealogist. The documents are organised by letter codes, class and piece numbers, to which there are class or descriptive lists briefly indicating their content and period. Some have been summarised in printed and indexed calendars. A published *Public Record Office Current Guide*, in three parts, is also widely available on microfiche. The third part consists of a subject index, the second gives brief accounts of the content and period of each class, listed sequentially, and the first contains administrative histories of the various departments and their records.

The archives are normally closed to the public for thirty years, though some material is immediately accessible; other confidential or nationally sensitive documents may be heavily weeded, or be withheld, like the census returns, for up to a hundred years, or until a prescribed period after the last dated entry in a book. You may also be asked to sign an undertaking that your research is for private study only. There are archives dating from the Domesday Book of 1086 to the present day chronicling the actions and decisions of people from all backgrounds. If you want to trace records about soldiers, sailors, merchant seamen, emigrants, immigrants, ships' passengers, lawyers, railway workers, Metropolitan Police, coastguards, customs and excise officers, civil servants, Crown employees and Royal Warrant holders, apprentices, nurses, teachers, dissenters, coroners' inquests, trials in the Assize courts, convicts and transportees, bankrupts, civil litigants, changes of name, taxation, records of the superior probate court before 1858, Poor Law Unions, land ownership, tithes, enclosures, births, marriages and deaths of Britons overseas, then there should be something here for you. The PRO produces a rich assortment of free records information leaflets and family fact sheets directed mainly at the family historian, drawing attention to record classes of greatest value on specific topics.

Scottish national archives

The two branches of the Scottish Record Office, in HM General Register House, and West Register House, Edinburgh, hold Scottish national archives. A reader's ticket is required. The Historical Search Room, HM General Register House, holds legislative and administrative records of

Scotland before the Union with England in 1707, those of the central and many local courts, kirk session minutes relating to Church of Scotland congregations, archives of other denominations, testamentary material from all of the Scottish commissariots, registers of sasines and deeds, valuation rolls, taxation lists, burgh records, those of customs and excise officers, and military musters, pedigrees, family, business and estate papers. West Register House concentrates on modern government department records and has a good map collection.

National archive repositories for Ireland

The National Archives of Ireland, in Dublin, and the Public Record Office of Northern Ireland, Belfast, are the places of deposit for material relating to their jurisdictions. Both issue reader's tickets. Besides housing surviving census returns, the National Archives of Ireland holds some parish registers of the Church of Ireland, marriage licence bonds, wills and administrations, tithe applotment books, Primary Valuation and various taxation lists, army and militia papers, pedigrees, and microfilmed material held by other repositories or in parish churches. The Public Record Office of Northern Ireland covers the six northern counties and has microfilm copies of sources kept in Dublin which date before 1922, as well as some parish registers, wills, land and manorial records, army and militia lists, family, business and estate papers.

National archives of the United States of America

The National Archives, Washington, DC, holds the following freely accessible federal material: the census, mortality schedules, records about Indian tribes, land transactions and awards, naturalisations of immigrants, incoming passenger lists, passport applications, births, marriages and deaths of American citizens abroad, details about government employees, military and naval personnel and veterans, their widows and dependants, coastguards, and wills of residents of British Columbia. They are subject to a seventy-five year closure rule, and many lack personal name indexes. There are self-service microfilm facilities on a first-come first-served basis, but many of the microfilms can also be inspected at National Archive Regional Archives, each of which serves several states. You can arrange to borrow them for more convenient use in other state libraries and research institutions within each region. Details about services and holdings are summarised in a series of publications, the best of which are probably *Guide to Genealogical Research in the National Archives* and *Using Records in the National Archives for Genealogical Research* and you can find more information and addresses on the Internet.

English local government records

Records of English local civil government are housed in county record offices, observing pre-1974 boundaries. As well as offering a safe place of deposit for historical material they continue to receive new acquisitions from councils and numerous local bodies and organisations, parishes and individuals. Many now have insufficient accommodation to admit searchers without an appointment, so branch offices have sprung up accumulating records for their own vicinity, with microform copies of other popular sources kept in the chief repository. The opening hours vary, some having a late-evening extension, or a Saturday service. Admission to record offices in over thirty counties is by a renewable county archive research network reader's ticket, obtainable on production of personal identification. It is valid at each contributing office, shown on every visit, surrendered when you begin to order documents and handed back to you at the end of the day. A few offices charge for the ticket and require two passport-sized photographs. Other offices operate independent schemes, whilst some have no restriction except that you sign the daily visitors' book.

County record offices

A typical county record office will contain the following:

- filmed copies of census records of the county;
- the International Genealogical Index;
- church registers and other parish records;
- nonconformist chapel records;
- marriage licence allegations and bonds;
- published indexes;
- parish histories;
- typescript and published work about the area;
- Poor Law Union material since 1834;
- wills and administrations;
- collections of family and estate papers;

- local authority cemetery registers, transcipts;
- maps;
- directories;
- electoral registers;
- poll books;
- newspapers;
- school records;
- rate books;
- tax assessment lists;
- County Police records;
- County council minutes;
- manorial documents;
- pedigrees and biographies;
- Petty and Quarter Sessions rolls;
- coroner's records;
- county court files;
- old deeds and charters;
- estate agents' sales catalogues;
- deposited records of local businesses, societies and organisations;
- a series of personal name and topographical indexes.

You can find out about many of the name indexes in the British Isles from *Unpublished Personal Name Indexes in Record Offices and Libraries*, compiled by J Gibson, updated in *Marriage, Census and Other Indexes for Family Historians*, by the same author with E Hampson.

A number of offices offer a limited research service. Most have free handouts about their principal holdings and some publish guides for family historians.

Corporation and borough archives

Corporation and borough record offices specialise in civic and town administrative and judicial material: deeds, charters, maps and town plans, apprenticeship and freedom registers of guilds, livery companies or burgesses, rates, rentals, tolls and taxes, some of which extend back to the Middle Ages. Access to these may be limited or only by appointment.

The National Library of Wales

The National Library, at Aberystwyth, is the place of deposit for Welsh public records, being mainly those of the civil, criminal and equity proceedings of the Great Sessions, but it houses much provincial, parochial and diocesan manuscript material, including microfilms of all the Welsh census returns up to 1891, bishops' transcripts of parish registers, nonconformist records, marriage licence allegations and bonds, wills proved in Welsh local ecclesiastical courts before 1858, later registered copy wills, manorial documents, maps, deeds, personal, family and estate papers, pedigrees, newspapers, and a number of parish and parochial documents to which there is a published guide. A reader's ticket is required.

Scottish regional centres

Scottish regional archive offices and libraries cover an area wider than a county; they contain local administrative archives, including school records, and those relating to poor relief, plus newspapers, electoral registers, maps, local history collections, transcripts, indexes and microfilms of the census, Old Parochial Registers of baptism, marriage and burial and other parish records.

Local Irish resources

Ireland is served by a government-funded network of more than thirty local history and heritage centres under the aegis of the Irish Genealogical Project in Dublin, set up in the 1980s. Its aims are to produce computerised indexes of parish records, and a commercial research service, as public access is not permitted. The project has been expanded to take in tithe applotment books, the Primary Valuation, civil records of births, marriages and deaths, gravestone inscriptions, and the 1901 and 1911 census returns.

American regional facilities

Individual American state archives, county courthouses, local libraries and historical societies, concentrating on local sources like land deeds and wills as well as microfilm copies of church registers, gravestone inscriptions, and other parochial material often overlap in their catchments so that you do not always have to travel to the state capital to carry out your searches.

Church records of England and Wales

Diocesan record offices, formerly the custodians of ecclesiastical archives such as records of the church courts, bishops' and archdeacons' visitations, licences, faculties, wills and bishops' transcripts of parish registers, have in many cases been merged with county record offices, though Lambeth Palace Library, in London, retains archives for the Province of Canterbury (except for probate material, in the Public Record Office), and the Borthwick Institute of Historical Research, in York, is responsible for the archives of the Province of York. Unfortunately diocesan boundaries do not always correspond with those of counties, so some ecclesiastical archives will be held in a county record office away from their immediate area. The National Library of Wales holds archives of Welsh dioceses.

Denominational libraries

Denominational libraries, besides possessing a fine collection of printed books and periodicals, will often have special archive collections and indexes relating to congregations, individual members and clergy.

Churches and chapels

Churches and chapels have custody of current working documents and minutes relating to parochial affairs, some retaining historical records such as baptism, marriage and burial registers, most of which have now been transferred to county record offices.

Private collections

Specialist archives include those accumulated by large public or limited companies and businesses, assurance societies, places of learning and professional training, trade and professional associations, private clubs, charitable foundations and trusts, historical and genealogical societies, and museums, a number of which may not be opened to the public or grant limited access. Nevertheless specific searches can often be undertaken on your behalf.

Society of Genealogists and family history societies

Organisations you ought to find helpful are the Society of Genealogists, in London, and your local family history society. A floor guide is issued to first-time users of the library of the Society of Genealogists, which is largely self-service. The card catalogue is divided into English counties or by country and then into six subject areas, which enable you to locate the shelf marks of individual items or to requisition them from the staff. There are:

- current editions of the International Genealogical Index, FamilySearch, British Isles Genealogical Register;
- microform indexes of births, marriages and deaths registered in England, Wales, Guernsey, Isle of Man, Scotland, Australia and New Zealand;
- paper- or microform copies of almost nine thousand British and overseas parish registers, an alphabetical published list of which, arranged by country and then county, is regularly updated;
- extensive collections of copies of gravestone inscriptions;
- publications about dissenters and immigrant congregations;
- printed school and university registers;
- census, marriage, marriage licence and probate personal name indexes;
- family, parish and county histories;
- published sources, passenger lists and biographies of emigrants and overseas residents;
- printed biographies and genealogies of nobility and gentry, peerages, books about royalty and heraldry;
- directories of professional people and officers in the Armed Services;
- trade directories;
- printed registers of apprentices and freemen of livery companies, indexes to masters and apprentices;
- poll books of voters;
- serial publications of kindred societies;
- reference books and guides.

Its special collections include the great card index, containing about three million names drawn from random disparate printed and manu-script sources, which is a good place to look if you are desperate. To find a specific person or event, or plot surname distribution try:

- Boyd's county and miscellaneous Marriage Indexes;
- Boyd's Inhabitants of London, containing more than 60,000 family group sheets of names extracted from City livery company records of apprentices and freemen, parish registers, wills and heraldic visitation pedigrees between 1530 and 1689;
- Boyd's London burial index;
- other specialist catalogued indexes. For example, the microfilmed Bernau index contains names of over four million suitors and

sworn witnesses extracted from Chancery and Exchequer of proceedings, actions in the Courts of Requests and Star Chamber, and other archives in the Public Record Office or elsewhere.

Family history societies concentrate on sources relating to their area and often have microform copies of centralised records such as birth, marriage and death indexes and the census, the 1881 census index and the International Genealogical Index for their county. Many of the societies have pages on the Internet.

Genealogical Society of Utah Library

In Salt Lake City, the library of the Genealogical Society of Utah is open to the public as well as operating a worldwide network of family history centres and branch libraries. *The Library: A Guide to the LDS Family History Library,* by J Cerny and E Elliott, summarises the extent of its holdings, which can also be accessed on compact disk on FamilySearch via the Family History Library Catalog. You are thus able to conveniently research ancestors in many different countries or who crossed state or ocean frontiers, without the expense or delay of hiring a local searcher or having to visit a number of archive offices. However, some resources, by their very nature, serve only as finding aids, for example indexes to births, marriages and deaths.

Genealogical Society of Utah research outlets

Whereas archives are unique and cannot be borrowed, paper- or micro-form copies are widely dispersed, for simultaneous use by readers in different places, most of which can be loaned out. The Society has the largest genealogical collection in the world, laying emphasis especially on American, Canadian, British and European sources, and you can borrow microforms of its listed records at any of its branch libraries and family history centres. You can also hire microfilms of many of the national archives. Access is free unless what you want is held off the premises, for which you pay a monthly or three-monthly hire fee. Look in your local telephone directory under 'Church of Jesus Christ of Latter-day Saints' for the nearest centre. A complete list of addresses of centres throughout the United Kingdom is obtainable from the British Isles Family History Service Centre, in Sutton Coldfield in the West Midlands. It is a good idea to telephone the centre beforehand as they open for limited periods and space may be small.

National Register of Archives

The National Register of Archives, part of the Royal Commission on Historical Manuscripts in London, is a central clearing house of information on the manuscript holdings of local record offices, national and university libraries, museums and other organisations in the United Kingdom and elsewhere. You can find the whereabouts of private archives, family and estate papers of major landowners outside the public records. You can search its computerised subject, personal, business and locations indexes to the numbered catalogues of the various collections on the Internet or by personal visit during opening hours. The search room also contains the Manorial Documents Register for England and Wales, and printed guides and catalogues of major repositories and libraries here and overseas. The Scottish counterpart is at West Register House, Edinburgh, the Irish Manuscripts Commission being in Dublin.

Using your local library

Try a large local library for general reference works and publications about your area, current local electoral registers, United Kingdom telephone directories, back-numbers of certain national and local newspapers and magazines. You can request books from elsewhere using the inter-library loan service. There should also be an on-line catalogue indexed under subject, author and title, and library staff will advise you about other networked on-line services. A local studies library, devoted to published material about the county or region, local newspapers, parish histories, maps, old photographs, serial publications, directories and microforms of archives in the county or Public Record Office, the International Genealogical Index, transcripts and indexes of parish registers and wills, is also worth seeking out. The opening hours may be longer than in the record office, everything is generally self-service, and the building itself more central. You can undertake a lot of preparatory work using the books and microform services in a library before visiting a record office, or even occasionally use it as a substitute. Sometimes, however, the local studies library is attached to the county record office.

National and internationally known libraries

National libraries, like the British Library in London, the National Library of Wales at Aberystwyth, those in Edinburgh and in Dublin, and the Linen Hall Library, Belfast, all require a reader's ticket or personal identification. They publish printed, microfiche or on-line catalogues of their holdings, which include important artificial manuscript collections made by scholars and antiquarians. The first two, with the Bodleian Library, Oxford, University Archives at Cambridge, and Trinity College, Dublin, are copyright libraries in which is deposited a copy of every book published in the United Kingdom. Besides its printed books, the British Library has departments for official publications, manuscripts, prints and drawings, maps, a newspaper library, India Office and Oriental Collections, and the National Sound Archive. The National Library of Wales, too, has a fine department of prints, drawings and maps.

The American Library of Congress in Washington, DC, has a local history and genealogy section, to which there is a family name index, and books can be ordered elsewhere by inter-library loan, or can be purchased from University Microfilms. It publishes a regularly updated *National Union Catalog of Manuscript Collections*, to which there are periodic indexes containing citations to names, places, subjects and occupations. The Newberry Library, Chicago, and the New England Historic Genealogical Library, Boston, also have renowned family historical stocks. The Library of Congress and many state libraries have made their catalogues available on-line.

—— Research planning: reading up ——

Here is a selection of useful guides to the whereabouts, contact telephone numbers, opening hours, search regulations and summarised contents of record repositories and libraries. All of them are regularly revised and updated so make sure you use the latest edition.

- *Record Repositories in Great Britain, A geographical directory*, issued by the Royal Commission on Historical Manuscripts, contains a handy list of institutions in the United Kingdom holding archives other than those of their own administration, arranged by county or region.
- *British Archives – A Guide to Archive Resources in the United Kingdom*, edited by J Foster and J Sheppard, gives more extensive coverage of national, university, major public and private institutions and libraries, societies and associations, arranged alphabetically by place. There is a good introduction to research methodology. There is a key subject index too.
- *The ASLIB Directory of Information Sources in the United Kingdom*, is organised alphabetically by library title, listing subject coverage and special collections of each institution.
- *In and Around Record Repositories in Great Britain and Ireland,* by J Cole and R Church, looks at record office holdings from the family historian's perspective, and is a simple reference guide to addresses, contact numbers and search regulations of national and local centres.
- *Record Offices: How to Find Them,* by J Gibson and P Peskett, contains clear maps to help you reach your destination by car or public transport, showing the proximity to each other of offices in the same city or town.
- *Guide to Genealogical Resources in the British Isles,* by DB Owen, concentrates on local studies collections, libraries, museums and historical societies.
- *Libraries in the United Kingdom and Republic of Ireland,* produced by The Library Association.

Titles and addresses of associations and societies can be gleaned from:

- *Directory of British Associations and Associations in Ireland,* edited by SPA Henderson and AJW Henderson.
- *Associations and Professional Bodies of the United Kingdom,* edited by J Ramscar.

For the United States of America consult:

- *The County Courthouse Book,* edited by EP Bentley.
- *Directory of American Libraries with Genealogical or Local History Collections,* compiled by PW Filby.

- *Directory of Special Libraries and Information Centers,* edited by JA DeMaggio and D M Kirby. This takes in Canada too.
- *American Library Directory* encompasses both the United States of America and Canada, as does
- *Encyclopedia of Associations,* for organisations and societies.

If you want to find out about repositories and libraries elsewhere, the following contain details about major national, regional and local archive offices and libraries worldwide, listed alphabetically by country and then by state:

- *Genealogical Research Directory,* 1995 and 1997 editions, edited by KA Johnson and MR Sainty.
- *The World of Learning,* which also includes learned societies, universities, colleges, research institutes, art galleries and museums.

GENUKI is a computerised genealogical information service about primary sources in the United Kingdom and Ireland available to users of the Internet. There are many other on-line public access catalogues of major repositories and libraries worldwide. Many provide E-mail addresses to deal with enquiries. Read *Internet for Genealogy,* by D Hawgood, for advice on its uses and limitations.

Local holdings and what has been published

You can learn about finding aids from the Gibson guides, a series of frequently updated inexpensive handlists to centralised, local and private holdings in the United Kingdom and Ireland of specific sources, copies and indexes. A complete list of titles is included in the Bibliography at the end of this book.

Using these, you can plan much of your work before visiting a record office or library.

Texts and Calendars; an Analytical Guide to Serial Publications, edited by ELC Mullins, and updated, 1957–82, contains a subject index of sources transcribed, translated, abstracted or indexed by official bodies, national and local historical, antiquarian and archaeological societies and associations in England and Wales. *Scottish Texts and Calendars; an Analytical Guide to Serial Publications,* edited by D and WB Stevenson, follows a similar pattern. They cite many records outside the scope of the Gibson guides.

Databases

A number of computerised databases and bulletin boards of nominal indexes are also now on the Internet; *A Guide to historical datafiles held in machine-readable form*, edited by K Schürer and SJ Anderson, covers the United Kingdom and summarises overseas compilations, with subject, place and source indexes.

Databases bring together published and private research material, contents of widely dispersed or out of print books and articles, but because the information is arranged out of context, coded or truncated, you do need to look at the original source to assess its genealogical value and relevance. Alphabetical strings of names can be meaningless or misleading without knowing their background.

A few words of warning

Transcripts and indexes are not above error, abbreviation, inaccuracy and omission, or may be incomplete versions of the original. Always find out the compiler's intention, the scope of the work, and what has been excluded. A transcript or index is no substitute, although often easier to read than the original, and it is much more clinical to handle than old documents.

Preparing for your visit to a record office

Time will inevitably be a constraint when you visit your chosen centres, so it is a good idea to think in advance about how best to go about your research.

- Find out their present location and opening hours.
- Always enquire about search room regulations, if a reader's ticket will be necessary and any fee.
- Check how many documents can be requisitioned at a time, the likely waiting period, about fixed delivery times, lunchtime closure or document delivery suspensions, and time for placing final orders, and the upper limit on document productions in a day.
- Some offices allow advance orders for documents, but you will need to be specific about exactly what you want to search.

- Many record offices require you to reserve a seat; if so be sure that if you are delayed it will still be available when you get there, or have a contact telephone number to ring in case you are held up.
- If you want to use a microform reader you may have to book in advance, and there may be a time restriction.
- It is not recommended that you take a friend – however well-intentioned, as their interest in your forebears will rarely match yours they can be both a distraction and a nuisance to others.

When you get there

- Take some means of personal identification or your reader's ticket.
- Restrict the amount you carry to an updated pedigree chart, your final checklist of items to search, plenty of A4 narrow feint file paper, sharpened pencils, a ruler, magnifying glass or sheet, and a map of the area you are searching.
- As you will probably have to leave your coat and bags in a cloakroom, have a secure place for loose change and any locker key.

Once in the search room you will be asked to sign the daily register, show or be issued with your reader's ticket, and may be asked the purpose of your visit.

- Many record offices supply free explanatory handouts to help you find your way around and locate the various catalogues describing the documents and special indexes. If in doubt, ask the staff to help you trace your first document reference so your order can be processed immediately.
- Some archives are now only accessible on self-service microform, and you can look at these whilst you wait for document productions.
- Browse through the nominal and place-name indexes and if you find a promising reference consult the main catalogue before requisitioning the document itself.
- Note down details of title, author, and the date of publication of any books or guides and where you found them in case you do not have time to read them in full, so you can obtain them on inter-library loan.
- Try not to be too ambitious and take regular, short breaks to offset mental fatigue and eye strain. The mind switches off unawares and you may find yourself turning pages or winding on reels of film totally oblivious to their content. If you miss a vital baptism entry,

you will never find it elsewhere, for it is a unique record. Once your concentration falters, stop immediately, get up and walk around or have a cup of coffee, and then double-check the last few pages or frames.

- Avoid being too hasty. A kind of panic descends towards the end of the day as you realise what remains to be done, when the brain is least able to cope. If you read slowly and steadily you will make fewer mistakes, be more thorough and accurate, and actually achieve more.
- As the day progresses regularly review and readjust your checklist, crossing off or adding items, not all of which will be there. This focuses your attention and structures your day.
- Avoid acting on assumptions, skipping from one random source to another in the hope of proving a hunch, or adapting their content so they apparently fit your theories.
- Every stated or suggested family link should be capable of standing on its own without need of further research, every piece of evidence corroborating or expanding your existing knowledge about the family. If not then any discrepancy or conflict should be resolved before you go further.
- Once assured of new facts, add them to your pedigree chart.

Plan B

- Have a contingency plan in case you reach a dead end; if you have come a long way you may never return to this office again, so make sure you make ample use of all its resources and seek out any special local collections which might assist your research.
- If you have a lot to do or run out of time and energy, plan for a two-day excursion. Many record offices will reserve material overnight for collection next morning. You will then be better acquainted with the search room layout and procedures, will have studied the handouts at length, revised your checklist, and be ready for more. If you cannot arrange this, some record offices offer a limited free or prepaid postal research service or provide a list of local professional record agents willing to act on your behalf. You may prefer to set aside another day and continue yourself.
- Try wherever it is realistic to combine visits to several repositories in a town on one day, but this requires careful planning. As an outsider I frequently underestimate walking distances between London record repositories and the long waits for public transport.

If you know their various opening hours and copies of certain items are in more than one place, these may be left for the one which is open the longest, but do not stockpile everything until the end of the day when physical and mental tiredness are taking their toll. Some sources too may be dependent on the successful outcome of searches higher up on the list. You may have to go backwards and forwards to one or two venues, adding further to your time.

Handling documents

Paper, parchment or vellum documents are unique and irreplaceable. Many will be very old, decayed, fragile or faded, and were never created for frequent handling. They have been carefully preserved and repaired for future use. Each has a unique reference number or catalogue mark for identification and retrieval.

Be sure you have enough space to spread out large documents, and unwrap them carefully, keep them flat with provided paperweights, place books on a rest, rolls over a stand. Never lean or take notes on top of a document, mark it in any way or touch it more than necessary. Unfold any corners and turn the document over to make sure you miss nothing. Use your ruler as a place marker in large repetitious documents. Once you have finished, replace the document as you found it, and return it to the production desk.

Using microforms

- Cramped workspace and poor light pose special hazards in designated microform areas. Always be quiet, tidy and perserverant. Sometimes the reader is to blame, so try another. If a microform proves intractable on most occasions staff will let you look at the original document, which is much quicker to flick through, the handwriting usually more distinct and the whole experience far more of a pleasure. However some original material is no longer held on site, so another trip may be necessary.

Problems with handwriting

- Handwriting styles vary over period and place, but working steadily back in time your eye becomes attuned to the ways in which words

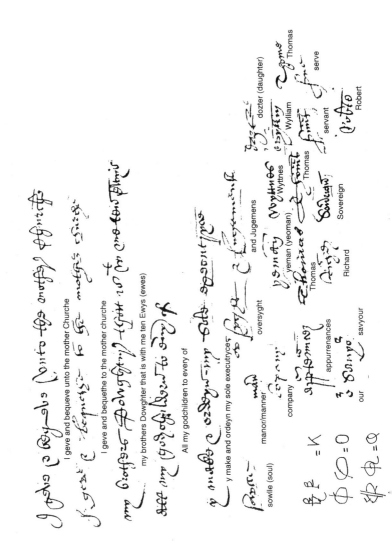

Figure 9 Samples of handwriting, showing capital letters and small characters abbreviations and suspended letters

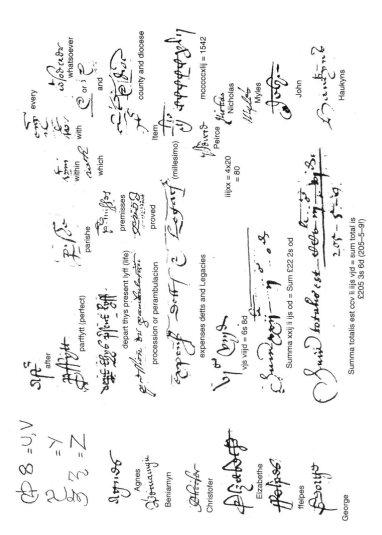

found in sixteenth- and seventeenth-century documents, common contractions,

and letters were formed. Some Victorian documents can be more awkward to decipher than Tudor sources, compiled three centuries before, and there have been good and bad writers in every epoch.

- Spelling was also haphazard, names often having several variations in the same document. If in doubt about a word, pronounce it, as it may have been written phonetically. Moreover, words were often abbreviated by contractions or suspensions, especially when office copies were made. Examples of contractions, where vowels or part of the middle of a word are omitted, may be indicated by a horizontal line drawn over the top. Where only a few letters of a word are written, the suspension of the rest is shown by a curved line over or through the last letter, by a flourish, or a full stop. Other words may run together, have double vowels or letters in superscript. Some letters were interchangeable, such as 'c' and 't', or were written in a different way, like the reverse 'e' and long 's'.

- If a specific word presents difficulty then its context may help: look for its occurrence elsewhere in the same document where it may be clearer or its meaning known; use a magnifying sheet or move your seat under different lighting; try to construct the word by identifying each letter in other words, leave a gap if you are making an exact line by line copy, and come back to it later; write the word as it appears so that you see how it was formed; and finally, ask a member of staff to help if necessary with individual words. You can gain practice by reading facsimiles and transcripts of diverse types of record which not only build up expertise, but also reveal from their content where names and dates will usually appear.

Meanings of words

You may need to consult a specialist glossary or dictionary to understand archaic or obsolete words, or those which have changed their original meaning, but some may be in regional dialect, especially in relation to domestic furniture or work tools.

Understanding Latin documents

Formal legal documents employ a set format and terminology, in which you can predict stock phrases, and appearance of names, relationships and dates. This is invaluable when the document is in Latin, which was the court language until 1733, although English was used between 1653 and 1660. Read any printed examples in translation first if Latin is not your strong suit. A rudimentary knowledge of Latin grammar and vocabulary is helpful, but you should be able to get by with a dictionary and Medieval Latin glossary. Often the scrivener's own grasp of Latin was shaky, so English words were given Latin endings.

Be careful with proper names in Latin, as in Medieval documents people may be described by their occupations or parentage rather than surnames. You can find out about Latin proper names in *The Record Interpreter*, by CT Martin, and try the translation exercises in *Latin for Local and Family Historians*, by D Stuart.

Working with numbers

Arabic numbers were not common in English documents until the late sixteenth century, Roman numerals being used, with pounds '*li, libri*', shillings '*s, solidi*' and pence '*d, denarii*' written after in superscript. A score is indicated by 'xx' in superscript above the appropriate number. Where numbers end in digits each is dotted and the final one 'j'. You can calculate money values today from *How Much is That Worth?* by LM Munby.

The dating of documents

Before 1752, in England and Wales, Ireland and the Dominions, the first day of the year was 25 March (Lady Day) according to the Roman Julian Calendar. Pope Gregory XIII introduced our present calendar in 1582. It was more quickly adopted by Continental Roman Catholic than Protestant states, Scotland enforcing it from 1 January 1600. This means that passing from one country to another, a traveller might go backwards and forwards in time, so always write down dates as seen and interpret later. Until the end of 1751, the whole of March counted as the first month, February as the twelfth. An unwary searcher might be deceived into thinking that a baptism in January 1741 was followed by a burial in October 1741, yet the latter had actually occurred several months before. A document dated January 1741 would be 1741 under the Julian (Old Style) Calendar, but 1742 under the Gregorian (New Style). If you interpret this to January 1741/2 the conversion is clear to any reader. Occasionally months are numbered, particularly in records of the Religious Society of Friends, so the seventh month in 1741 was September, and the eighth October, rather than the ninth and tenth months from 1752 onwards. Old and new dating schemes present problems to the user of the International Genealogical Index, where you may encounter a mixture of original and converted dates in extracted sources.

Archives of a legal and fiscal nature were dated by regnal year, which since 1307 has commenced on the day of the current monarch's accession, numbered sequentially at every anniversary and ending on the day of death. Deeds and charters were often dated using the number of days or day of the week before or after a fixed religious festival or feast day, whilst others were tied to moveable Holy Days such as Easter and Trinity. Consult a perpetual calendar, or *Handbook of Dates for Students of English History*, by CR Cheney, to work out precise dates.

Taking notes

When taking notes always use separate numbered sheets of file paper for each source and write only on one side. Head each with the document reference number or catalogue mark, title, period or date and where you read it. If continuation sheets become detached the references reunite them. The first sheet should also record the period searched, any gaps, and name variants found. Even if a search proves negative, you will still need to record it to prevent repetition. Try to avoid abbreviated or shorthand notes which may be open to misunderstanding. Keep extracted information in its original order, leaving unaltered the spelling of names and places (in Latin if necessary). It helps to pick out people's names in capital letters. Retain descriptions of family relationships as written, 'my' in preference to 'his', to avoid later confusion or misinterpretation. Indicate any part of the document which is too indistinct to read or queried words, names and dates, which might be double-checked another time or against information in other sources. Record office staff may be able to advise on odd words, but not in reading an entire document.

You can use commercial standard record sheets and workbooks to fill in details under headings. Their major drawback is that the headings take no account of idiosyncracies in a document and as a result information is filed out of sequence and out of its original context. For example, an illegitimate child's surname may not be clear from a baptism register when the surnames of the parents but not the child are given, so copy out the exact entry which then can be compared with other evidence, rather than jump to the wrong conclusion.

Interpreting your findings

At this stage you are sifting and gathering information, extracting names, relationships, dates, places, occupations and other details from disparate sources. Your assessment of their relevance and genealogical value comes afterwards. Sometimes you will have looked at the wrong place, or taken too short a time-span, have overlooked other superior material, or documents which would have expanded or completed the picture, misread, misunderstood or missed out vital details. Always be prepared to search a document again when it does not seem to make sense. Archives are your raw material, and it is up to you to analyse them effectively and accurately.

Reliable analysis is only possible if you have sufficient relevant, valid information, regularly filed and easily retrieved, but do not be tempted to leave this until you have collected so much that the task becomes overwhelming.

Do not read into a document what is not there. Your evaluation will be modified by limitations of scope, period, content, condition and availability of records, the knowledge, purpose, honesty and accuracy of their creators. They may not tell you all or indeed any of what you want to know, or they may tantalise you with their ambiguity. Ask yourself who was the informant, what was his or her role: as official recorder, participant, or witness, and how contemporary was the person to the event described as this may result in bias or unreliability. Is the given information consistent with that of other sources of the period and place? Does it contain clues to other events or connected sources, clarify relationships, name other people and places? If there are discrepancies were they due to original clerical error, late recording or poor copying, was there a mistake on your part, or does the document not relate to this family branch, generation or individual?

Filing and storage systems

Having transferred your discoveries onto your pedigree chart, file away your notes carefully and safely. Keep your system simple, and stick to it. The best test of a filing system is: can a total stranger understand it unaided and can you quickly and easily retrieve information from it? Never destroy any notes, for they may later be of use. File paper can be placed in a ring-binder, under subject or date order, with a checklist or research log at the front. You can keep a separate correspondence log.

Never store material in airtight containers, but in dark, cool, dry conditions or under cover above floor level away from direct heat and the fading effects of direct sunlight. Ventilation is important as it prevents mould. It is worth spending a little money to ensure safe preservation of your family's archives. Acid-free high-strength corrugated self-assembly archive boxes are ideal for storing loose papers and documents. Unique documents and photographs kept in transparent acid-free or Melinex sleeves will guarantee their condition does not deteriorate and obviate the need for handling. They can be filed in an album. Avoid using polythene bags and brown envelopes, as the first are prone to sweat and absorb ink and print, envelopes leave a brown stain and cause deterioration as they degrade. Remove any rusty clips, elastic bands and pink tape, and replace them with brass clips and white tape if necessary. Damaged items should be repaired with wheat starch or special archival tape, not glue or cellotape which are unsuitable and cause further harm, but seek expert advice first from your record office, to avoid costly mistakes.

You might want to keep information about individual people in an alphabetical card index or about a couple and their children on family group sheets. The card or group sheet for the latest born person of the same name is placed in front of earlier ones, each of whom is accorded a unique number, his parents' names and date and place of birth or baptism. The number is used as an identifying tag to the corresponding numbered people on the pedigree chart. A card can record much more biographical detail than the chart, adding comments and remarks you may not want made public.

Family historians sometimes prefer to feed their data on to computer, using a specially devised program. You can buy or hire commercial demonstration videos featuring a variety of programs which help you decide; the reviews and updated lists and titles, addresses, contact names, telephone numbers and prices in *Computers in Genealogy*, published quarterly by the Society of Genealogists, enable you to shop around for what suits your individual requirements. Some packages alert you to unlikely family links, and offering a choice of pedigree chart styles and sizes, you can quickly and regularly amend them and print out multiple copies for family circulation. Computers are more versatile than a card index, instantly sifting and displaying information, in any number of permutations, producing professional-looking printouts, and downloading copies of data on to disk for sharing with other searchers. You can edit, merge and move information, and the disks take up less storage space than a card index, though always ensure you have updated back-up disks stored elsewhere in case of accidental loss or damage.

10

EXPLORING ENGLISH
AND WELSH PARISH REGISTERS

Census returns tell you people's approximate birth years and places.
You can look for a birth certificate if it occurred after civil registration
began. Sometimes births were not registered or are difficult to identify
from the indexes, perhaps because the mother's confinement took
place away from home, or the child was registered under different
names from those by which it was later known, or as an unnamed
male or female birth. If you know where the parents were domiciled,
then it may be easier and cheaper to look for the baptism in the local
church registers. Before the commencement of civil registration in
England and Wales on 1 July 1837, 1 January 1855 in Scotland, and 1
January 1864 in Ireland, it is to these records that you must turn for
evidence of birth and parentage. But a child's birthplace was not necessarily where it was baptised, nor does the census indicate anyone's
religious denomination, so you may have to look at registers of chapels
and congregations outside the Established Church. Baptism did not
always promptly follow birth, delayed until several children in the
family were taken together, perhaps years after the eldest was born.

Formal registration of baptisms, marriages and burials began in
England and Wales in September 1538, since when every church has
preserved a written record, the weekly entries being read out during
Sunday service. The entries were intended to avoid disputes about
age, title or lineage, and to determine whether a person was the
king's born subject.

Baptisms and marriages are still registered today, but since 1853
(1852 in London) there have been fewer interments in churchyards

for reasons of health and sanitation. The volumes therefore represent only a sample of the true total, for the vast majority of burials were recorded by the local authority or private company responsible for the cemetery concerned, or from 1902, the crematorium.

Where to find them

Originally stored in a locked chest in the church, completed parish registers are now mostly in county record offices, the incumbent retaining those still in use. If you want to consult these, you will need to write to the church concerned for an appointment. Addresses of Anglican clergy can be found in *Crockford's Clerical Directory*, but do not write to a named individual, who may have moved on. A fixed scale of fees is applicable. If you are unable to examine the records yourself the incumbent may be willing to do it, although he or she is not obliged to, and the fee will be different. An offer of a reasonable donation to church funds may be welcomed. Always check in advance how much you are likely to have to pay. An urban register crammed full of scrawled yearly entries will take much longer to search than a rural volume, so you may have to limit your scope to conserve funds.

The Phillimore Atlas and Index of Parish Registers, edited by CR Humphery-Smith, contains county parish maps and a complete listing of deposited English, Welsh and Scottish original registers. From this you will see that nearly all the Welsh parish registers are at the National Library of Wales in Aberystwyth or in county record offices in the principality. Most record offices have published lists of their holdings and a telephone call will give you up to date information. Because of their fragile state and heavy use, many of the deposited registers are no longer available for public use and can only be seen in microform. Microfilms of numerous parish registers can also be hired for use at family history centres of the Church of Jesus Christ of Latter-day Saints, from which extracted baptisms and marriages are filed in the International Genealogical Index.

Thousands of parish registers have been copied or indexed, and should be available in the record office or library of the area. Probably the most important collection is held by the Society of Genealogists, in London, and some can be borrowed by members. Its published catalogue, *Parish Register Copies in the Library of the Society of Genealogists*, is mostly integrated into the *Atlas* mentioned above, which also cites other known transcripts. *National Index of Parish Registers: Parish Registers of Wales,* edited by CJ Williams and J Watts-Williams, lists the whereabouts of Welsh originals, copies and indexes under both Welsh and English place-names.

The history of parish registers of England and Wales

Although parish registers theoretically began in 1538, in practice very few survive from that date or were continuously kept. In 1598 each parish was ordered to purchase a parchment register book into which all preceding baptisms, marriages and burials were to be copied up, particularly those after the start of the Queen's reign in 1558. This meant that many older books were discarded and the first twenty years ignored. A professional scrivener was often employed for the task, so the handwriting for at least those forty years is neat and consistent, even if the entries are probably truncated versions of the originals.

Record-keeping was disrupted over the Civil War and Commonwealth period, spanning 1643–60. A special officer, elected by the parish ratepayers, was given custody of the registers from 1653, when the Established Church was Presbyterian. The volumes were frequently taken into private care, and not returned at the Restoration of the Anglican Church in 1660, so all earlier contents vanished with them. From 1645 until 1660 the registers noted births and deaths as well as baptisms and burials, and publications of intent of marriages, conducted by a justice of the peace rather than a priest from 1653 until 1660. Some parishes have gaps for the whole period, whilst other registers were combined for convenience with those of adjacent places. After 1660 Anglican clergy retrospectively and incompletely recorded baptisms, marriages and burials from the hiatus years, possibly to provide legal evidence of age and paternity. Thus the erratic under-registration of those eighteen years represents almost a generation, and previous and later entries of a surname may have to be supplemented by other sources for proof of direct family relationship.

After the Act of Toleration in 1689, dissenting congregations were permitted to erect their own places of worship, and as a result began to keep their own records of baptism, marriage and burial, so that not every inhabitant of a parish will be registered in the Established

Church registers until marriages of every couple, regardless of creed, became mandatory in the Anglican Church between 25 March 1754 and 30 June 1837, excepting Quakers and Jews.

Registration was also affected by a tax on births, marriages and deaths, between 1694 and 1706, and stamp duty on baptisms, marriages and burials, 1783–94.

In Wales, poor record-keeping and ineffective supervision of remote country churches and their thinly scattered parishioners, has meant that the survival rate of parish registers is patchy.

The arrangement of the entries

At first, baptisms, marriages and burials were written up in one book, but from 25 March 1754 marriages were recorded in a separate printed volume, and baptisms and burials followed suit after 1812. Until then the entries might be arranged chronologically by date, list all the baptisms, then the marriages, and finally burials during each month, record baptisms on one page, or at the front of the book, and burials on the facing page or running from the back, with marriages scattered among each. They soon ceased to be contemporaneous if baptisms exceeded burials, or vice versa. Occasionally too, stray entries were inserted out of date order. From 1813 separate printed baptism and burial registers were used.

Baptisms

Until 1812, baptism entries reflect the whim of the clerk. At best they provide the day, month and year, baptismal name, surname and parentage, father's abode and occupation, at worst merely the exact date and name of the infant. There is often no cohesion in the way the entries are written, the surname coming after the child's or parents' names, making searching laborious. Between 1798 and 1813, parish registers in the diocese of Durham and some other places note not only the names of the child and his or her parents, his date of birth, and birth seniority, but the birthplaces of each parent, grandparents' names and the occupations of the father and paternal grandfather resulting in a single entry extending the family's history back two generations.

From 1813, baptisms were copied into standardised pre-printed books, organised under headed columns, giving exact date, forename of the child, the names of both parents, surname, where they lived, father's occupation and the signature of the officiating priest. They are easier to read because all you have to do is scan the surname column for your family.

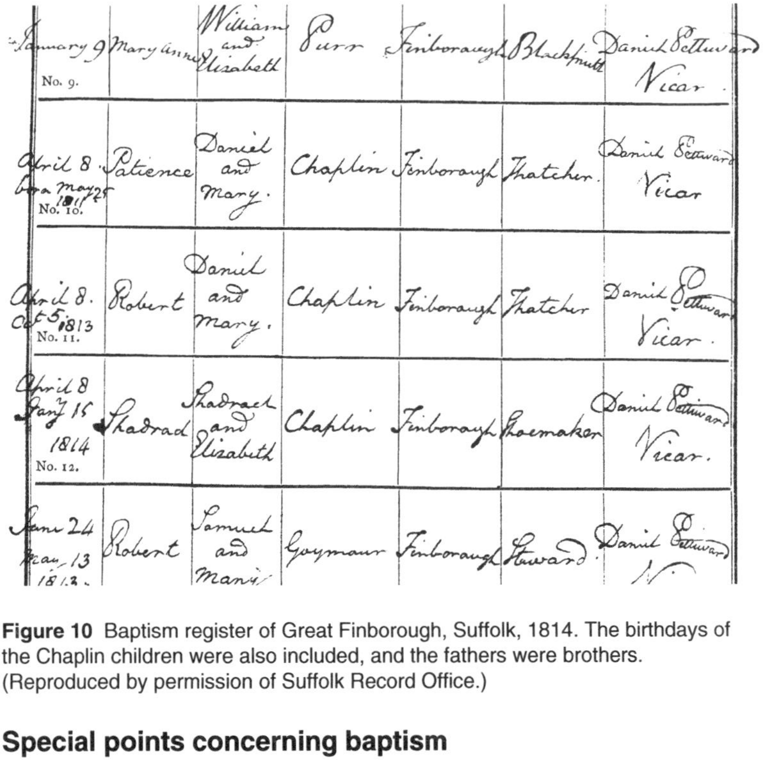

January 9 No. 9.	Mary Anne	William and Elizabeth	Purr	Finborough	Blacksmith	Daniel Pettiward Vicar.
April 8. born May 25 1811 No. 10.	Patience	Daniel and Mary.	Chaplin	Finborough	Thatcher.	Daniel Pettiward Vicar
April 8. Oct 5 1813 No. 11.	Robert	Daniel and Mary.	Chaplin	Finborough	Thatcher	Daniel Pettiward Vicar.
April 8 Jany 15 1814 No. 12.	Shadrad	Shadrach and Elizabeth	Chaplin	Finborough	Shoemaker	Daniel Pettiward Vicar.
June 24 May 13 1813.	Robert	Samuel and Mary	Goymour	Finborough	Steward.	Daniel Pettiward V

Figure 10 Baptism register of Great Finborough, Suffolk, 1814. The birthdays of the Chaplin children were also included, and the fathers were brothers. (Reproduced by permission of Suffolk Record Office.)

Special points concerning baptism

- Although baptism was supposed to be on the first Sunday after birth, or on the next Sunday thereafter, you will find in the few instances where dates of birth are given, this was rarely so. It may have been strictly adhered to at the outset but weeks, months or years often elapsed before baptism. It seems too that there was a falling-off of baptism in the nineteenth century, so the registers are not an accurate record of all births within a parish.

- Dual entries were made of children 'privately baptised' at home by a licensed midwife, surgeon, physician or priest, and later 'received into the church'. This might be because they were sickly, or due to severe weather conditions, absence of a resident parson, or temporary church closure. The entry may also refer to a Catholic family.
- Whenever possible the putative ('reputed') father of an illegitimate ('base born') child was named, so the vestrymen or local justices could enforce maintenance against him. Before 1813 the entries are frequently unclear as to which parent's surname was taken by the child.

How best to utilise the registers

- If you are doing a specific search, broaden the period to fifteen years surrounding an ancestor's possible birth in case of faulty information, late or missing baptism, so that you know if the family was present in the parish from entries relating to brothers and sisters.
- If you extract every entry of the surname and its variants from the beginning of a register, especially in rural areas, entire generations, family groups and unconnected strays will reveal themselves.
- When people cannot be linked, or vanish, consult a local map and look at registers of parishes within a walking radius, as many families did not move far, often in a series of circular movements spread over one or two generations. In urban centres you might have to look at a cluster of parishes serving a small densely populated area, and at its environs. An itinerant might have his offspring baptised in a variety of parishes along the way. You can also try regional personal name indexes like the International Genealogical Index for isolated references.
- A large-scale Ordnance Survey map showing contours, natural features, field names, and their relative proximity is helpful where an apparent change of residence occurred. But premises may be renamed, a person disappear from the registers because his family was complete, he moved away or died, coinciding with the appearance of a newcomer or new parent of the same name.

- Parish boundaries were also redrawn and new churches erected as populations expanded, so a family staying put might be recorded in a register of a recently created parish. Conversely, the clerk of a mother church frequently noted baptisms in its outlying chapelries in both records.

Some likely obstacles

- Several couples of identical given names producing children of the same name at the same period, place or locality pose a special problem, particularly in rural communities where there were relatively few surnames. Sometimes the registers will distinguish fathers as 'senior', 'junior', 'elder' and 'younger', or connect them with their township, farm or house. Burial registers and wills may eliminate a few of the young and parental demise may be indicated when the adjective is dropped, any posthumous offspring being so described.
- Look for any forename pattern over successive generations. In the past a fairly limited range of names seems to have had currency. Systematic naming of children after the father, paternal grandfather, maternal grandfather and so on are clues to filiation, birth seniority and possible gaps. Sometimes a younger child was named after one who had died or several were given the same name as older surviving siblings. By the early nineteenth century surnames, especially maternal maiden names, were frequently adopted as forenames, and two or more given names were common. The Bible, popular contemporary literature and heroes of the day were also name sources.
- Continuity of occupation within a family may be a clue, the eldest son being the most likely to follow his father's trade or work.
- If you cannot find the baptism of a forebear it may be because the child was a product of the mother's previous marriage, who took on the stepfather's name, obscuring his or her original identity. Young children taken into the families of married older sisters, or childless relatives, might also adopt their surname. This may partially explain the use of aliases.

Where all three factors, of name, residence, and occupational pattern exist, your lineal descent should be easier to prove, provided that the relevant records are adequate and continuous.

Points to bear in mind when using Welsh records

- In Welsh parish registers you will find patronymic strings of first names prefaced by 'Ap' or 'Ab', each person labelled by his genealogy over three or more generations, using a small range of Biblical and saints' names, and it is continuity of homestead which is all-important, rather than heredity of surname. Place-names and personal names were recorded in the native language, the rest of the entry being in English.

Marriages

Once you have tracked the baptism of the earliest known child of a couple and there are no previous entries spanning at least fifteen years, you can look for the parents' marriage. As many as a third of all marriages started with the bride already pregnant, some after birth had taken place. If the birth was before marriage, the child would be baptised using the mother's surname, perhaps recording also the name of the father, her future husband.

Weddings were usually solemnised in the bride's church, so search for the eldest child's baptism there too, for it was common to return to the maternal home for the first confinement. Sometimes couples chose the nearest market town or ecclesiastical centre to marry, the baptisms of their progeny scattered in the registers of churches in and around the town.

What the registers reveal

Until 1754, precise date, forenames and surnames of both partners may be found, or only those of the husband. Where one party was widowed or lived in another parish this too might be mentioned. From 25 March 1754 marriages were written up in a separate printed book. The name of each party, marital status, parish of abode, the date of the ceremony and whether by banns or licence invariably appear, each entry being signed or marked by the couple, at least two witnesses and the officiating clergyman. The witnesses might be the churchwardens, or relatives and friends of the pair. Their traced kinship to the family may provide leads to your ancestor's own earlier or later whereabouts if you get stuck.

If you find a marriage after 1754 but no baptisms of children, it may

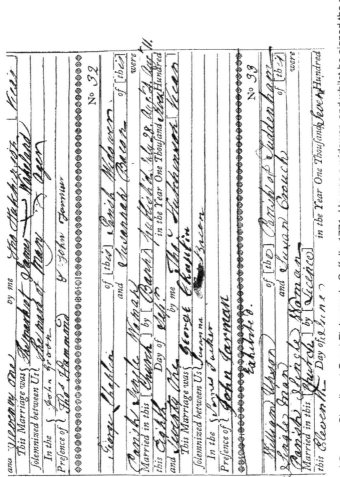

Figure 11 Marriage of George Chaplin at Great Finborough, Suffolk, 1771. He was a widower, and whilst he signed the register his bride, Susannah Bacon, made her mark. They were the parents of Daniel and Shadrach Chaplin, whose own children were baptised at the church there. (Reproduced by permission of Suffolk Record Office).

suggest one partner was nonconformist, until chapel marriages were permitted in 1837.

From July 1837 registers were kept in duplicate, one being sent to the superintendent district registrar when full; the duplicates are identical in content to the certified entries produced by the General Register Office, except that the originals contain signatures. You can search such marriage registers at the church or county record office free of charge, whereas you have to pay for a certified copy at the General Register Office (The Family Records Centre from 1st April 1997), where you can only consult the indexes.

Clandestine and irregular marriages

Before 25 March 1754 a number of urban and rural centres earned a reputation for clandestine and irregular marriages. The registers of such 'lawless churches', claiming exemption from ecclesiastical control, 'peculiars', and rural chapels contain far more weddings than can be justified by the number of inhabitants. A clandestine marriage was one without banns or licence, usually performed by a clergyman in a church or chapel of a place where neither party was resident, or in a marriage-house, tavern or prison. An irregular marriage took place in the parish of one of the partners, without banns or licence, or in a church other than where banns had been published, or for which a licence had been granted though neither party was a parishioner, or had not resided for at least the obligatory previous four weeks.

Many surviving registers, notebooks and indexes of clandestine marriages at marriage-houses, taverns and prisons, compiled by clergymen or register-keepers, are now at the Public Record Office at Kew. Some were destroyed, found their way into other repositories, were filed as evidence in legal proceedings, or remain in private hands. Entries might be fabricated, duplicated, recorded incompletely or erratically out of date order, and occasionally baptisms may be included. Places of residence and occupations may be given as well as the wedding date, names and marital status of the parties, providing vital clues as to where they came from.

Some couples were local, others journeyed from all over the country, attracted by their secrecy and speed, because no prior residential requirement had to be fulfilled, and they could save on church expenses and social entertainments. It particularly suited runaways from disapproving parents, military and naval personnel with no permanent fixed abode, and the marriages were valid in common law.

It has been reckoned that in the early eighteenth century between a quarter and a third of all weddings were contracted in such places. After 25 March 1754 clandestine marriages continued in the Scottish border country until declared illegal in 1856 unless one party had been a resident for at least twenty-one days.

Banns books

From 1754 marriages were valid in England and Wales only if by banns or licence. Banns, signalling a couple's intention to marry, were published and read out during services in each of their churches on the three Sundays preceding the ceremony, so if any of the congregation knew of a legal impediment they had ample time to object. The dates banns were read and the names and parishes of the parties were recorded as part of the marriage registration, on separate pages in the same volume or in a banns book. If you cannot find the marriage of parents of children baptised in a parish, the banns may reveal the bridal home. However, even though banns were read, it does not always mean that marriage followed promptly if at all.

Indexes, transcripts and extracts

Besides scanning the International Genealogical Index for a particular marriage entry, county marriage indexes can prove invaluable, especially if arranged alphabetically under surnames of grooms and brides. Not all are fully comprehensive, some may be limited by period or area, others privately held. Look at *Marriage, Census and Other Indexes for Family Historians*, by J Gibson and E Hampson, for details about your county of interest.

Printed copies of many marriage registers end in 1812, leaving a gap of twenty-five years to civil registration, and often exclude names of witnesses, and whether the couple signed the register. Before his death in 1955, Percival Boyd used printed transcripts, extracts, marriage licence allegations and bonds to compile a county by county marriage index for England between 1538 and 1837. The 534 volumes are lodged in the library of the Society of Genealogists, but copies for individual counties are on microfilm in local record offices, and a complete microfilm set can be seen at family history centres. Almost seven million names, representing between twelve per cent and fifteen per cent of total marriages in 4,300 English parishes, are recorded in the indexes, which are organised in three series. It does not extend to every county, however, nor are dates consistent, or run from start to finish, unbroken, for each parish but *A List of Parishes in Boyd's Marriage Index*, outlines the percentage of coverage for each county as well as dates and places.

The Main Series is divided into sixteen county runs, then under ten twenty-five year periods, (except 1538–1600 and 1801–37), with double entries for men and women excluding Yorkshire which is indexed by males. Only the year, surnames and abbreviated forenames of each couple, the place of marriage or licence issuing office are recorded, so you have to examine the original source for full details. The First Miscellaneous Series extends from 1538 to 1775 (double indexed up to 1700), drawing on published marriages in other areas, and contains additional entries for counties in the Main Series. The Second Miscellaneous Series, 1538–1837, covers marriages from all English counties, with double entries in strict alphabetical surname order. The first two Series are phonetically indexed, for example names beginning with GN- and KN- appear under N-, so caution is needed.

If you know the approximate year of a male antecedent's birth, but have failed to locate his baptism or marriage, weddings of females of the same surname and generation may be a pointer to his origins, as brides tended to marry in their native parishes. The indexes can also be used to plot surname distribution over area or period, as well as to pick up stray name references.

Another important marriage index for family historians is the Pallot Index, held by the Institute of Heraldic and Genealogical Studies, Canterbury. It runs from about 1780 to 1837, and contains duplicate entries of every marriage in all but two of the hundred-and-three City of London churches, plus some in other counties. There is also a less extensive index of baptisms. Places and periods are listed in *The Phillimore Atlas and Index of Parish Registers*. Although not open to the public, searches can be made for a specific marriage or for up to twenty references to a surname for a fee. As some London registers were destroyed by enemy action this index may be all that remains, and for people with ancestors living or moving around London it is immensely time-saving.

What to do next

Having found a marriage, your next step will be to locate the groom's baptism, taking his given parish first, deducting ten years off the marriage year to allow for late baptism, and to pick up younger siblings. You will need to cover a wide period if you do not know an approximate birth year from other sources like the census, a death certificate, gravestone inscription or family knowledge, but if he died after 1812 the burial register will invariably give his age.

Burials and what the registers may tell you

Burial registers are frequently neglected by family historians. Up to 1812, at best they yield the precise date, deceased's name, abode, occupation and age. If the deceased was under twenty-one, parents' names may be cited, and whether death occurred in infancy; if a woman, her current marital status and husband's name help place her in her family context. At worst merely date and name appear.

In time of crisis or epidemic such as 'pox' or plague under-recording was inevitable, the reason for increased mortality usually being recorded. Some late eighteenth- and early nineteenth-century registers in and around the City of London and other parishes note cause of death, exact place of interment in the church or churchyard and age of the deceased. 'P' was written against the names of people given a pauper's funeral, probably with latitude when duty was payable between 1783 and 1794.

From 1667 until 1814 corpses were to be wrapped in sheeps' wool to keep the woollen trade buoyant. The burial registers note when an affidavit was sworn to confirm this had been done and these were sometimes accompanied by the person's name and relationship to the deceased. Where the burial registers are deficient, notes about affidavits can prove invaluable as they were sworn within eight days of interment.

Some entries record bodies that were 'hurled', 'interred' or 'tumbled' into the ground, indicating burial of a dissenter without benefit of Anglican rites, or an unbaptised person, excommunicant or suicide. Burials of executed felons abound in parishes where the Assize Sessions sat.

From 1813, the printed burial registers are arranged under headed columns for date, forename and surname, age and abode, and the signature of the officiating minister. Ages are often unreliable, marital status and family relationships omitted, making positive identification difficult. Other nineteenth-century sources like a death certificate, gravestone inscription or will may corroborate the burial entry. Conversely, you may find a burial for which there is apparently no related death certificate. From 1853 (1852 in London) only burials actually in the churchyard are recorded in the registers, so if you know when and where a person died you may have to track his or her burial to a public cemetery.

Indexes of burials

Very little attention has yet been paid to indexing burial registers, unless as part of a larger project embracing a whole parish register. However, in 1996, the Federation of Family History Societies launched a plan to compile a computerised national database of deaths and burials, initially for the period 1813–50. It will supplement the International Genealogical Index which is largely devoid of these.

Percival Boyd's index of over a quarter of a million London burials between 1538 and 1852 includes interments of dissenters in Bunhill Fields from 1823, and is on microfiche, the original volumes being kept at the Society of Genealogists. Other local burial indexes are listed in *Marriage, Census and Other Indexes*.

Why burials are important sources

Burials complement baptisms and marriages in a variety of ways:

- by identifying people by their ages and relationships, revealing what became of them and when;
- by defining a person's occupation, abode and marital status;
- by marking the end of one attachment and availability of the widowed partner for remarriage;
- by giving a start date at which to begin looking for a will: any further reference to the same name in later – dated records cannot relate to the same individual, unless described as deceased;
- by indicating where newcomers came from if they were isolated surname references;
- by providing a clue to continuity of residence before the period of registration began in 1538 when names appear sporadically in early registers, so that you can consult other contemporary documents about the place in which they and their relatives might be recorded.

Gravestone inscriptions

The registers should wherever practicable be used in conjunction with gravestone inscriptions. Because the majority of parish registers have been removed from churches to county record offices, this may involve a special journey. Many churchyards have been cleared but not before a plan of the numbered plots and a transcript of the inscriptions was made. Copies may be found in the county record office, the church itself, or at the Society of Genealogists for which there are published handlists. Inscriptions copied years ago from gravestones which are no longer legible or in place, or in a crowded churchyard or cemetery can be more easily found in a book or microfiche.

Gravestone inscriptions became popular and widespread from the late eighteenth century, using local stone, metals or wood. Each headstone style was selected by the family, erected and inscribed perhaps some years after the first interment. Family groups often lie in a single grave or adjacent plots. At best dates of birth and death, residence, occupation, and names of the grave's occupants will be given, details of husband and wife, children and their spouses which may be lacking in the burial register; at worst name, age and date of death will be given, the details not always corresponding with those in the burial register. An inscription before 1813 may be the only evidence you have about approximate year of birth.

Earlier tombs, tablets, brasses or stained glass windows commemorate local nobility, gentry, merchants and clergy. Many are in inaccessible family vaults or inconveniently situated inside the church, but often they are enriched with coats of arms, striking and colourful effigies and provide a range of detail about the deceased, his or her forebears, family connections and near descendants which would otherwise be difficult to reassemble. A short printed guide to the church will usually draw attention to those of special interest, as will a published county or parish history.

Bishops' transcripts

The earliest register copies are the yearly or biennial parchment or paper bishops' transcripts of baptisms, marriages and burials sent by English and Welsh parishes to diocesan registrars from 1598 until well into the nineteenth century. At first the year began at Easter, but from 1603 was fixed at 25 March (Lady Day). The transcripts are now lodged in county or diocesan record offices, but there is no complete unbroken run for any diocese nor are there any English returns between 1645 and 1660. From 1837 marriages were excluded from the returns. Some transcripts predate 1598 and occasionally duplicate archdeacons' transcripts (or register bills) can be used to fill gaps. The transcripts are normally arranged in parish bundles, but Norfolk and Suffolk register bills are organised by year, then by deanery and parish. If you know when, but not where someone was born this arrangement allows several neighbouring parishes to be tackled at once, taking care to note those places for which years are missing. In Wales, though many start in the early eighteenth century, transcripts extant only from 1661 are in the National Library at Aberystwyth.

The transcripts are a ready substitute if you want to search a number of parishes, if the registers remain at the church, no longer exist or are too indistinct for the period required. They are often complementary as the churchwardens or clerk often corrected errors or omissions in the original registered entries. But they also missed out or truncated others, so they are not entirely reliable, surnames and forenames may be spelled differently, dates and occupations vary, possibly because the copyist was not the original scribe. You cannot be sure which of two conflicting entries was actually correct without checking other sources.

Other copies to look for

Modern, printed, typescript or manuscript transcripts of parish registers are the fruits of someone else's decipherment of old handwriting, making widely available records which are perhaps now too badly decayed or damaged to be read, or are held a long way from where you live. Transcribers make mistakes, misread names, omit, mix, transpose and abbreviate entries, so use them as a guide and consult the originals wherever possible, even if in microform. Some may actually amount only to selected extracts rather than a complete copy.

Copies frequently end in 1812, almost thirty years before civil registration began, and until recently tended to concentrate on baptisms and marriages to the exclusion of burials, thus providing but a partial picture.

International Genealogical Index (IGI)

An example of an index with few burial entries is the International Genealogical Index, comprising the names of over two-hundred million deceased people worldwide who were born or married before about 1885. The Index was first produced on microfiche as the Computer File Index by the Church of Jesus Christ of Latter-day Saints in 1968, with updated editions in 1976, 1978, 1981, 1984, 1988 and 1992. The 1993, 1994 and 1996 versions are computerised as part of a program called 'FamilySearch'. A copy of the 1988 Index is also on CD-ROM.

Until 1992, this was compiled from parish registers, bishops' transcripts, vital records and other sources of births, baptisms and marriages as part of a 'controlled extraction program', but not every register nor every entry from a register was included. Since 1992, the Index has been put together from 'compiled records', being family history sheets of deceased ancestors submitted by patrons of the Church, but the reliability of the entries depends entirely on the contributors. It is widely available in family history centres and branch libraries of the Church, many local record offices and libraries possessing at least a microfiche edition for their own area, a few, like the Society of Genealogists, having CD-ROM. An explanation of *Finding an IGI Source* and *International Genealogical Index Reference Guide*, is available on microfiche or CD-ROM with each edition.

It is arranged under country, then by county for England, Wales, Scotland and Ireland, and by state for other countries like the United States of America. There are companion given name indexes for Wales and some European states. You can find out what places and periods are covered by the index from the microfiched *Vital and Parish Records Listing* accompanying each edition.

The index of surnames runs alphabetically using a standard phonetic spelling though retaining the original variant within each, cross-referenced where appropriate; this means that similar sounding, though distinct surnames were wrongly grouped together. Given names appear strictly alphabetically in original full or abbreviated form, followed by the names of cited parents, spouse (or for pre-1970 temple records the family representative, heir or other relative), sex, type of event, its date, town and parish. Where there are several people of the same given name, the entries run sequentially by date, the earliest first. You should take care with prefixed surnames, and also when looking for variant abbreviated forenames like Bill, William, Willm and Wm, each filed separately.

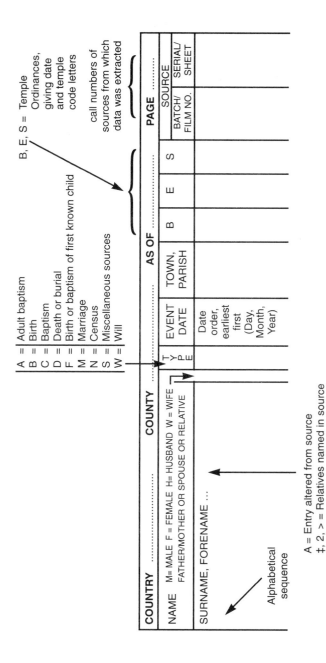

Figure 12 What the IGI contains

The Welsh indexes are straightforward for events after 1813 as surnames are extracted from the baptism register or bishop's transcript surname columns; before this the index generally assumes a child took the given name of the father as a surname, the entries ignoring the rest of the genealogical patronymic string in the original record. But sometimes a hereditary name was already in use, yet does not appear in the index on every occasion. If you know the approximate year and parish of birth or baptism it may be easier to search the given name index first. If you know the father's name, the surname index might be preferable first, and you should be able to pick up his other offspring.

Recent editions substituting submissions made by patrons for individual source-extracted entries have led to multiple duplicated and varied contributions about the same person. Entries submitted after 1990 often contain estimated dates and places of residence taken from sources like the census or wills, rather than exact details of birth, baptism or marriage, relying too perhaps on unverified personal information rather than documentary evidence.

FamilySearch and Ancestral File

Individual names are not linked on the IGI into family groups or pedigrees, but these may be found in Ancestral File, another computerised index in FamilySearch, with names and addresses of contributors for temple ordinances after 1990. Names and addresses of submitters between 1970 and 1990 can be gleaned from the original source sheets, quoting the cited batch or film number, though they may now be out of date and not always is the contributor willing to share or exchange his or her information. You can obtain a printout of baptisms or marriages extracted from a specific parish, arranged alphabetically by name, quoting the batch number. A more detailed explanation can be found in *Genealogy in the computer age: understanding FamilySearch*, by EL Nichols.

Advantages and drawbacks of computerisation

The CD-ROM editions are much more versatile as you can select a specific region, individual name, marriage, or parent search, within a set timescale, or try the browse option for speculative searches of a surname or locality. You can obtain a printout (or download the information onto disk purchased at a family history centre or at the Society of Genealogists) for analysis at home.

Specific searches take no account of surname variants or other ways in which the entries appear, for instance a request for a screen view of children of 'John and Mary Smith' would yield their issue not those recorded for 'Jn and Mary Smith', 'Jn and My Smith', 'John Smith', or other permutations, although they were the same parents, so you have to select a wide range of options. Identically named parents and children may reveal themselves at the same place and period, but actually belong to distinct family groups, and as the details are not a complete copy of the original entry, may miss out vital distinguishing details of abode and occupation. A methodical search of an original register prevents this situation arising.

Special attributes of the IGI

The Index has revolutionised the family historian's approach to tracking people born or married out of area, or moving around several counties and has revealed family linkages which might otherwise have lain undetected.

Few families were static over a long period, members of each generation often migrating to and fro in a circular way around the countryside, or in and out of urban centres, all within a small compass, but some travelled greater distances to larger towns and cities or to the capital.

Whilst an entire family unit might uproot itself, the most mobile group was probably aged between twelve and thirty: apprentices, domestic servants, landless labourers and single people. Their movements will not feature in parish registers at all until marriage or demise, perhaps many miles away from where they were born. This was especially true of professional people. You may be able to identify them in the Index by process of elimination, not forgetting to look at burial registers, which lie outside its ambit. The Index is also a ready short-cut for pinpointing dates and places of events found in civil registration indexes, people's births and baptisms from clues in the census, and for identifying the names of their parents, siblings and marriage partners. It is, however, only as good as the information fed into it, so should be used as a key to the full entries in original records, not as a primary source.

11

ENGLISH AND
WELSH NONCONFORMISTS

An important group of people who might be excluded from the parish registers of places where they lived were religious dissidents. As successors to the Elizabethan Puritans, parishioners dissatisfied with the Anglican Church began to meet together informally for worship. Known collectively as The Old Dissent, they soon ramified into three distinct movements, the General and Particular Baptists, the Presbyterians and Unitarians, and the Independents or Congregationalists. In the mid-seventeenth century the Religious Society of Friends also broke away from the Established Church.

So strong was their influence that during the period 1643–60, episcopally ordained clergy were ousted and supplanted by Presbyterians, and between 1646 and 1660 the authority of Anglican bishops and archdeacons was abolished and replaced by that of self-regulating parish presbyteries. From 1662, however, a series of enactments under the Clarendon Code led to the ejection of priests occupying a church living who refused ordination or acceptance of the Anglican Book of Common Prayer. Consequently many evicted clergy roamed the countryside to preach or emigrated with their congregations.

Tolerance of Protestant dissenters

From 1672, nonconforming preachers and householders were permitted to apply to their bishop for a licence to 'teach' or hold meetings in their homes within the diocese. A list of their names, addresses and denominations, taken from sources at Lambeth Palace Library in

London and among State Papers at the Public Record Office, has been printed in *Original Records of Early Nonconformity under Persecution and Indulgence*, by G Lyon Turner. The Act of Toleration in 1689 went further, as henceforward meeting houses or chapels could be erected by Protestant dissenters, so long as they were registered with the archdeacon, bishop or Quarter Sessions of the county, thus granting official sanction and a local focus. Although many chapels were established around this date they did not always flourish. Originally, most meeting houses served a wide radius, or were shared by different denominations which were locally too small on their own to run a place of worship. As the number of adherents increased daughter chapels were erected, but births and baptisms might continue to be recorded in the records of the mother chapel some distance away. Some preachers travelled around on circuit, whilst others became so popular that their fame attracted people to their chapels from far afield. There was also a two-way flow of allegiance between the Church of England and dissenting congregations, and between the denominations themselves, especially the Presbyterians and Congregationalists. Returners to the Anglican faith are frequently described in parish registers as 'Anabaptists' when baptised or buried, and in any event where they had no burial places of their own the parish churchyard was utilised. Mostly, though, it is difficult to distinguish from parish register entries who was and was not a conformist.

Gradually, splinter sects, whose beliefs diverged from the mainstream, hived off to form their own meetings. From the mid-eighteenth century, Calvinistic (Primitive) and Wesleyan Methodist preachers travelling from one circuit to another, drew most of their converts from transient and densely populated mining and manufacturing communities which sprang up in ancient sprawling rural parishes whose churches were situated far from the homes of inhabitants, but until about 1790 they continued to be baptised and buried by the Established Church. Each denomination had areas where its influence was particularly strong.

In Wales, the spread of nonconformity was slow until about 1780, after which it gathered pace.

Denominational registers

Because of early persecution, the first known surviving English

Protestant non-parochial register starts only in 1644, but few begin so soon. As all births and deaths were recorded in parish registers between 1645 and 1660, civil marriages took place before a magistrate from 1653 until 1660, and births of nonconformists were supposed to be notified and entered in parish registers up to 1706 under a statute of 1695, separate records might have seemed unnecessary, especially since they could not be used as evidence of paternity or age in a court of law.

In 1840 and 1857, the Registrar General ordered the surrender of non-parochial registers up to 1837 in England and Wales for authentication, with those of foreign congregations (Walloon, Huguenot, Lutheran, Dutch, Swiss and other churches). These, and deposited unauthenticated registers (including private chapels and premises where clandestine marriages had been performed before 1754) are now preserved in the Public Record Office where the authenticated volumes can be seen on microfilm at The Family Records Centre, the unauthenticated books at Kew. The authenticated entries are included on the International Genealogical Index under the appropriate counties. Microfilms and copies of the registers are also widely available in family history centres and at the Society of Genealogists in London, local ones being accessible also in county record offices.

Some registers which were withheld by chapels may still be there, in the denominational headquarters library or in county record offices. Most denominations publish *Year Books* of addresses of current local chapels and meetings. *My Ancestor . . .*, is a series of booklets produced by the Society of Genealogists about the major denominations, containing alphabetical lists arranged by county of known United Kingdom chapels and meeting houses, registers, other records, copies and finding aids. *Nonconformist Registers of Wales*, edited by D Ifans, is a survey of the principality, the National Library of Wales at Aberystwyth having an extensive collection of material generated by the Welsh Calvinistic Methodist Church (the Presbyterian Church of Wales), whilst the Glamorgan Record Office at Cardiff has records of Welsh meetings of the Religious Society of Friends from the 1660s onwards.

Points to consider

- The denomination at the time of deposit may not have been the same as at the outset.
- A chapel's foundation date and that of the first register entry may be many years apart.

- The books were not uniformly kept, with gaps, incomplete scrappy entries, retrospective baptisms jumbled up amongst those of a later era, and erratic recording of burials.
- Under-recording was least likely between 1785 and 1794 when stamp duty on baptisms and burials was extended to nonconformist registrations.
- Because the registers were treated as the priest's personal property, he might take them from chapel to chapel, entries from entirely different parts of the country being mixed up in his book.

Register content

The dated birth or baptism registers usually disclose the names of both the child and his or her parents, the mother's maiden name, where they lived, and the father's occupation, so are more informative than their Anglican counterparts, and of course there are fewer of them. Baptist registers record births and adult baptisms of members. Certain family names dominate the entries, among which the mother's maiden name may be traced, her surname also identifying her as marriage partner, especially useful after 25 March 1754, when all weddings became obligatory in the Anglican Church save for those of Quakers and Jews. As people journeyed as much as thirty miles to have their infants baptised at a chosen chapel or by a favourite priest, their given places of abode are also invaluable.

Burials

As already mentioned, oblique references in parish registers to bodies 'interred', 'hurled' or 'tumbled' into the ground may imply that they were dissenters, for whom the incumbent refused to perform funeral rites, especially for unbaptised Baptists and Quakers, and excommunicants. From the eighteenth century, meeting houses began to set aside land for burials, but the registers are frequently defective until 1864, when all burying grounds were legally obliged to keep records of interments. After 1880, dissenting ministers were allowed to conduct funerals in parish churchyards too, which were registered by the church.

The burial entries in nonconformist registers state the date and name of the deceased, and sometimes the place of residence and age. Registers of public burial grounds of dissenters in large urban centres, for example Bunhill Fields in London, contain references to people of all denominations, and some Anglicans, the partially indexed records of which, 1713–1852, are at The Family Records Centre in London, the indexed registers of Gibraltar Burying Ground, Bethnal Green, 1793–1826, being at Kew.

Gravestone inscriptions

Monumental inscriptions may fill gaps left by the registers, many of which they predate. Transcripts of a number have been published, and there is a good collection at the Society of Genealogists.

Other records kept by dissenters

Surviving minute books recording the conduct of church business and discipline, membership lists and church rolls should also be helpful, as they incorporate members' baptisms and burials, addresses, dates of admission and cessation through death, transfer elsewhere, or other reason. When a person or family moved their destination was often recorded. The church rolls were amended with married names of female members. Trust deeds relating to chapel property may also be annotated with the dates of death of trustees and their replacement by new nominees. Denominational magazines and year books should be scanned for obituary notices and biographies of ministers and nationally or locally prominent members. All the foregoing may be found at the chapel, at the denominational headquarters, local record office or library.

Two London birth registries

In 1742, a centralised birth registry was set up for the three denominations at Dr Williams's Library, in London, in the hope that its certificates might be admissible in courts of law, and to make up for the deficiencies of local record-keeping. Anyone paying the requisite fee could register their children's births, and as it was not limited to Londoners, births of people from all over the British Isles and overseas can be found until 1837 when the register was closed. Duplicate certificates completed by the parents and signed by them and two witnesses testified to the child's name, date, place and parish of birth, parentage and at least the maternal grandfather's name. One registered and numbered copy was filed at the registry and written up in a book, the other was handed back endorsed with the registration date and number. Particularly after 1768, baptisms were also registered.

Consult the initial indexes of surnames first, as registration did not always follow promptly after birth, completed families often being registered together. Parents registering their own births at the same time were consecutively numbered with those of their offspring. The photocopied or microfilmed registers and duplicate certificates are at The Family Records Centre in London, and Public Record Office, Kew, respectively, with similar indexed birth registers of the Wesleyan Methodist Metropolitan Registry, in London, 1773–1838.

Religious Society of Friends

Minute books of English and Welsh regional monthly and quarterly meetings of the Religious Society of Friends, to which births, deaths and burials of Quakers were reported, and meetings at which public declarations of marriage were exchanged up to 1837, are in the Public Record Office, Kew, or county record offices. You can search county digests of deposited books at the Public Record Office on microfilm at the Friends Library in London, on payment of an hourly fee. As already mentioned, records of Welsh meetings are kept at the Glamorgan Record Office at Cardiff.

Later central registers of births to 1959 (when birthright membership was abolished), deaths and burials to 1961, and of marriages of Friends throughout Great Britain to 1963 are also available in the library, arranged chronologically by initial letter of surname. They may be used as an alternative to civil registrations, but are not fully comprehensive for births or marriages, and from 1843 announcements in *The Friend* (discontinued after 1913), or *British Friend* may be better sources.

The county digests greatly simplify the extraction of all surname references in deposited records for any county or area from the seventeenth century to recent times. The digest entries are not full copies of the originals, so you should check these too. The marriage digests have two entries for each wedding, but omit fathers' occupations and the names of witnesses. You need to look under surnames of both partners for details of parentage, which are given separately for groom and bride.

What the minutes tell you

The birth entries in the registers of minutes reveal the child's name, when and where born, parentage, parental residence, and father's occupation, some early minutes retrospectively recording the parents' births too. The death entries provide in many instances both dates and places of death and burial, name, age, residence, occupation and parentage, whilst the dated marriage entries set out the names and abodes of the couple, their occupations, parentage and father's residence and occupation, followed by the names of everyone present, commencing with relations. As the same surnames constantly recur in the minutes, it is possible to reconstruct the various extensive family links over several generations.

As Quaker burials were in private gardens, orchards, or in a parcel of land designated as a sepulchre, and headstones were denounced as idolatrous in 1717, memorial inscriptions are sparse before 1850, when the rule was relaxed.

Some points about identifying dates

When using the digests and registers, you will see that the months and days are allotted numbers rather than names. Before 1 January 1752 the first day of the year fell on 25 March, which was also the first month, February being the twelfth and January the eleventh. Sunday was the first day of the week.

Details about Quakers in other sources

Look for baptisms in Anglican parish registers of adults born as Quakers, marriages of Friends to outsiders, and burials in the churchyard, especially during the first fifty years after the implementation of the second Burial in Woollen Act in 1678.

The Friends' own archives about members

Other useful Friends' records include the minutes of men's and women's separate or joint fortnightly preparative and larger monthly meetings dealing with church affairs. They note: admissions to membership, circumstances leading to disownment or disciplinary action taken against members; the two or three monthly public notifications by prospective couples of their intention to marry, subsequent enquiries made by the meetings about their suitability (they were not closely related, not remarrying in haste, and before 1859, both were

Friends), and freedom to marry with parental consent. The minutes testify to care of the poor, issue of removal certificates as character references and letters of introduction for people moving to specific meetings at home or overseas, receipt of certificates for incoming migrant Friends, and contain testimonies about recently deceased members. Sometimes these are the only extant record of a particular marriage or an individual's activities or mobility, and as a marriage partner from another meeting had to produce a certificate affirming its enquiries had been satisfactory, you can find out about their place of provenance. Many of the books are lodged in county record offices, if not retained by the meetings, a complete list of which, and some microfilm copies, are held at the Friends' Library in London.

The county quarterly and London yearly meetings of local elders and representatives also contain testimonies about deceased members and 'ministering Friends', to which there are indexes for the yearly meetings covering the period 1672–1906 at the Friends' Library.

Sufferings books kept by monthly meetings list names and abodes of Friends whose goods, crops or stock were distrained by county sheriffs, or who were imprisoned at Quarter Sessions for non-payment of tithes or for refusing to serve or pay for the hire of a substitute in the county militia. These document members in time and place, and the value of their seized property. The early United Kingdom ones to 1697 have been published in *A Collection of the Sufferings of the People called Quakers*, by J Besse, arranged by county, to which there is a personal name index. The original Sessions rolls of the magistrates, in Latin to 1733, are in county record offices, and some have personal name indexes, as outlined in *Quarter Sessions Records for Family Historians: A Select List*, by J Gibson.

Most monthly meetings have kept membership books of admission and cessation since 1 July 1837, and these are with the relevant meeting house.

Roman Catholics

If your antecedents were Roman Catholic, their baptisms, marriages and burials are likely to have occurred using Anglican rites, though they continued to worship secretly in private chapels or houses of local Catholic gentry in spite of severe penal laws. From 1606, you may discover registrations of private baptisms, avoiding the necessity of an Anglican church ceremony, as baptism was required within a month of birth on penalty of fine. Catholic landowners' children were usually publicly baptised in the Established Church to protect their rights of future inheritance. Otherwise, Catholic recusants may be under-recorded or difficult to identify as such in Anglican registers, and their own early records were deliberately sparse in case they should be seized as incriminating directories.

Roman Catholic registers

Although rough notebooks of baptisms were kept by priests and house chaplains, registers became prevalent only from the mid-eighteenth century, principally after the passage of the first Catholic Relief Act of 1778, and from 1791, when their places of worship were registered and thus became legal. Like their Protestant dissenting counterparts, non-resident Catholic clergy treated their registers as their personal property, so many were lost or contain baptisms of people from different areas.

Roman Catholic registers are mostly still in private hands, though a minority up to 1837 were deposited with the Registrar General in 1840 or 1857, chiefly from Yorkshire, Northumberland and Durham, and are now in the Public Record Office. Authenticated entries are on the International Genealogical Index. A few registers from other counties such as Hampshire and Lancashire have been published by the Catholic Record Society. Lists and whereabouts of *Catholic Missions and Registers 1700–1880*, in England, Wales and Scotland, have been edited by MJ Gandy together with a separate *Atlas* marking out Catholic parish boundaries. You can obtain the names and addresses of parish priests from the current edition of *The Catholic Directory*.

What the registers disclose

Baptisms may have been retrospectively recorded in the registers, and surname spelling is idiosyncratic and often phonetic. Details were usually written in Latin, dated baptisms giving the name of grandparents and godparents ('sponsors' or 'gossips') as well as those of the child and his or her parents, mother's maiden name, their abode and father's present occupation, and sometimes the child's date and place of birth and parents' birthplaces were noted.

Marriages between Catholics may have been clandestine, or by licence, followed by a private ceremony conducted by a Catholic priest, even after 25 March 1754.

Catholic registers of their own consecrated burying grounds usually supply age at death as well as name and date of demise of the person, though they were not legalised until 1852.

Other sources about Catholics

It is more common to find burials in Anglican registers, unless refused by the incumbent because the person had been excommunicated by a church court. They may be described as 'papists', 'recusants' or 'privately interred', indicating that Anglican rites were not performed.

Monumental inscriptions on headstones in churchyards prior to 1830 are likely to belong to Catholics if they are incised with a cross or the monogram 'IHS', but thereafter their attribution is less certain.

Lesser used Catholic archives

Other Catholic records you may find productive are the lists of dated conversions, and confirmations of adherents from 1687, which appear among the baptism registers or in the records at Archbishop's House, Westminster. If a member of your family was admitted to the priesthood or a religious order, biographical details about them and their parentage may be gleaned from college, seminary and institutional archives in this country or abroad. Particulars about their places of origin can then be tapped to trace your sibling ancestors.

Nominal records about Catholic recusants

As anti-Catholic legislation imposing civil and fiscal penalties was applied to convicted or proven Catholics until full emancipation in 1829, periodic dated parish lists show geographic spread and local concentration of known or suspected papists in England and Wales, but none is a complete country-wide directory, often merely representing a sample of dioceses or counties.

Some sixteenth- and seventeenth-century lists have been published by the Catholic Record Society.

Names, domiciles and occupations are frequently included in commissioned mandatory papists' returns now lodged in the House of Lords

Record Office, London, diocesan or county record offices, covering the years 1680, 1705, 1706, 1767 and 1780. Those for 1767 are especially useful as they give ages and length of residence of people in their current parish, and are dispersed among the above repositories, those for the diocese of London being at Lambeth Palace Library in London.

Spasmodic seventeenth- and eighteenth-century diocesan censuses, and presentments supplied by incumbents and churchwardens at the archdeacons' biannual and bishops' triennial visitations, also provide evidence of unbaptised or excommunicate inhabitants, and names of recognised or suspected papists, a collection of which are in the House of Lords Record Office. Proceedings instituted against recusants in the church courts contain testimonies under oath of local inhabitants about their accused neighbours, each deposition being prefaced with the name, abode, age, occupation and birthplace of the witness.

County Quarter Sessions rolls up to about 1782 contain presentments by churchwardens and parish constables of named recusants from 1570, and court minute books of the county Assizes from 1581, of those who were summonsed or indicted for non-attendance at church, acquitted or convicted, fined and bound in a recognisance for good behaviour during the following year. The former records and finding aids are described in Gibson's guide *Quarter Sessions Records for Family Historians: A Select List* whilst gaol calendars, court minute books and bundles of indictments of county Assizes are in the Public Record Office, Kew, organised under their respective regional circuits.

Registrations of papists' estates with the county clerk of the peace between 1715 and 1791 are also to be found among Quarter Sessions records, some of which have been printed; alternative central enrolments, in the custody of the Public Record Office, Kew, were abstracted and printed for the year 1715 in *The English Catholic Non-Jurors of 1715*, by EE Estcourt and JO Payne. You may also uncover enrolments of deeds and wills of Catholics during the same period in the Public Record Office or county record offices.

From 1625 until 1660, and 1689 until 1830, convicted Catholics aged seventeen and upwards were liable to pay double tax or a poll tax if their wealth fell below the assessed tax threshold. Indicted papists were similarly penalised from 1640, as were Catholics over sixteen refusing to swear prevailing statutory oaths of loyalty and allegiance to the Crown. Chronological parish lists of assessed taxpayers, exempt residents or absentees, people in arrears, or paying double levies are organised under hundred or wapentake within each county, by regnal year until 1688 (except for the Civil War and Commonwealth period). A complete list of places covered by each surviving roll or file is being prepared for publication by the Public Record Office.

Parish lists of Catholics double-charged for the land tax from its introduction in 1689 until at least 1794 when relief was granted, are noted in yearly county bundles with other concurrent assessed taxes of the period. The county files of appeals to the Exchequer between 1829 and 1831 against erroneous double payments are valuable because they often reveal genealogies of families since the last decade of the seventeenth century, stating how much was paid on the lands they owned or occupied. You can find out about dates and where-abouts of tax assessments and returns in England and Wales from the Restoration of the Monarchy in 1660 until the end of the century in *The Hearth Tax, other later Stuart Tax Lists, and the Association Oath Rolls*, by J Gibson, and for England, Wales and Scotland from the late seventeenth century onwards in *Land and Window Tax Assessments*, by J Gibson, M Medlycott and D Mills.

In February 1641/2 all males over the age of eighteen were expected to subscribe their allegiance to the Crown, the Protestant succession and faith against Popery, the primacy of Parliament and the liberty of the subject, on pain of bar from public office for refusal. Surviving parish Protestation returns of names (including some of women) taken down by the minister or churchwardens and transmitted to Parliament are in the House of Lords Record Office, with appended lists of absentees, known and suspected papists refusing or failing to comply. *The Protestation Returns 1641–42, and Other Contemporary Listings*, edited by J Gibson and A Dell, contains a complete county survey of England and Wales, identifying published lists and local copies. Other rosters of papists subscribing or declining to swear statutory oaths may be found among Quarter Sessions records and Public Record Office sources.

Family profiles

Biographies about convicted recusants and their immediate family circle were also furnished by the Exchequer and county Quarter Sessions to the Commissioners for Compounding with Recusants, appointed at intervals between 1614 and 1642, to discover concealed sources of revenue which could then be taxed. The records of the Northern Commissioners for 1629–32, in Ushaw College Library in Durham, have been published by the Catholic Record Society, revealing names of wives, children, in-laws, parents and grandparents of summoned people, in addition to their abodes and whereabouts of their lands. Seized estates were often then leased back or let to their former owners at a higher rent with the promise of no further action.

You can likewise discover family details about recusants from the papers of the Parliamentary Committee for Compounding with Delinquents (Royalist Compositions), which between 1643 and 1660 dealt with known or suspected supporters of Charles I, receiving voluntary inventories or informations valuing their goods, rents and estates before and after hostilities commenced, in order that the appropriate fine could be assessed, the severity of which was determined by the level of help rendered to the King. The filed evidence and correspondence frequently contain references to collateral branches of the family, dependants, tenants, employees and local inhabitants who were fellow-sympathisers or gave written testimony. There are indexed printed calendars to the records, which are in the Public Record Office at Kew.

After the Jacobite Rebellion of 1715, the Forfeited Estates Commission was set up to administer lands surrendered by papists tried and convicted of treason. A nominal alphabetical list, arranged by county, shows who was attainted, and the disposition of their lands, the documents themselves including depositions and petitions for compensation for lost or damaged property submitted by people in the northern counties. These too are in the Public Record Office at Kew.

Family and estate papers of known local Catholic landowners or sympathisers may also mention recusant relatives, tenants and neighbours, but as anything written could be used as incriminating evidence, they are likely to be less productive than government or diocesan instigated records. The National Register of Archives, at the Royal Commission on Historical Manuscripts, in London, has copies of catalogues of many such collections, plus on-line computerised subject indexes to principal names and estates covered by them.

Recusant rolls

Names, abodes, status or occupations and length of recusancy of dissenters of all creeds in England and Wales sent to the Exchequer by county clerks of the peace may be gleaned from annual recusant rolls running between 1591 and 1691, at the Public Record Office, Kew. They are deficient during the Civil War and Commonwealth periods, and because they were written in abbreviated Latin except for 1653–60, they are sometimes difficult to decipher. A few county rolls have been printed. Arranged alphabetically in Latin by county and then for Wales, the rotulets give details about people indicted, convicted, fined, suffering distraint of goods or forfeiture of land, or gaoled by dated meetings of Quarter Sessions or Assizes for persistent recusancy, non-attendance at church, or hearing mass, though rarely is their denomination given. As forfeiture was somewhat tardy, you may have to look at rolls for a number of years after a court appearance, but once found, you can examine the indictment or court minute books of the appropriate place of trial for more information.

Summing up

It is likely that at least one branch of your family had a connection with nonconformity, however brief, so the above sources should not be ignored, especially if you have failed to find your ancestors in parish registers.

12

LOOKING AT PARISH REGISTERS IN THE REST OF THE BRITISH ISLES, IRELAND AND THE UNITED STATES OF AMERICA

It is worth looking first at the International Genealogical Index of the Channel Islands for references to your name, and indexed births, marriages and deaths of islanders between 1831–1958 are included in the microfilmed Registrar General's Miscellaneous Foreign Returns at the Public Record Office, Kew. A transcript of baptisms, marriages and burials of native Channel Islanders at the 'French Church', Southampton, running from 1567 until the eighteenth century, is in the library of the Society of Genealogists in London.

On Jersey, the rectors of each of the Anglican parishes have custody of registers of baptisms, marriages and burials prior to civil registration in 1842, the earliest entry being in 1540. Manuscript copies and incomplete indexes in the library of the Société Jersiaise, St Helier, are open to members and bona fide searchers. Later marriage registers, up to the current year, are kept by the Superintendent Registrar, St Helier, but there are no public research facilities. A microfiche index to marriages as far as 1900 is available at the above library. The Channel Islands Family History Society is preparing an index of the registers of all twelve parishes and of the Methodist, Independent and Roman Catholic congregations up to 1842, all of which can be inspected at its research room in St Helier.

On Guernsey, you can inspect microfilm copies of parish registers at the Priaulx Library, St Peter Port, by appointment.

Details about Roman Catholic residents are among the records of the Bishop of Portsmouth, on the mainland.

Isle of Man

Abbreviated pre-civil registration baptisms and marriages from deposited Anglican registers at the General Registry in Douglas, are incorporated into the International Genealogical Index. For full details you would need to examine the original records of baptisms, 1611–1878, marriages, 1629–1883, and the burials, 1610–1878, or the bishop's transcripts of them, which cover the periods 1734-67 and from 1786 until the end of the nineteenth century, by appointment at the Registry.

Scotland

Old Parochial Registers of births, baptisms, proclamations of banns, marriages, deaths and burials kept by ministers and kirk session clerks of the Established (Presbyterian) Church of Scotland from 1553 until 1855 are available on microfilm at the General Register Office, in Edinburgh. Births, marriages and deaths between 1801 and 1854, registered as 'Neglected Entries' when civil registration began in 1855 are found at the end of the appropriate filmed parish register. Microfilm copies can also be hired at family history centres and branch libraries of the Church of Jesus Christ of Latter-day Saints worldwide, and microfilms of local registers are held by Scottish regional record offices and libraries. A number have been transcribed and many of these are lodged in the library of the Society of Genealogists in London. Kirk session minutes, mostly in the Scottish Record Office in Edinburgh, record dates and fees paid by parishioners for baptism, proclamation of marriage banns and burial, but contain only the briefest information about the parent, groom and bride, or informant. These may be useful where the registers themselves are deficient.

Starting with civil registration and the census

You can discover the birthplaces and dates and places of marriage of parents of people born after 1855, the parentage, approximate birth years and places of marital couples, and information about births and deaths of older brothers and sisters from civil registration records. Because they are housed in the same building as the Old Parochial Registers, the switch from central to local sources is straightforward, and you can also refer to the census returns for information about ages and birthplaces of family members.

Problems with surnames

As there were relatively few surnames in Scotland, identification of both parents in post-1855 civil records gives you an immediate headstart. In the Border counties, nicknames and diminutives were frequently used to distinguish inhabitants of the same name, whilst in coastal communities of the north-east the name of a person's boat might be tacked on to his surname. The use of patronymics instead of hereditary surnames in the Northern Isles up to the nineteenth century and adoption of different surnames by siblings are other features of Scottish family history. If you find an alias, it might be indicative of a territorial Highland clan or sept name, a man's wife's maiden name, or a wife's maiden and married names, though women were usually known by their maiden names throughout their lives and were recorded as such at their burial.

Indexes

The Old Parochial Registers of baptism and marriage are accessed via a computerised surname index, of which there are microfiche copies at family history centres and the Society of Genealogists. Arranged alphabetically by county, and usually under its original spelling, each person's surname, forename, sex, parent or spouse, event type, date and parish are given, with the number of the microfilm. Where mass migration or dislocation of inhabitants of cleared coastal villages and Highland settlements occurred, especially in the nineteenth century, these indexes can prove invaluable.

If your surname begins with Mc— or Mac— be sure to check under both, indexed separately, and consider the use of interchangeable letters such as 'Qu' for 'W', and Gaelic renditions of forenames.

The baptism date is inserted in the index when both birth and baptism appear in the register, and only the first parish is named in cases where several were combined. You can identify these from the maps in *The Phillimore Atlas and Index of Parish Registers*, or a gazetteer.

There are paper indexes to a few of the death and burial registers.

Background to registration

The bulk of the registers commence in the seventeenth century or later, but there may be extensive intervals when no entries were recorded, and deaths and burials may be lacking until 1855. This may be explained by the custom of taking bodies to ancestral or native burying grounds, or by the existence of several graveyards in a parish. The entries are in English or Old Scots, the latest-starting and least complete registers seeming to have been kept by more remote communities.

Births and baptisms

The best registers are those of dated births and baptisms, which usually provide the names of the child and its parents, the mother's maiden name, parental abode and father's occupation. Birth seniority may be stated too, especially when baptism was delayed and several siblings were baptised together. There was a widespread practice of naming the eldest son after the paternal grandfather, the second after the maternal grandfather, the third after the father, whilst the eldest daughter took the name of the mother's mother, the second that of her paternal grandmother, and the third her mother's name, though there were variations. Children might be called after the minister, or their sponsors (whose names and family connections might be entered in the register), though it has been suggested that sponsors were sometimes chosen because their names matched those of the grandparents. Surnames began to be used as forenames from the eighteenth century, but were not always associated with the family itself. A few male and female forenames were interchangeable, particularly in the Highlands, and Gaelic names, diminutives and latitude with forename variants were common, making positive attribution difficult.

Illegitimate children normally took the father's surname, in the nineteenth century the mother's, and were legitimised if the parents subsequently married provided both were single or of widowed status at the time of the birth. The child then assumed the father's surname. Kirk session minutes reveal details of investigations into the paternity of base born children so are worth exploring for more information.

Marriages

Dates of proclamation of banns or contract of marriage rather than the actual ceremony may be recorded in the marriage register or kirk session minutes. Although banns may have been proclaimed marriage did not inevitably follow. Kirk session minutes note the marriage money pledged by the groom as surety for the couple's good behaviour and marriage within forty days. The proclamation identified the parishes of each partner, the bride's father's name and groom's occupation, and if the groom was a minor, his paternity. If you look at the registers of both churches, you may find extra details about the wedding.

Irregular marriages

Irregular, but nonetheless valid, marriages in Scotland took four forms until 1939, since when only marriages by cohabitation and repute have been allowed, for which a declaration of marriage is required from the Court of Session in Edinburgh. Besides this, irregular marriages were by betrothal followed by consummation, by consent in the presence of witnesses, or without proclamation of banns though taking place in the Established Church. Payment of fines for the last can be found in kirk session minutes. Other places for irregular marriage were Tolls, such as at Lamberton and Mordington, at Halidon Hill and Coldstream, and at matrimonial offices like Gretna Hall, but from 1856 at least one of the couple had to have been resident in Scotland for twenty-one days prior to the ceremony, which was a deterrent for runaways. When nonconformist weddings were forbidden in 1661, Scottish dissenters crossed into England to marry up to 1753, though members of the Episcopal Church were married by their own clergy, under certain conditions, after 1712. After the passage of Hardwicke's Act Anglican ceremonies only were permitted in England, by banns or licence, so nonconforming Scots resorted to irregular marriages until the prohibition on their own denominational rites was removed in 1834. From 1834 proclamations of banns of dissenters' marriages were recorded in the Old Parochial Registers. Conversely, English Presbyterian dissenters travelled to centres like Edinburgh and Haddington in East Lothian to be married between 1754 and 1837.

Deaths and burials

The sparse recording of deaths and burials may be partially overcome by looking for details of fees paid to the kirk session clerk for hire of the parish mortcloth or pall with which to drape the coffin, though the impoverished and children under ten were excluded. In larger towns and burghs registers of non-denominational burial grounds were better kept, and are in the custody of the municipal authority or the General Register Office, Edinburgh.

Scottish memorials

The durable quality of many Scottish granite and slate headstones has ensured their survival from at least the sixteenth century. The Scottish Genealogy Society in Edinburgh holds an extensive collection of transcripts of monumental inscriptions from all over Scotland, further copies being lodged in regional record offices and libraries, including those at New Register House, Edinburgh, and the Society of Genealogists in London. The inscription may yield not only the name of the deceased, but his or her dates of birth and death, occupation, place of origin, croft, farm or toun of residence, parentage, spouse's full name and native parish, and the names of their children. The preposition 'of' indicates a landowner, 'in' a tenant, and 'at' a landless person. Occupations are sometimes signified by symbols carved on the stone.

Dissenters in Scotland

The Old Parochial Registers encompass people of other denominations, but unlike their English and Welsh counterparts, nonconformist registers were never centrally collected up. Incomplete series of listed volumes of baptisms and burials of Episcopalians since the seventeenth century, of Methodists from a century later, of members of the Free Church from 1843 and of nineteenth-century baptisms and marriages of Roman Catholics are in the Scottish Record Office in Edinburgh, though a number are still in local hands. Baptisms of many Methodists can be traced in records of the Established Church of Scotland.

The Scottish Established Church became Presbyterian when Roman Catholicism was proscribed in 1560, except for 1610–38, and 1661–89, when it was displaced by the Episcopalians. Sometimes births, baptisms and banns of marriage of the last group will be found in the Old Parochial Registers, especially since their clergy were driven underground and their meeting houses closed or destroyed in 1716 and 1746 after the Jacobite rebellions. Toleration was only restored in 1788 on condition that the ministers swore to acknowledge the thirty-nine articles and the Book of Common Prayer. Roman Catholics, however, continued to be persecuted until the first Relief Act of 1793, and few registers survive before this for protective reasons. Even when virtual full emancipation was granted in 1829 many Catholics continued to marry by cohabitation and repute.

The influence of English soldiers garrisoned at forts in Scotland led to the establishment of short-lived dissenting congregations which did not long outlast their stay, but nonconforming immigrant itinerant and seasonal workers from England and Wales after the Treaty of Union in 1707 made a more profound impression. Exchange of labour is reflected in the census returns of Scottish and English Border parishes. Catholic Irish arrived by sea from Donaghadee and Larne in large numbers during the nineteenth century for employment as railway navvies and shipworkers, and when the steamboat service started between Belfast and Glasgow in 1818 this gave added impetus, to the point at which Roman Catholics were second only in number to members of the Church of Scotland. Unfortunately the registers fail to give their places of provenance.

A comprehensive list of Quaker births, marriages, deaths and burials from 1622 until 1890 is held at the General Register Office, Edinburgh, and there is a microfilm copy at the Friends' Library in London, together with a Scottish digest up to 1837 and thereafter central registers of all births up to 1959, deaths to 1961 and marriages to 1963 of Friends in Scotland and elsewhere in Great Britain. The Society of Genealogists in London has a transcript of births registered between 1647 and 1874, marriages, 1656–1875, and deaths 1667–1878, for all Scottish meetings.

Ireland

Although in the minority, the Church of Ireland was paramount until disestablishment in 1869. Parish registers of baptisms, marriages and burials officially started in 1634, though one dates back to 1619. Few begin so early, and mostly commence after 1770. Nearly a thousand registers of baptisms and burials up to 1870, and marriages to 1845, collected up as public records, were consumed by fire in 1922, leaving less than half the original total, fortuitously kept back by churches, incidental transcripts made by priests on surrendering their records in 1845 , and compiled extracts made by historians and genealogists utilising them before the fire. As civil registration of non-Catholic marriages did not commence until 1845, and of births, marriages of Catholics and deaths until 1864, this was disastrous, especially as there were no bishops' transcripts and few census returns exist before 1901. However, these sources can bridge the gap up to 1870, and as length of marriage was indicated for married women in the 1911 census returns, this is a useful pointer to the date, though merely a person's age and county of birth were noted in 1901 and 1911, rather than the actual place. Do not rely on these ages being accurate, so search a spread of ten years either side of a projected birth year. You can find local surname distributions using the International Genealogical Index and the indexes to the tithe applotment books and Primary Valuation papers over half a century before. As with Scotland the limited range of surnames and forenames may make positive identification difficult.

The present whereabouts of surviving registers

A list of all known surviving registers is held by the National Archives of Ireland in Dublin, and there is a published *Guide to Irish Parish Registers*, by B Mitchell. Deposited originals, microfilm and other copies are dispersed in the National Archives of Ireland, the Representative Church Body Library in Dublin and for the northern counties in the Public Record Office of Northern Ireland in Belfast, although some registers remain with the clergy. The prior written permission of incumbents is required to examine microfilmed registers of the dioceses of Kildare, Glendalough and Meath, on deposit in the National Archives of Ireland. Names and addresses of local priests can be gleaned from the *Church of Ireland Directory*.

What the registers reveal

The registers were erratically kept up and badly written, the spelling in them being inconsistent or phonetic. You can expect baptism entries to state the date, child's name, and those of his or her parents, and occasionally their townland of residence, and from about 1820 the father's occupation. The marriage registers contain dates and names of couples, citing parishes of non-residents. Between 25 March 1754 and 31 March 1845, all weddings, except those between Quakers and Jews, were celebrated in the Established Church of Ireland by banns or licence, the entries being annotated accordingly. Irish irregular marriages during that period may be traced at Portpatrick, in Wigtownshire, and at Gretna Green, Dumfriesshire, both reached by the sea crossings to Scotland. The burial registers usually provide the date, name, age and townland of deceased local inhabitants of all denominations.

Headstones commemorating the dead

Gravestone inscriptions are a vital resource for details of birth, marriage and death and family relationships when parish registers are deficient. Many have been transcribed and indexed. There is a surname and place-name index up to 1910, and integral indexes thereafter to those published in the *Journal of the Association for the Preservation of the Memorials of the Dead,* 1888-1934. Indexed details are held on computer at local heritage centres throughout Ireland, which offer a commercial research service. There are also extensive collections of transcripts in The Genealogical Office in Dublin, and at the Society of Genealogists in London.

Tracing nonconformists

Baptisms, marriages and burials of Presbyterians are frequently found in Church of Ireland registers, though some records of congregations survive from the late seventeenth century. Presbyterian register contents are similar to those of the Established Church. The originals are in church custody (especially for the southern counties), in the Public Record Office of Northern Ireland, or at the Presbyterian Historical Society, Belfast. The Public Record Office in Belfast also has microfilmed copies of most locally held registers for the northern counties, and a list of those deposited with the Presbyterian Historical Society. Unfortunately, the present local whereabouts of registers of a particular church may be difficult to ascertain as many congregations merged, moved or vanished.

Like the Presbyterians, early Irish Methodists will be found in Church of Ireland registers between 1747 and 1816, rather than records of their own creation. During the split between 1816 and 1878, Primitive Methodists continued to use the Established Church but Wesleyan Methodist ministers kept circuit registers of the baptisms they performed making it difficult to track down specific entries without knowing their movements. As many local heritage centres now have indexed copies of surviving registers, the problem has been somewhat alleviated. A list of extant registers, arranged under each of the nine historic Ulster counties, is held by the Public Record Office of Northern Ireland, but there is nothing similar for the rest.

Microfilmed minutes of monthly meetings, recording births, marriages deaths and burials, and of documentary evidence about the Sufferings of the Religious Society of Friends are held in the Society's libraries in Dublin and at Lisburn, Co. Antrim, Northern Ireland, and in the Public Record Office of Northern Ireland. Some date from the seventeenth century, and the first has indexed records of births, marriages and deaths of Friends throughout Ireland between 1859 and 1949.

The earliest known surviving Roman Catholic register of baptisms and burials dates from the 1680s, but many only commence in the last century as a precaution against seizure as relaxation of civil and religious restrictions only began in 1793, and full emancipation was not granted until 1836. Burial registration was uniformly patchy. Late start-dates may also be connected with the creation of smaller parishes carved from sprawling densely populated urban ones, so you should not neglect older records of churches nearby. In order to identify which Catholic church served a civil parish look at *Topographical Dictionary of Ireland*, edited by S Lewis; county maps showing contiguous parishes and first register entry dates are included in *Tracing Your Irish Ancestors*, by J Grenham.

The registers are in Latin or English, baptisms noting the date, child's and parents' names, the mother's maiden name, where they lived and names of godparents or sponsors. Marriage entries reveal the date, the couple's names and those of witnesses, but may include each of their addresses, age, occupation and paternity of the bridal pair. The registers also record marriage dispensations, granted when partners were blood relations (*'consanguinati'*), and specify their degree of kinship as first cousins (second degree), second cousins (third degree), or if the two families were connected by an earlier marriage (*'affinitatus'*).

United States of America

Because commencement of civil registration of births, marriages and deaths may be as recent as the twentieth century in some southern states, church registers of baptisms, marriages and burials assume great importance as a genealogical tool.

Identifying a congregation

The myriad sects and lack of overall federal or state uniformity of worship reflect the predominant creeds and native languages of leading pioneers, planters and later immigrant families and groups congregating in counties or states with their fellow countrymen. Some assemblies soon withered or could no longer sustain a chapel and preacher, so amalgamated. As with British dissenters, adherence to one denomination was not always strict, so settlers might be found in records of various local chapels and churches. Often though, the congregation's denomination may be an indicator of the European state or locality of first-generation settlers, who frequently sailed to the colonies with their priest or local gentry: the chronicled place of origin of the latter two can provide a vital clue to that of other settlers. If family or other archives identify the priest concerned, his denomination and church should be known to the library of the appropriate county, and you can trace ministers in towns and cities in contemporary directories.

If you have found names of later ships' passengers, nineteenth-century immigrants may be traced back to their place of provenance via their death certificates, naturalisation papers and dated lists of alien arrivals at Ellis Island, New York. Death certificates may give the name of the clergyman officiating at the funeral, and a marriage certificate the denomination of the church or chapel of at least one of the bridal couple.

The International Genealogical Index is also worth tapping for references to your surname in various states, as the entries record parishes and counties where birth, baptism or marriage occurred.

Tracking down the records

Original registers may be studied in state and local historical libraries and societies, or remain at the church, where access may be restricted. You can obtain addresses of current clergy and church elders from computerised telephone directories. Microfilm copies and transcripts of many church registers may be widely seen, and hired for use at family history centres or branch libraries of the Church of Jesus Christ of Latter-day Saints worldwide. The Society of Genealogists in London, has published a list of its collection of copies.

Addresses of libraries may be found in the current edition of *The Directory of Archive and Manuscript Repositories* and of local historical societies in *Directory of Historical Societies and Agencies in the United States and Canada*, which is updated every five years. If you cannot search yourself, or public access is not permitted, a paid research service is often available. State or county genealogical societies may offer help too, and are listed in each annual edition of *Genealogical Research Directory*.

What the registers may tell you

The earliest registers commence in the 1620s, each year beginning on 25 March until 1751 inclusive, and thereafter on 1 January in line with the modern Gregorian Calendar. Written in the vernacular, baptism entries contain the date, names of the child and his or her parents, their residence, and sometimes the names of godparents, and the infant's date of birth.

As the early Puritan settlers were married in civil ceremonies, the clerk was not obliged to record them. Marriage details vary in fullness from noting the date and the names of both parties to a statement of age and birthplace, where they were living, the groom's occupation, parents' birthplaces, and the couple's denominations, usually encountered in registers of Catholic, Lutheran and German Reformed Churches. Irregular marriages were contracted in large American cities, so look for an elusive wedding in records of the one nearest to the place of domicile. The length of a person's marriage can be gleaned from the 1900 census schedules, and clues about marriage date and place extracted from veterans' and widows' applications for Civil War military pensions, in the National Archives, Washington, DC.

Burial registers frequently specify date and place of birth as well as death, vital to people trying to track the overseas origins of settlers, or newcomers trekking from other states.

Continuing migration west in the eighteenth century, and after the Revolutionary War makes for difficulty in tracing family movements and upheavals, but the International Genealogical Index may again prove helpful, albeit minus burials.

Gravestone inscriptions

Where death registrations and burial registers are wanting or deficient, gravestone inscriptions may prove invaluable. Though there are headstones dating from the early seventeenth century, a number of which have been transcribed and printed, most stem only from the eighteenth century or later. As the decennial federal censuses did not name everyone in a household until 1850, headstones can identify people whose existence and family relationships might be unrecorded anywhere else, especially women.

Immigrants were commemorated under the original spelling of their names, rather than ones later assumed by their offspring, and the headstones thus provide important clues to their native identity. The stones also often give details of date and place of birth, absent from any burial register.

In rural areas it was common for families to have their own burial plots close to their farm or homestead. Some have been well attended and the headstones remain in good condition, but many have been lost or destroyed, or their whereabouts are unknown. Most churches had attached graveyards, using new suburban sites when they were closed or filled up. Public civic, county or local authority cemeteries permitted burials of people of all denominations, as do the more recently established commercial memorial parks. You can often determine place of interment from death certificates.

Sextons' books, registering burials in public and municipal cemeteries and memorial parks, are augmented by cemetery deed books listing sales, transfers and bequests of plots. The sextons' records contain names, dates, and causes of death, relationship and name of the next of kin, and sometimes birth details about the deceased, which may be missing from or illegible on the headstone. These are in the custody of the appropriate cemetery office, whose address can be obtained via a telephone directory.

13

DELVING AMONG THE CONTENTS OF THE PARISH CHEST

Using parish registers, you can track your ancestry back three hundred years before civil registration to the reign of King Henry VIII in the sixteenth century. Concomitant with these were other parochial records chronicling the activities of parishioners, from which you can learn about their interaction with each other and the role they played in running parish affairs. Like the parish registers, such material has now mostly been removed from the parish chest, inventoried and placed in the care of county record offices (or for Wales, in the National Library at Aberystwyth), where you will find listed minute books of vestry meetings, churchwardens' accounts, overseers of the poor rate books and accounts, bastardy bonds, indentures of poor apprentices, signed examination papers about legal settlement, settlement certificates and removal orders of outsiders, constables' and highway surveyors' accounts. Sometimes a town book was used for all the accounts, which with numerous other amorphous volumes and loose material, form a formidable extra genealogical resource. Rarely do any stretch in an unbroken sequence from inception, and as they were compiled by a succession of annual officers of varying education, literacy, and conscientiousness, their legibility, spelling and thoroughness are uneven.

Vestry meetings

The vestry meeting, with its roots in the fourteenth century, deliberated over both ecclesiastical and civil matters affecting the parish and its inhabitants, regardless of denomination, under the chairmanship of the incumbent, until most of its civil duties passed to parish councils created after 1894. An open vestry was a general meeting which every parish ratepayer could attend; a select or closed vestry consisted of twelve, eighteen or twenty-four co-opted principal inhabitants and became a self-perpetuating elite, whose decisions and nominations often reflected their religious leanings, social connections and prejudices. You can tell who was present from the signatures at the foot of the minutes.

The minutes of the monthly and fortnightly vestry meetings set down the collective resolutions about parish by-laws, administration of communal parish property, disciplinary action taken against parishioners for moral misconduct, encroachment on or abuse of the commons, or non-attendance at church, and the Easter elections of parish officers.

The vestry applied to the bishop for a faculty granting consent to their sanctioned expenditure on substantial repairs and alterations to the church or churchyard, examined the ledgers of parish officers on completion of their service, and supervised distribution of poor relief and apprenticeship of poor boys and girls in other parishes.

Parish officers

Besides electing the churchwardens, the vestry was responsible to the mid-nineteenth century for nominating to the justices of the peace names of parishioners for approval as overseers of the poor, highway surveyors and constables for the parish. A property qualification determined candidacies for these posts. Sometimes the various offices devolved by 'house row', according to occupancy of particular properties, or certain people were repeatedly elected to office, whilst others held several posts simultaneously. Occasionally dated house row agreements come to light, identifying current occupiers or owners of affected properties and their successors, each taking a turn at parish service. Provision was usually made for a male substitute should a woman become liable. They form a virtual parish survey of land ownership and tenancy at a prescribed date, and in the absence of a map they locate and name individual homesteads, farms and plots of ground.

Service as a parish officer could be onerous and until the nineteenth century only expenses were refunded, though it conferred a legal settlement on the holder, and thus entitlement to parish support should he become destitute or unable to work through sickness or old age. The vestry minutes may record how many votes each nominee received, and when paid officers like a sexton and organist were employed, details about applicants, appointments, salaries and resignations may be found too.

What happens today

Minutes of vestry meetings recording annual Easter elections of churchwardens are still kept today, together with those of parochial church council meetings conducting business relating to communal parish property outside the scope of the parish council. Parish ratepayers may attend vestry meetings, but only baptised parishioners over the age of eighteen and not belonging to another congregation may attend the second. Their names and addresses are listed alphabetically on an electoral roll displayed at the church.

The role of the churchwardens

The office of churchwarden dates back at least to the fourteenth century. In parishes made up of more than one township, it was usual to elect two representatives for each, with responsibility for the upkeep and repair of designated parts of the church building and fabric. The following tasks fell within their remit:

- After 1538 they purchased and preserved registers into which they or the incumbent wrote down parish baptisms, marriages and burials, and after 1598 compiled annual transcripts of the entries for transmission to the bishop.
- Under threat of excommunication for neglect, they made twice-yearly written presentments to the archdeacon on his visitation to the parish, and when the bishop visited every three years, on the condition of the church and churchyard, religious conformity and performance of his duties and divine services by the incumbent, the moral conduct and any irregularity of parishioners such as recusancy or persistent non-attendance at church.
- They acted as sequestrators when the living fell vacant.
- They were expected to raise finance for the parish through their efforts. Accounts of their daily income and expenditure were laid before the vestry meeting at the end of the year, and contain dated

receipts of donations, church rates, pew rents, special collections of alms and offerings, fees for funerals and hiring-out the parish hearse, balanced by outgoings on quarterly wages to the parish clerk, bell ringers, sexton and organist and disbursements for the general upkeep of the church, and rewards paid for pest control.

- Sometimes the churchwardens acted as overseers of the poor, so their accounts contain entries of expenditure on outdoor relief paid to the elderly, sick and infirm at home or boarded-out.

Overseers of the poor

Overseers or collectors of the poor were first formally appointed under a statute of 1597, though voluntary contribution of alms began much earlier. Each parish had at least two for every township and from 1819 the vestry was empowered to pay one overseer a salary. The office was finally abolished in 1925, though its function was vestigial after 1834, when civil Poor Law Unions were set up. Their responsibilities included the following:

- Fixing the six-monthly poor rate and drawing up property valuations with advice from the vestry and local magistrates, from which they compiled jurors' lists and until 1918 electoral registers.
- Handing out nomination papers for local elections.
- Posting parish notices and militia lists of able-bodied men of the parish within the statutory age limit.
- Organising the regular perambulation of the parish boundaries ('beating the bounds').
- Acting as the first census enumerators.
- Until 1834 they fulfilled their responsibility for putting the able-bodied poor to work, paying outdoor relief to paupers remaining at home or placing them in the workhouse, arranging for burials of the poor or unknown travellers at parish expense, apprehending wandering lunatics, rogues and vagabonds, and organising the examination and removal of strangers without obvious means of support.

Overseers' rate books, from about 1601 until 1834, record the six-monthly collections of the poor rate, each contribution calculated at so many pence in the pound based on the specified annual value of named occupiers' properties. The running account books, from 1691 until 1834, contain:

- Dates, names, ages, weekly support, rents and pensions paid to permanent recipients.
- Intermittent medical, nursing or midwifery expenses.
- Funeral bills.
- Weekly upkeep of orphans or pauper children boarded-out for the year with relatives or other householders after 1782.
- Maintenance of single parents.
- Apprenticeship of poor or orphaned youngsters.
- Provision of fuel and clothing to old, needy or disabled parishioners no longer capable of work.
- Purchase of raw materials to create industry for fit poor.
- Removal costs of unwelcome newcomers back to their established last parish of legal settlement.
- Travel expenses of pauper emigrants.

Thus their pages record confinements, illnesses and epidemics, harvest failures, personal disasters and tragedies, unemployment and migration, all of which help to build up a picture of community life, and can be linked to baptisms, marriages and burials in the parish registers. The rate and account books were surrendered annually to the vestry meeting and a local magistrate for inspection and approval.

Bastardy orders and bonds of indemnity

From 1733, a person charged on oath by two magistrates or by the county Quarter Sessions with being the father of an illegitimate child was apprehended and jailed unless he gave security under a bastardy order to indemnify the parish against all expenses for his offspring's upkeep, by paying a one-off lump sum or regular fixed contributions. The dated bastardy bonds, signed by the acknowledged father and his surety, the churchwardens and overseers, accepted responsibility for the named infant born in the parish, and payment of a specified weekly or other sum during its infancy (until eight). The names, residences, occupations or offices of all parties, including the mother, were given, plus the marital status of both parents. These were recorded in the vestry minutes, any appeals going first to the vestry and then to Quarter Sessions.

In many instances, though, there is no formal record of how base-born children were cared for, so presumably agreement about future support was somehow reached between the alleged father and the overseers. The best outcome was to coerce him into marrying the mother to make the child legitimate, especially if he belonged to another parish, since this conferred both mother and child a settlement there.

Pauper apprentices

Pauper children and orphans were frequently apprenticed at about seven or eight as domestic or farm servants of householders within the parish or elsewhere. Parishioners might take their turn by house row, with a penalty for refusal, or the vestry arrange their binding-out to a craftsman or tradesman in another parish, by paying a premium. From the eighteenth century, London parishes often off-loaded unwanted children to factories and mills in manufacturing centres, whose own registers describe their names, ages and parishes of origin, dates of arrival, discharge or death, conduct, employment, education and health. Where such survive they may have been placed in county record offices or remain with the present-day representatives of the business or factory-owning family.

Duplicate indentures set out agreed terms and conditions. They cover the period 1601 until the twentieth century, although compulsory binding-out ceased in 1844, and sometimes from 1802 a special apprenticeship register was substituted. A copy of the dated indenture was kept in the parish chest, signed by the overseers, two magistrates, consenting parent or guardian and the parishioner or non-resident prepared to house, feed, clothe and employ the named child until the age of twenty-four (reduced to twenty-one in 1767) or marriage, and setting out the terms and any money paid by the parish. Complaints about abuses during servitude were heard initially by the vestry meeting or referred on appeal to the county Quarter Sessions.

The Old Poor Law and gaining a legal settlement

The Poor Law Act of 1601 was designed to maintain and set the poor to work using the funds of parishioners. Later legislation secured them a settlement, so preventing their perishing and restraining migration to places where they might squat, lay waste, burn the wood and destroy the best or largest commons before moving on. Up to 1876, the grounds on which a person established a legal place of settlement were governed by a series of statutes from 1662. Initially, strangers renting a tenement worth less than £10 a year could be removed within forty days of arrival on the order of two magistrates unless they could offer sufficient security discharging the parish from any expenses likely to be incurred on their behalf. After this had elapsed they were granted a settlement. Temporary residents possessing a certificate from a previous parish of residence agreeing to take them back were considered acceptable. In 1685 the forty-day period commenced when the newcomer submitted a written notice of arrival to the overseers, so they could no longer hide during the qualifying period for residence. From 1691, the qualifying period was deemed to start when the notice was read out in church and registered in a parish book.

After 1691, legal settlement was determined in one of the following ways: by parish of birth; by indenture of apprenticeship to a parishioner once forty days of it had expired; by hire in service for a year in the parish; by intermarriage with a male parishioner; by contribution to the parish rates; by holding a parish office; or by residence for the full forty days. Whichever was the most recent conferred a settlement.

Many parishes shunted pregnant single mothers on until the child's birthplace granted it a settlement, so from 1744 the mother's settlement became that of her illegitimate offspring.

Settlement certificates

After 1697, as restriction of mobility of labour had raised unemployment levels, the poor were allowed to enter any parish in search of work so long as they had a settlement certificate signed by the churchwardens and overseers of their place of provenance and two magistrates guaranteeing to receive them back should they become chargeable. Thenceforward until 1810, paupers suffered the indignity of being badged on the right shoulder with the initial letter 'P' and that of their place of settlement (thus being known as badgers), on penalty of loss of relief or placement in the house of correction for refusal.

Parishes were authorised to transport rogues, vagabonds and sturdy beggars to the Plantations after 1662, and lists of names drafted by the overseers and sent to Quarter Sessions for approval may be found in the vestry minutes and Sessions rolls.

Examinations and removal orders

The caches of signed examinations of persons under oath before a local magistrate disclose the background, movements and purported last legal place of settlement of strangers looking likely to become a burden, and against whom a complaint had been made within forty days by the churchwardens and overseers. The potted autobiographies are about people whose lives would otherwise have remained lost to us. They contain details of every event having a bearing on settlement from cradle to present circumstances. Age, parentage, birthplace, apprenticeship, employment, marriage, names and ages of children were all written down. They were preserved by the parish as evidence of settlement somewhere else. When settlement was refused, a removal order was drafted and signed by the churchwardens, overseers and two magistrates, with a duplicate for presentation by the parish constable escorting the person or family out to the officers of the parish where they were deemed legally chargeable. Appeals concerning settlement and removal may be found among the records of county Quarter Sessions.

Unfortunately, because examinations, settlement certificates and removal orders were prepared individually, their survival is patchy and they probably represent only a small fraction of the thousands of original records. Many county record offices have produced personal name indexes to their collections, from which you can track a person's life history and mobility within the county, about the country or abroad. Look at *Marriage, Census and Other Indexes for Family Historians*, cited earlier, for their whereabouts.

Records of the New Poor Law

Poor Law Union Records, compiled chiefly by J Gibson and C Rogers, contains a complete survey of post-1834 records of local Boards of Guardians and central administration up to 1948 in England and Wales, to which there is a *Gazetteer* of parishes within each Union.

The parish constable

The office of parish or petty constable (also known as headborough, borsholder or tithingman) probably stems from before the thirteenth century, and continues to the present day in a few instances, though gradually replaced after 1829 in London and after 1839 in counties when paid police forces began to be set up. As the office may have originated in the manor, there was some overlap of function with that of manorial constables, and their annual appointments may therefore be found in manorial court leet minutes rather than those of the vestry meeting. From 1842, however, only the vestry nominated candidates and recommended their salaries for approval by the Quarter Sessions, before whom the new constables were sworn in.

Constables' accounts, dating from the 1660s, like those of the overseers of the poor and highway surveyors, were placed before the vestry meeting and a local magistrate at the end of each year.

The constable's major duties revolved around crime prevention and included a power of arrest. He held the keys to the parish stocks, pillory or cage used as punishment for misdemeanours. Through him the paid justices sitting in county Assize Sessions learned about local felonies and misdemeanours. He supplied to the Assizes or Quarter Sessions names of recusants, persistent non-attenders at church, drunkards, and licensed badgers, and reported unlicensed alehouses, illegal or riotous assemblies so they could be dealt with. He convened parish meetings and local petty sessions, summoned the coroner's inquest jury, and drafted lists of freeholders from which the county clerk of the peace empanelled juries at the Quarter Sessions.

- He enforced local regulations regarding licensing, weights and measures;
- collected county rates and national taxes;
- cared for the parish armour on behalf of the county militia;
- mustered, fully equipped and paid for the upkeep during training of militia men chosen by lot from his list of liable men in the parish, and hired substitutes using discharge money of those excusing themselves from compulsory service;
- remitted weekly pensions fixed by the county to sick or maimed impressed soldiers and seamen, and gave succour to itinerant soldiers making their way home.

Until overseers of the poor were appointed he was responsible for the welfare and housing of destitute parishioners. He apprehended beggars, whipped vagrants and moved them on, and executed removal orders of strangers out of the parish.

The constable also had charge of the parish pound for the custody of stray livestock, purchased and looked after the parish bull.

The highway surveyors

Signed highway surveyors' or waywardens' accounts record outlay on road upkeep and repairs, and moneys received to hire substitutes in place of parishioners liable for annual free statutory labour. Two officers were normally elected, though there might be more if the parish was a large one. Dating between 1555 and 1834, when civil highway districts took over, their books are the least likely to survive, if kept at all, as the officers were often ill-educated or negligent, allowing roads to become ruinous in spite of their triannual reviews and reports to Quarter Sessions.

What else to look for among parish records

Other documentation originally stowed away in the parish chest included:

- eighteenth- and nineteenth-century maps and awards of applotments of land to compensate landowners deprived of future use of enclosed commons and open fields;
- a copy of the nineteenth-century tithe map and apportionment commuting payment in kind by householders to a yearly rent charge;
- sporadic dated terriers from about the early seventeenth century onwards, inventorying the church contents, the churchyard, its fences and hedges, followed by a detailed description of the construction of the parsonage house and outbuildings, the nature, extent and use of the glebe, and abutments on other named properties, identifying each owner or tenant, tithe income, Easter offerings and other customary revenue of the incumbent;
- a survey of 'ring fences', marking out the parish boundaries;
- signed and sealed dated deeds and wills of benefactors mentioning the mechanism under which trusts and charitable endowments were to be set up and managed, their purpose, names of trustees and intended group of beneficiaries.

If the local school was endowed by the church, the chest might contain minute books of meetings of school governors, at which the priest presided. You might also turn up marriage allegations, bonds and licences in parishes which were peculiars, correspondence relating to requests for interment in the churchyard after 1853, faculties from the bishop permitting church alterations or churchyard clearance, and more recently, copies of parish magazines announcing or reporting local events and news about inhabitants. You may even find indexes or transcripts of parochial records and gravestone inscriptions, a churchyard plan, and less often for obvious reasons, a visiting book into which the incumbent jotted down dated comments and remarks about the health or current status of his flock.

Nominal lists

You may also find out about parishioners from discarded electoral rolls, lists of communicants and candidates for confirmation. When the clergy were census enumerators, draft decennial returns of heads of household between 1801 and 1831 may be found too. Many known ones appear under their respective counties in *Local Census Listings 1522–1930: Holdings in the British Isles*, by J Gibson and M Medlycott.

Details of pew rents collected from parishioners allocated seats by the churchwardens may accompany church seating plans. Rosters of seventeenth- and eighteenth-century contributors to appeals under Royal mandates or briefs, and special collections by the parish clerk or churchwardens for specific deserving causes take you back to an earlier era of charitable fund-raising.

When the incumbent was the patron of the living or his relative, and happened to be a tax commissioner and lord of the manor, copies of dated tax assessments, manorial court rolls and rentals might also be stored in the parish chest.

Scotland

Although kirk session meetings of parish elders of the Church of Scotland were first instituted in the mid-sixteenth century, minute books do not seem to have been kept by session clerks until the next century. These and recorded minutes of the meetings of parish presbyteries, like the English and Welsh vestry meetings, cover all aspects of parish administration and discipline, under the chairmanship of the minister as moderator. They note receipts of pledges for proclamations of marriage and mortcloth fees, moneys paid in support of the poor, identify fathers of bastard children, inhabitants summoned and punished by public confession or fine for moral misconduct or slander, recommendations for divorce or nullity of marriage of couples seeking to petition the commissary court, and paint a vivid picture of community life. Burgh and sheriff courts could enforce their decisions and imprison miscreants, so where parochial records are defective the loss may be made up by consulting the court act books, many of which are now in the Scottish Record Office in Edinburgh, and some of which have been published. You can read more about them in *Candie for the Foundling*, by A Gordon.

Looking for names and dates

Parish lists of communicants, catechism rolls of young people examined on their religious knowledge, of children and residents of other denominations, and occasional rosters compiled by the minister setting out the names, ages, marital status, family relationships, occupations, health, educational level and moral conduct of his congregation each serve as a directory of inhabitants at a specific date. Filed and dated certificates of testimonials from the minister or kirk session of a newcomer's former parish provide a vital link to place of origin.

Most of the above parish records are now in the Scottish Record Office, though some remain with individual churches. Consult *Local Census Listings*, 1522–1930, for the whereabouts of the nominal lists.

Ireland

Extensive collections of minute books of parish vestry meetings are held by the Representative Church Body Library in Dublin, and of the northern counties in the Public Record Office of Northern Ireland in Belfast, though some have been retained by local clergy. Searches can be made of indexed microfilms of a number by local heritage centres, though public access is prohibited.

United States of America

Some of the early vestry minute books and records of church elders in seventeenth-century colonies on the Atlantic seaboard have been printed. Their business closely resembled that transacted by English and Welsh vestry meetings, including annual elections of officers, responsibility for law and order, moral discipline, and the mustering of able-bodied men into the militia. You may be able to trace overseas origins of settlers from dated confirmation lists, as they give the name, age, place of baptism and parentage of candidates. Membership and communicants' rosters signify a person's joining and leaving dates. When cessation was by death, the burial register, gravestone inscription, or probate packet might tell you more about the person and his or her family. If the person moved away or was a newcomer, the dated testimonial sent ahead by the minister or church elders will disclose place of origin and destination as well as a character assessment. This is particularly helpful if the testimonial was dispatched from overseas, as was the case with the Religious Society of Friends, because an immediate connection can then be made with the immigrant's place of provenance.

You can discover the dates and whereabouts of known parish records from local genealogical or historical societies or local libraries of the area, but if they are in private hands, there may be access restrictions.

Church clerks tended to write their minutes in the vernacular language of the immigrant group or dominant nationality, so this may pose a problem for the modern reader. However, the entries were often very full and spelled the names as originally used by settlers before obscured by subsequent Americanisation or alteration. When parish registers of baptism, marriage and burial are wanting or deficient, such records at best can supply evidence of first arrival, residence and continuity, and where family or social groups arrived together, serve as a bridge to their transatlantic origins.

14

NECESSARY STEPS BEFORE MARRIAGE

Prior to 1 July 1837, the only alternative to the protracted publicity of banns read out to church congregations on three consecutive Sundays was the purchase of a marriage licence permitting the ceremony in a specific church or chapel.

History and types

Spasmodic references to Medieval marriage licences, written in Latin, are found in bishops' registers, but their wider usage originated in the mid-sixteenth century and the break with Rome, interrupted only during the Commonwealth years of 1653–60 when the church courts were suspended and marriages were performed by magistrates without religious ceremony.

The procedure was speedy and private, but one of the parties had to be resident in the appropriate parish for four weeks preceding the applcation (reduced to fifteen days in 1823). Although the residential rule was laid down in a canon of 1604, it was not always strictly applied before 1754, as shown by the popularity of irregular marriages between outsiders in certain parishes, notably peculiars (parishes owing no direct loyalty to the local bishop). From 25 March 1754, however, no marriage was valid in England, Wales or Ireland without banns or licence, unless the couple were both Quakers or Jews, so irregular marriages came to an end.

Who granted licences?

Where at least one of the pair lived in the chosen parish the chancellor of the diocese supervised issue of a licence through his registrar or deputy. In large dioceses archdeacons were delegated similar powers, often acting through surrogate parish clergy who sent them their bundles of signed and sworn documentation for registration and safe-keeping.

The Vicars General of the Archbishops of Canterbury and of York sold licences to couples who came from different dioceses, whilst the Faculty Office of the Archbishop of Canterbury exercised overall licensing authority over marriages between residents of separate Provinces. There was nothing to prevent application to a superior office, which might be more convenient and carry greater social cachet, though it charged higher fees. Some places exempt from this hierarchy had peculiar jurisdiction over licensed marriages in their own churches.

By far the most licensed weddings were and are by common licence, but to 1754 the Vicars General, and thereafter the Faculty Office, were empowered to grant special licences 'to marry at a convenient time or place' which until 1866 did not need to be defined. After 1759, they were limited to certain social categories unless the applicant had strong and weighty reasons which he could prove to the registrar, for example, a connection with a specific church or a death bed ceremony.

Marriage allegations and bonds

The licence was presented by the couple to the priest authorising him to perform the wedding service in his church. It is most unusual for the licences themselves to have come down to us, unless lodged in the parish chest of a peculiar where it was issued. Sworn and signed preliminary marriage allegations and bonds were filed in the arch-diocesan or diocesan registry and brief details entered in separate act books or registers of licences, in Latin up to 1733.

The allegations, bonds, act books and registers can be inspected in diocesan or county record offices, those of Welsh dioceses in the National Library of Wales at Aberystwyth. Allegations and bonds in the Faculty Office and Vicar General's Office of the Province of Canterbury are kept at Lambeth Palace Library in London, those of the Vicar General of the Province of York at the Borthwick Institute of Historical Research at York.

The allegations and bonds were filed together chronologically, and many collections have been indexed or summarised in calendars. Printed or microfilm copies of indexes or calendars are widely available, especially in family history centres and branch libraries of the Church of Jesus Christ of Latter-day Saints, and the Society of Genealogists in London has a good run, to which there is a published catalogue. The Welsh allegations and bonds have been indexed up to 1837. All known English and Welsh records and finding aids are included under counties in *Bishops' Transcripts and Marriage Licences, Bonds and Allegations: A Guide to their Location and Indexes*, edited by J Gibson.

As a licence was valid for three months, look for the allegation and bond during that interval before a marriage, and conversely in parish registers during the subsequent months after the application date. You can tell if a marriage was by licence as the parish register notes it, usually shortened to 'by Lic.'. The indexes and calendars of all offices appropriate to the parish should be consulted, and you can also trawl them for elusive marriages of people away from their place of residence, and track a surname's geographic distribution over time. As diocesan boundaries are rarely coincident with civil counties, you may have to search ecclesiastical material extending over several counties or of more than one diocese serving a particular locality in a record ofice well away from the majority of the relevant parish records.

What the records contain

Few collections survive in an unbroken series, but where the allegation is missing, usually the accompanying bond may be present. The allegation was always sworn under oath by the groom or by both partners, asserting there was no lawful impediment to the marriage. The dated document stated the names, abodes, current marital status and age of the couple and the groom's occupation, identifying the church or churches for which the licence was valid. It was then signed by the parties present and the ecclesiastical representative.

'Twenty-one and upwards' indicates that the person claimed to be of full age. Unless the party was widowed, a canon of 1579 required prior parental consent, regardless of a couples ages, which had to be in writing for persons under twenty-one. From 25 March 1754, a minor's marriage became null and void without it, so the parent or

In the Archdeaconry Court of Suffolk.

The *27th* day of *October* 185*4*

Appeared personally *Spencer Chaplin*
of *the parish of St Margaret in Ipswich* in the County
of *Suffolk* a *Bachelor*
of the age of *19* Years *but under the age of 21 Years*
and prayed a License for the solemnization of Matrimony, in the
Parish Church of *Saint Margaret in Ipswich aforesaid*
in the County of *Suffolk*
between him and *Ellen Smith*
of *St Nicholas in Ipswich aforesaid* in the County of
Suffolk a *Spinster* of the age of
19 Years *but under the age of 21 years* and made Oath that
    he believeth that there is no impediment of Kindred or Alliance, or
of any other lawful Cause, nor any Suit commenced in any Ecclesiastical Court, to bar or hinder the proceeding of the said Matrimony,
according to the Tenor of such License. And he further made Oath
that he the said *Spencer Chaplin*
hath had her usual place of abode within the said Parish of *St Margaret*
in Ipswich aforesaid for the space of Fifteen Days last past. *And*
he further made oath that the consent of Shadrach
Chaplin the father of the said Spencer Chaplin and also the (Signed)
consent of William Smith the father of the said Ellen
Smith hath respectively been obtained to such
marriage

Spencer Chaplin

Sworn before me

Licence issued same day
Charles Howard
Registrar

Figure 13 Spencer Chaplin's marriage allegation, 1854. Because both he and his bride Ellen Smith were under twenty-one, their fathers, Shadrach Chaplin and William Smith, were required to give their consent to the wedding. (Reproduced by permission of Suffolk Record Office).

guardian normally attended with the applicant or furnished a sworn affidavit or other documentary evidence signifying consent. For orphans, a copy of the church court warrant or Court of Chancery order of appointment of guardianship had to be produced too. On some
occasions, couples undoubtedly evaded the regulation, alleging majority by adding on years, but from September 1822 until March 1823 a certified baptism entry from a parish register or sworn affidavit was mandatory as proof of age, so providing crucial information about parentage and place of origin. Evidence of divorce, freeing a partner to remarry, detailed the date, place of marriage, spouse's name and alleged lover, plus the various stages of its dissolution from church to civil court to eventual private Act of Parliament.

Between 1579 and November 1823, bonds were demanded of applicants sworn with a relative or friend willing to act as surety for the allegation and performance of the conditions outlined in the licence. The dated and signed bond was in two parts, the obligation (in Latin until 1733) set out their names, domiciles, occupations and groom's marital status, and the condition (in English) stated that there was no lawful impediment to the marriage with the named bride, whose parish and marital status were inserted, that neither partner lived in parishes or were of better estate than alleged, and proper consents had been obtained.

Thus age was the only item in the allegation absent from the bond, which had the name of a third party willing to be bound in a sum forfeited if its conditions were not met. Allegations and bonds complement the parish registers because they frequently reveal ages and occupations, and if consent affidavits were affixed, the names and parishes of living parents or guardians.

Applicants for licences

Licences were not confined to the upper classes: a glance through any calendar will show names of people of relatively humble station. As they were paid for, licences lent kudos, but were also preferred by nonconformists after 25 March 1754 as a means of avoiding attendance at Anglican services to hear banns proclaimed. Their other main attractions were promptness and confidentiality, an advantage when couples were of markedly different social backgrounds or age groups, when parish officials had persuaded a putative father from another place to marry a pregnant woman and thus off-load liability for supporting her and her child, when soldiers, sailors and travellers overseas were anxious to marry at short notice, or when families were eager to spare expense on entertainments and wedding celebrations. People could become temporary residents in order to marry in a chosen church. Licences offered flexibility in permitting marriage during prohibited periods in the church calendar, such as Advent or Lent and on fasting days, and outside the canonical hours of eight o'clock and noon (extended to three o'clock in 1886). Couples married abroad, and uncertain of their status in English law, often sought licences to marry again upon their return.

Summing up

Although a licence might be granted, marriage might not be the invariable or immediate outcome, and although a particular parish might be specified, by no means was the ceremony always conducted there, especially before 1754.

Scotland

As Scottish marriage registers are often incomplete, you can trace in kirk session minutes proclamations of marriage banns and receipts of money pledged as surety for the couple's good behaviour and marriage within the prescribed period of forty days. Affidavits sworn by grooms attesting there was no lawful impediment to the wedding were sometimes filed by grooms requesting proclamation of banns, and registers of such 'blotter' marriages in Edinburgh and Glasgow are held by the General Register Office in Edinburgh. Ceremonies without banns rendered them clandestine unless, after 1638, there were special circumstances where presbyteries or kirk elders gave consent. Marriage licences were issued by bishops only when the Episcopalian Church was paramount between 1610 and 1638, and from 1661 until 1689. Kirk session minutes and certificates of proclamation are now mainly in the Scottish Record Office in Edinburgh, or are held locally. Licences are kept in the Scottish Record Office.

Marriage contracts

Copies of marriage contracts, often located in family archives, may also be preserved as abstracts among the indexed registers of deeds of the Court of Session in Edinburgh, at the Scottish Record Office, running from 1554 to date. They set out the names of the contracting parties, their residences and status, parentage or guardianship, the terms and conditions of the marriage settlement, as well as the date the document was signed and sealed when marriage was imminent. When marriage registers are defective, such registrations may be your sole evidence of a particular union and its likely date.

Ireland

Until 1746, marriage licences were only applied for when both parties belonged to the Church of Ireland, but later ones include attachments to people of other denominations. However, from 25 March 1754 until 31 March 1845, all weddings were performed by banns or licence in the Church of Ireland unless both parties were Quakers or Jews.

Unfortunately, all the marriage bonds were burnt in 1922, though you can search incomplete indexes to extant records lodged in various diocesan registries (excepting Derry) and those once filed in the superior Prerogative Court of Armagh at the National Archives of Ireland in Dublin. There is a card index to the latter based on Sir William Betham's genealogical abstracts up to 1810 and of bonds issued by the diocese of Dublin to 1824, a microfilm copy of which is at the Society of Genealogists in London. A list of existing records and finding aids is reproduced in Gibson's *Bishops' Transcripts and Marriage Licences, Bonds and Allegations*.

United States of America

Written declarations of intent to marry, dating from colonial times, including banns are filed with parish registers. Public notices of intention are now kept with town or county clerks' records. These were gradually superseded from the mid-nineteenth century by marriage licences sold by probate judges or county clerks, and stored among county court probate records at county courthouses with signed and posted marriage bonds, which are usually annotated with the date of the actual ceremony.

In some states the bond was the sole requirement for a licence, in others it was dispensed with altogether. All the records relating to a specific licence are usually indexed at least under the groom's surname. The Genealogical Society of Utah has amassed for consultation in its main library in Salt Lake City or for hire at family history centres or branch libraries worldwide, a large number of microfilmed copies of applications, bonds, consents and licences, including copies of the collections of the National Society of Daughters of the American Revolution, and of the Works Progress Administration, set up under the New Deal in the 1930s, which were derived from local and private sources.

What you can expect to discover

The contents of the signed marriage licence applications were not uniform, but if you are lucky you may discover the date, the couple's names and ages, residences, occupations, number of the intended marriage, date and place of birth and parentage, parents' state or country of birth and fathers' occupations, and planned church of marriage, but you may have to settle merely for the application date and couple's names. The application may also specify the state's minimum age for marriage, usually fourteen for grooms, twelve for brides, though parental consent was generally necessary for the former until twenty-one, for the latter until eighteen, and where appropriate, the parental affidavit signifying approval was affixed. Consent documents were particularly prevalent in areas where early marriage was legal. The licences themselves were filed by the relevant probate judge or county clerk, with the date and place of the ceremony inserted by the officiating minister.

Marriage contracts

Marriage contracts to protect family wealth, property or inheritance rights may occasionally surface in family archives, in court records and among other deposited deeds. In states applying French or

Spanish law codes, formal marriage contracts were standard, from which you can glean details about extensive family networks and native places of settlers.

Where original church registers no longer exist or are scanty in detail these civil records are of great value, and they provide much more personal information about a couple, their background and parentage than the wedding entry.

15

TRAWLING PROBATE RECORDS OF ENGLAND AND WALES

A will, expressing a person's final wishes for the distribution of his or her land and possessions after death, can be a telling summary of emotional preferences, prejudices, bonds of loyalty, duty and affection for family and friends. If you have located an ancestor's death certificate or date and place of burial, are curious about when and how property was acquired, the ultimate financial status and eventual disposal of your ancestor's estate, or you want to establish approximately when and where a person died, then this may be your best source. It may reveal who the closest living relatives were, clarify family relationships, narrow the field or indicate which of several possible candidates might be your forebear. As they predate parish registers, wills are your main platform to the Middle Ages.

Limitations and strengths of wills

Although not everyone made a will (possibly as few as six per cent of the population), and seeking the formal sanction of an official probate grant was a matter of conscience on the part of the executors, nonetheless the existing body of wills can settle links of kinship and marriage, and demonstrate a family's geographic spread over time and place. As binding legal documents they are far more reliable than census returns or other sources where the person was informant.

Where wills were taken to be proved before 1858

Until 1857, wills of people leaving property in England and Wales were proved in church courts. In ascending order, the archdeacon's court was utilised when the personal estate was confined to a single archdeaconry; if scattered in more than one, both within the same diocese, then it was to the bishop's consistory court that the will was taken to be proved; the Prerogative Courts of York and Canterbury had jurisdiction over property (*bona notabilia*) in several dioceses within their own Provinces worth more than £5 (£10 in London). Dioceses covering the civil counties of Cheshire, Cumberland, Durham, Lancashire, Northumberland, Nottinghamshire, Westmorland and Yorkshire and the Isle of Man fell within the Province of York. The Prerogative Court of Canterbury exercised overall authority over estates left in both Archdioceses, and over property owned in England or Wales by residents abroad and by military or naval men on active service overseas. When people left estates in both Provinces you may find probate grants in both courts. The Prerogative Court of Canterbury was widely used after the outbreak of the Civil War in 1642, and when church courts were suspended between 1653 and 1660 it was converted into a Court of Civil Commission, and all wills were taken there to be proved. There were also myriad peculiar and secular courts outside the above framework, controlled by Royal patronage, boroughs and city corporations, lords of manors, the chancellors of the Universities of Cambridge and of Oxford, bishops with jurisdiction over places outside their own dioceses, deans and cathedral chapters or parishes.

Where to find them

Wills were made in ancient times, but regular series of original or registered copies of those proved in England and Wales date only from 1383 for the Prerogative Court of Canterbury, and 1389 for York, though some diocesan court probates can be traced from the previous century.

Original or registered office copies of wills proved locally before 1858 will be found in diocesan or county record offices, for Welsh dioceses in the National Library of Wales at Aberystwyth. Wills proved in the Prerogative Court of York (PCY) are at the Borthwick Institute of Historical Research, York, whilst probate material of the Prerogative Court of Canterbury (PCC) is in the Public Record Office at Kew. Registered copy wills and administrations and yearly lists to them can be inspected on microfilm at The Family Records Centre, London.

Lists and indexes

Indexes and lists of wills, grants of letters of administration over estates of people dying without having made a will, and probate inventories of goods, specify the named person's place of abode and date of the document or copy. Many have been microfilmed, so these and other printed probate indexes can be widely searched in places other than where the records are kept. The Society of Genealogists in London has a published guide to its collection; you can also hire microfilm copies at family history centres and branch libraries of the Church of Jesus Christ of Latter-day Saints. There are printed indexes of PCC wills running up to 1700, administration grants to 1660, of wills between 1750 and 1800, and a cumulative index for 1701–49 is in preparation on microfiche by the Friends of the Public Record Office drawing on the yearly index compiled so far. A slip index of administration grants, 1750–1800, awaits publication by the Society of Genealogists. An alphabetical calendar covering the years between 1853 and 1858, can be found in a number of county record offices, of which there is a microfiche edition. Published indexes of wills and administrations in the PCY extend as far as 1688.

Finding the boundaries of each court

County maps in *The Phillimore Atlas and Index of Parish Registers*, cited earlier, depict ancient boundaries of ecclesiastical parishes before 1832, over which are superimposed in colour the ambits of relevant probate courts serving England and Wales before 1858. As with applications for marriage licences, executors could take wills to the most locally convenient court in the chain, provided the estate was large enough, so you should always scan the lists of each one having jurisdiction over where your antecedents lived. When a person lived close to a county or diocesan boundary, for instance, his property might cross over the borders, so affecting where his will was proved.

Wills proved since 1858

On 12 January 1858 ecclesiastical authority over probate ceased. Thereafter wills were taken to be proved in civil district probate registries, or in the Principal Probate Registry (PPR), in London, and this is still the case today. Until 1926, the local jurisdiction of district registries was rigidly applied, but since then any office may be used to suit the convenience of executors.

At the Principal Probate Registry you can examine and purchase photocopies of registered copies of wills proved there and originals proved in district registries more than twelve months ago. You can also make a prepaid postal application for a three-year search of the PPR calendars and issue of a copy-will or grant by writing to The Chief Clerk, at the Probate Subregistry in York, using an application form supplied by the Principal Probate Registry, and quoting the person's name, address and date of death. Registered copies of wills proved in the Welsh district probate registries up to at least 1941 are also kept at the National Library of Wales at Aberystwyth, the originals and later material being held locally.

Using the calendars

You can help yourself to the yearly printed alphabetical calendars of wills and administration grants from 1858 on the open shelves at the PPR. To 1870 wills and administrations are listed separately. Besides recording name, last address, status or occupation, date and place of death of the deceased, they identify the current address, occupation and relationship to him or her of the named executors or administrators, the probate or administration date and registry, and before 3 August 1981, the gross value of the estate, or latterly, the amount it was sworn under. You can thus glean a lot of free information, extracting details about individuals of a particular surname leaving property in England and Wales over a long time-span, as well as discovering their exact dates and places of death, whose apparent ages or dates of birth can then be culled from the Office for National Statistics death indexes from January 1866 and April 1969 respectively.

Searching these alphabetical yearly calendars is a lot quicker than the quarterly ONS indexes, especially if your surname was a common one, and you are not sure precisely when and where somebody died. If your search is speculative, it would be worth checking first if someone has registered your surname with the Guild of One-Name Studies, for then every death, will and administration entry will have been extracted.

Copies of many of the consolidated calendars to wills and administrations earlier than fifty years ago are locally available, but you should verify the cut-off date, as it tends to vary, especially at family history centres. The National Library of Wales has yearly calendars up to 1972, and a microfiche edition of the calendars to at least 1935 is widely held by county record offices and libraries. The Society of Genealogists currently has microfilm copies of calendars up to 1930 for surnames beginning A–V.

The whereabouts of wills and indexes

You can find out about the dates, nature and whereabouts of probate records and finding aids for all church and civil courts to recent times in *Probate Jurisdictions: Where to Look for Wills,* by J Gibson. As diocesan boundaries rarely correspond with those of civil counties, access to centralised collections of indexes and calendars makes life a lot easier.

Making a valid will

A testator must be twenty-one or over, of sound disposing mind, must date and clearly declare the will and testament as his or her last, revoking all previous ones, in order to render it a legal binding instrument. He or she then initials the foot of each page, signs or marks it at the end in the presence of at least two witnesses, who themselves sign in each other's presence and that of the testator. A will conveys real estate (realty, comprising freehold land, and between 1815 and 1925, manorial copyhold tenancies), whereas a testament makes provision for the disposal of personal estate (personalty, including land held by lease). Until 1837, personalty could be bequeathed at fourteen, thereafter only on reaching twenty-one as was always the case with realty, but today soldiers and sailors of sixteen on active service may will their personal effects.

Marriage and wills

Wills of single people become invalid on marriage, unless explicitly linked to a specific forthcoming union which actually materialises, just as they become void on the birth of subsequent children, if no specific provision is made for issue as yet unborn. The former rule does not apply to soldiers and sailors on active service.

Married women rarely left wills before 1882, unless with their husband's written consent, and from then until 1892 wills of women married after 1 January 1883 were re-executed on the husband's death. A means of circumventing this was for her to be given personalty or land by her own family for her exclusive use under a dated pre-nuptial settlement drawn up in anticipation of her marriage, to which her future husband was a party. This afforded her a measure of independence, though usually the land was held by trustees on her behalf. If the agreement allowed her to dispose of her gift without restriction she might bequeath it, but her will had to specifically refer to the settlement, naming the various parties, the date and details about the property or land involved. Her husband's will might also mention the deed to ensure her property remained untouched after his death. Even if the original document no longer survives, you should be able to learn sufficient from the will about what was in it concerning her maiden surname, her father's name, residence and status, and those of her intended spouse, the terms and conditions of such a settlement and the date around which the couple married.

Devising freehold land

Until 1540, inherited freehold land in England in fee simple was not all freely disposable by will, to protect the interests of the heir at law (the nearest blood relative, starting with the eldest son) and the revenue and services due to the feudal overlord. However, land which the testator had himself purchased, been granted or held for a term of years could be devised. A way round the prohibition was for the landholder to set up a kind of trust by deed of enfeoffment, whereby named trustees or feoffees held his land as legal owners for the benefit of a specific person (usually himself), and after his death for individuals identified in the deed or for uses as instructed in his will. After 1540, all freehold land was disposable by will, except for that in fee tail, unless held directly as a tenant-in-chief of the king, in which case only two-thirds could be distributed, the remainder being reserved for the heir at law until feudal tenure was abolished in 1660.

Any land excluded from a will was treated as passing on intestacy, so automatically went to the heir at law, unless it was in fee tail (male, general, special or female), in which case the original deed of entailment predetermined its lineal descent over many generations.

If you can find such a deed, you can trace the family's fortunes and chain of inheritance over a long period, into collateral branches if a particular line became extinct. They may surface among family and estate papers, as subjects of disputes or exhibits in legal proceedings in the Courts of Chancery, or Requests, whose records are both in the Public Record Office at Kew.

Sometimes a will set up a chain of alternate life estates and entailments, known as a strict settlement, and these were common from the second half of the seventeenth century. Within two centuries about half the land in England was protected in this way for future generations of landowning families.

As it might be a long time before heirs became entitled it was important to know exactly where in the family tree a particular individual was placed in order of precedence in case of any dispute.

In Wales, until English law was introduced under the Acts of Union of 1536–43, the ancient custom of partible inheritance was applied, under which a landowner's estate was divided up equally among all his sons or grandsons at his death. It next devolved among his male heirs in the male (agnate) line as far as the fourth degree after which it escheated to the lord. Sometimes daughters inherited. The land could however, be disposed of with the consent of the heirs if the landowner wished to sell it. Partible inheritance lingered on in some parts of Wales until the seventeenth century.

Copyhold land and manorial records

An abstract of a will leaving copyhold land was enrolled in the minutes of the first meeting of the lord of the manor's court baron after the tenant's death so the will itself invariably identified the manor. Manorial records, disseminated in private or public custody, are not continuous or complete, but like wills, many date from the early Middle Ages. They were written in Latin until 1733, except during the Commonwealth period of 1653–60. You can find the known whereabouts of manorial court baron rolls or books, rentals and customals of England and Wales via the dual indexes of manors and parishes in the Manorial Documents Register, at the Royal Commission on Historical Manuscripts, in London. A local nineteenth- or early twentieth-century trade directory of the county will also name individual manors, for a parish might belong to several, or several parishes be part of a single manor.

Copyhold tenure was abolished in 1925, though after 1844 it became possible to convert it to freehold by paying a lump sum as compensation to the lord of the manor for his loss of future rent and other dues.

The contents of a will

The name, abode, status or occupation of the testator come first in any will, followed by the date, though this might be deferred until the end. Reference might be made to sickness or old age, indicating that it was probably composed not long before death. Instructions for burial in a particular parish or graveyard may suggest where the person came from or had family connections, but such aspirations were not always fulfilled. Medieval and early Tudor wills often contain elaborate instructions about funeral procedure and ceremonial, money being set aside to expend on masses and obits commemorating the deceased and named ancestors on certain days or anniversaries by a paid priest at a specific church, or funds were donated to construct a chantry chapel.

Distribution of the estate

After authorising payment of funeral expenses and all other debts, the remainder of the will concentrated on the distribution of the balance of the testator's estate, and the appointment of executors and trustees to carry out his or her wishes.

The chosen fate of articles of special sentimental or intrinsic value might be intended to cement close emotional bonds, though some heirlooms descended according to predestined family tradition.

Names of elderly kinsfolk and relatives by marriage, and the present whereabouts of family members who had moved away might additionally be mentioned, but sometimes people were identified merely by their forename and family connection. If you are unsure about your forebear's parentage or place in a particular family, details in the will about his or her continued survival or decease, spouse and living children at the date the will was made, together with references to other family marriages, offspring and deaths, may prove decisive or exclusive.

Changes in meaning

Unfortunately the meaning of some terms of family relationship has changed over time, so be wary of 'nephew' which might also indicate a grandson, 'cousin' a nephew or niece, 'natural son' a lawful legitimate child, 'step-son' a son-in-law, 'son-in-law' a step-son or adopted son, 'son' a son-in-law or step-son, 'father' a father-in-law (but not necessarily the father of the testator's present wife). 'My now wife' indicates he had been married before, 'my wife's child' that it was a stepchild. 'Cousin' and 'kinsman' were loose terms applied alike to blood relatives and people connected by marriage.

Changes of name

Sometimes a legacy or estate was left to a person on condition that he changed his surname to that of the testator, thus ensuring its continuity if the male line would otherwise become extinct. The usual method by which this was done was for the beneficiary to obtain a Royal Licence, which was registered after 1783 at the College of Arms in London as quite frequently the family was armigerous and its coat of arms was also assigned to him and his descendants. You can find out about name changes by Royal Licence announced in the *London Gazette* or deed poll enrolments on the Close Rolls in the Public Record Office published in *The Times* in *Index to Changes of Name 1760–1901*, by WPW Phillimore and EA Fry.

Gifts to places or selected groups

Legacies entrusted or gifted to parishes or certain categories of people suggest an existing personal, family or business link worth pursuing. Dates and terms of land purchases, leases or gifts of estates can lead you to other sources such as title deeds, charters and indentures. When friends, neighbours and associates benefited you might find such generosity reciprocated, or that the testator was returning a favour, so it is a good idea to examine their wills too for references to your family. Have a look at any place-name indexes to wills so you can study those of contemporary inhabitants, or select wills of local people following similar occupations to your antecedent if you cannot find any for your own family in a particular generation, as they might be named as kinsfolk, tenants, apprentices, friends, servants, creditors or debtors.

Wives and children

Although a wife might be named in a will, she might predecease her spouse, or die before the will was proved, which could be many years after it was drafted. Wives usually received land, the marital home and furniture, or part of it, for their lifetime or until remarriage, but had no say in its ultimate ownership, although the will might provide for it to be sold and the proceeds divided in a prescribed way. When this was among the children in equal portions, it might be many years before their mother's death or remarriage, so a *per stirpes* clause was commonly inserted whereby any deceased child's share was to be equally divided among his or her children. Some children might not feature in the will at all as they had been provided for, for example the eldest son, who was next in line to inherit a landed estate, sons and daughters already receiving trust income, or who had been allotted portions on attaining eighteen, maturity or marriage, whereas the future financial security and maintenance of dependent unmarried or under-age siblings remaining in the parental home was of paramount importance to the testator. A small token might therefore signify acknowledgement of affection rather than disrespect, married daughters occasionally being left a gift exclusively for themselves.

Appointment of executors

It was customary for the testator to appoint family or local friends as executors, who might be left a sum of money or the residue of the estate once all the debts and legacies had been paid. It is important to note who they were, for the attached probate act will record who actually took out the grant, as an executor might die before the testator, be under the minimum age of seventeen, or have changed a surname on marriage (for example, the widow, or a daughter).

Codicils

If probate was a long time after the will was drawn up, children mentioned as infants might by then be adults, married, dead or out of the country, the testator's personal or financial situation might have improved or deteriorated. Any number of codicils containing later modifications or new instructions reflecting changing circumstances could be annexed to the will at any time without the necessity of a completely new draft, but were required to include the date of the will to which they were then physically attached, being dated, signed and witnessed in the same manner as the will itself.

Oral wills

Wills were not always written. Up to 1837, in emergencies such as grave illness, where no scrivener or writing materials were to hand, a dying testator could declare his intention and dictate final instructions for the distribution of his or her personal estate as a nuncupative (oral) will before at least three witnesses, and appoint executors, and this was duly recorded as a memorandum by the appropriate court.

The role of the executors

After the testator expired, the executors took the latest dated will to the relevant court to be validated. They swore on oath to faithfully and honestly carry out its directions and a dated endorsement of probate was appended authorising them to act. When an executor declined responsibility, was not available, had died or was under the minimum age, or the will had failed to make a nomination, the court intervened and usually appointed the residuary legatee, the will being listed as an administration with will annexed.

Contested wills

If the will's validity or its interpretation was challenged, a caveat was lodged by the plaintiff, and probate suspended for up to three months by the court pending a decision or judgement. The probate court index entry of the will was annotated 'by sentence' after a hearing before a church court, 'by decree' when the Court of Chancery was used, as was the case with all matters affecting realty. The eventual registered copy of the probated will was endorsed with the names of the litigants and a brief summary of the case outcome. The church court records are in Latin until 1733, but Court of Chancery proceedings are in English from their date of commencement in the late fourteenth century.

You can read about family disharmony and conflict over property in the filed documentation and depositions of witnesses, the circumstances, undue influence and state of mind under which a will was alleged to have been composed, bearing in mind the likely bias of the contestants. They lend unique insight into descent of possessions and land within a family retrospectively over several generations, and ancillary court exhibits like draft wills and correspondence may further clarify people's motives, changed intentions, movements and kinships.

Original wills and office copies

Once the will was proved, a copy was handed to the executors, another was written up in the office register, the original being filed among the court's archives. Until 1733, excepting 1653–60, the dated probate act was written in Latin, giving the names, residences and relationship to the testator of the sworn executors. As probate might occur any time from a few weeks to many years after the testator's death, you may have to scour lists and indexes for up to twenty years, noting down as you do so all entries of the surname and its variants for future reference. Generally though, six months to two years was the interval. You can thus place a person's death to the period between the last dated document and when probate was granted.

Sometimes only registered office copies of wills are available, because the originals have been lost, destroyed, or are too fragile for production, the main difference being that the seal and signatures of the testator and the witnesses only appear on the latter, where clerical copying errors will not have arisen. You may be able to obtain a photocopy of a registered will, but this may not be permitted for the original.

If the document was entirely written by the testator, it was known as a holograph will, and did not require the presence of witnesses. Persons familiar with the handwriting attended the court, examined the script and swore an affidavit acknowledging it as such. Their names, domiciles, occupations and length and nature of acquaintance-ship with the deceased were recorded with the will.

If you are interested in collecting family signatures, or want to compare an ancestor's on a variety of documents, remember that he or she may have been in extremis when the will was made, and the autograph then bear little relation to one when the person was in full vigour, or much younger.

Administration grants and bona vacantia

When a person died intestate, or no will was found, the distribution of personalty was formalised by a grant of letters of administration by the probate court on application by the next of kin. On intestacy, a person's real estate automatically passed to the heir at law until 1925, when, like personalty, it became the property of the next of kin.

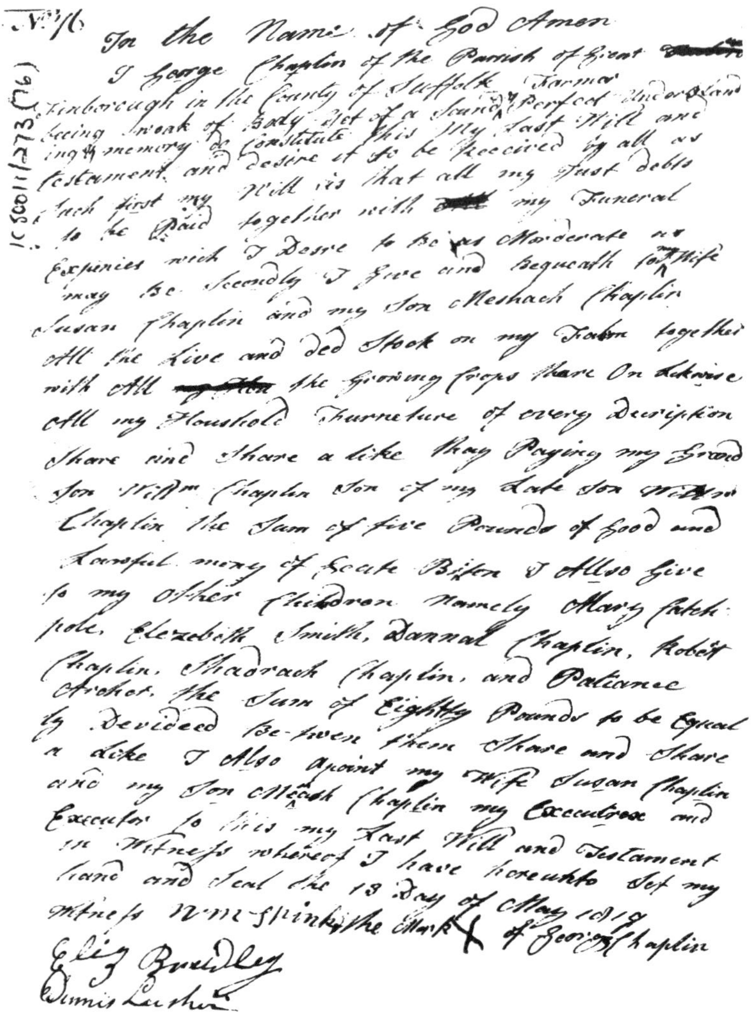

Figure 14 George Chaplin's will, 1819. According to his gravestone inscription at Great Finborough, George died the day before he made his will! He left his stock, crops and furniture on his farm to his wife Susan and son Meshech. (Reproduced by permission of Suffolk Record Office)

After the eldest son, birth seniority as next heir vested in his eldest son, followed by the second, third and so on, lineal male descendants first, then if there were no sons, any daughters of a dead heir at law shared equally as co-heiresses, the estate finally reverting to the descendants of the nearest direct ancestor of the deceased, if his own line of descendants was extinguished.

Because next of kin are determined in strict order of precedence by the degree of proximity of relationship to the deceased, you can learn from the grant who was the closest living relative willing to act as administrator. Here, the spouse comes first, then the children equally (any deceased child's children taking their parent's place), then the parents, followed by brothers and sisters jointly (their children or grandchildren stepping into their shoes if already dead), then half-brothers and -sisters, then the grandparents, then uncles and aunts equally (their descendants taking their place as before), then the chief creditor, and ultimately, for the want of any of these, the estate passes as *bona vacantia* to the Crown. Up to thirty years after an intestate's death, next of kin proving relationship may lay claim to *bona vacantia* held in England and Wales by the Treasury Solicitor, or by the Solicitors for the Duchy of Cornwall, and the Duchy of Lancaster, all based in London.

What the grant includes

The dated administration grant recorded, in Latin to 1733 (except for 1653–60), the name, abode, occupation and marital status of the deceased, followed by the name, residence and relationship to him of the administrator of his personalty, and the name and relationship of any nearer or equally entitled next of kin declining to act. From the early nineteenth century until 2 August 1981, the gross value of the estate was inserted, thereafter the amount it was sworn under. As the printed yearly indexed calendars of civil grants from 1858 onwards virtually replicate the original documentation, you can freely extract their total contents, plus the intestate's date and place of death.

If an administrator dies without distributing the whole estate, the court appoints a replacement, granting an administration *de bonis non* (d.b.n.).

Probate inventories

Between 1529 and 1782, mandatory 'true and perfect' probate inventories were filed in the court with wills and administration grants, but subsequently only at the special request of the next of kin or legal representatives. Inventories are usually listed with the wills or grants to which they relate, and a number have been published. You can find out about surviving series and finding aids from Gibson's *Probate Jurisdictions: Where to Look for Wills* mentioned earlier. They were appraised within a few days of the owner's death by at least three of his relatives, friends or neighbours, at the behest of the next of kin, to safeguard the interests of the executors and legatees, and to prevent fraud or theft.

The dated list of personal items was headed by the names, residences and occupations of the deceased and appraisers. All the house contents were surveyed and apportioned an estimated sale price, down to every piece of furniture, soft furnishings, books, pictures, kitchen equipment, domestic utensils, trade tools, debts and cash. This might be done room by room for the house, each of which was frequently named according to its function, and then the barns and outbuildings. Beds might be described by their type of construction, whilst some items may now be unrecognisable because they are obsolete, in dialect, or obscurely spelt. You can find out what they were in *A Glossary of Household, Farming and Trade Terms from Probate Inventories*, by R Milward. Quantities of growing and harvested crops, timber, animal carcasses and livestock were also evaluated, plus leasehold properties, the deceased's indebtdness or money lent out on credit.

The accumulation, range, quality and comparative value of individual pieces in proportion to the total assets, the amount of ready money let out or borrowed under security of a bond, and loose cash in the house, reveal much about a person's lifestyle, contemporary taste, degree of refinement and status in the local community. You can visualise house size and the way it might have looked inside, though empty rooms were obviously omitted, as were certain items such as wearing apparel (paraphernalia) traditionally set aside for the widow. Listed work tools may indicate the scale and sophistication of a business enterprise, or suggest a secondary occupation. If you analyse probate inventories of other family members or local contemporaries, you can discover whether his belongings and economic status were typical or atypical of the period or area.

Probate accounts

The total inventory assessment was usually less than the true market value of a person's assets and may have borne little relation to what was left once all the debts and liabilities had been settled, so the final probate accounts present a more accurate summary. They were submitted from at least 1540 by executors or administrators when compelled by the court or when requested after 1685, especially if the estate was likely to be in debt or subject to dispute. Drawn up within a year of death, they noted deduction of administrative costs, medical, nursing and funeral expenses, taxes, rent arrears, rates, discharged debts and other disbursements, and estate receipts including proceeds of sales of property on the direction of the deceased, the balance then becoming the residual estate once the various legacies had been distributed. If there were insufficient funds to pay these, the beneficiaries received an abatement, on a *pro rata* basis.

They survive much less frequently than inventories, but a survey of all known extant probate accounts (numbering about 30,000) in English church courts to 1857 has recently been completed for the British Record Society, and a printed microfiche index is forthcoming. Like inventories, they are generally filed with wills and administration grants.

They are particularly useful because they name the deceased's wife and children, sometimes their ages, places of residence and occupations, and creditor and debtor relatives. They may also identify children excluded from the will, on whom money or land was already settled, an annual income provided, or for whom a marriage portion had been set aside. Purchases of clothing, schooling costs, apprenticeship premiums and payment of maintenance for infant children, minors or orphans in accordance with the deceased's instructions may be detected nowhere else. You can also find out about outlay on funeral entertainments, mourning rings, and other gifts in compliance with the will, the names of suppliers and recipients.

Tutors, curators and guardians

The probate court's approval of tutors and guardians nominated in wills or appointed as next of kin to manage the goods of infants, unmarried minors and orphans until twenty-one, or of mentally or physically incapacitated persons was registered in a special book. The dated and signed tuition bonds set out their names, abodes and kinship to their charges, with the names and domiciles of sureties willing to be bound with them as guarantors of faithful performance. An inventory of the child's personal possessions was prepared and lodged by the appointed tutor with the court, and whilst these could be sold if necessary, any inherited land was unalienable.

Boys, on reaching fourteen, and girls at twelve could apply to the court via a proxy to overturn the arrangement and assign guardianship to a person of their choice. The dated and signed deed of assignation gave the child's name, age and relationship to the new guardian, whose curation bond (similar to a tuition bond) was filed with the original documentation, and the court's consent recorded.

Between 1258 and 1724, the probate Court of Husting of the City of London supervised control over the personalty and person of unmarried orphan children of city freemen, appointing nominees when their wills failed to do so. Records about tutors and guardians are in the Corporation of London Records Office, and there is a printed calendar of freemen's wills up to 1688. At least two other cities, Bristol and Exeter, exercised similar powers.

Death duty registers

Less well-known records about wills and administrations are the annual death duty registers of the Inland Revenue between 1796 and 1903, available on microfilm up to 1858 at The Family Records Centre in London and thereafter in book-form, at Kew. The yearly indexes up to 1811 are organised in three series, for PCC wills, PCC administration grants, and lastly for wills and administrations in all other country courts of England and Wales. From 1812 the will indexes are merged, but PCC administration grants and those of country courts each continue to be indexed separately up to 1857. There is a consolidated annual index of civil district and Principal Probate Registry wills from then onwards, but a separate series of administration grant indexes to 1863, after which there is a gap until 1881 when union indexes of wills and administrations were compiled up to 1903. The indexes, held in London, are arranged alphabetically under the first three letters of each surname, state the forename and residence of the deceased, names and addresses of executors or administrators, the probate or administration grant date and court, giving a page reference to the entry in the register. Where the original will or registered copy no longer exists, as is the case with many of those destroyed by enemy action belonging to West Country dioceses, the death duty registers offer a ready substitute about estates over a certain value, and they can be used in conjunction with available printed indexes of the courts' records compiled before World War II.

The scope of the various duties

Where individual legacies or intestates' goods were of sufficient worth (£20 at first, increased to £100 in 1853), legacy duty was payable, the percentage depending on the degree of kinship of the beneficiary to the deceased. Until 1804, legacies and residual estates bequeathed to spouses, children, parents and grandparents were exempt, limited between 1805 and 1814 to spousal gifts and those to parents, and from thereon to spouses only. Real estate was taken into consideration from 1805 until 1852 only if the will directed that it should be sold to pay legacies or be used as residue. Thereafter both personalty and realty were subject to succession duty on the owner's death. In 1894 legacy duty and succession duty were replaced by estate duty. The estates of soldiers and seamen on active service, and property left in England and Wales by overseas residents were excluded by the statutes.

Not every will or administration grant was caught, perhaps as few as a quarter before 1805, increasing threefold by 1815, so not all grants are registered, and not always was duty collected if the sum was considered insignificant.

What the registers tell you

The registered entries about liable estates are headed by the name of the deceased, last address, occupation and date of death, the dates when the will was made and proved, at which probate court, the names, addresses and occupations of the executors, and the value the estate was sworn under before deduction of debts and expenses. In the case of intestacy, the date of the administration grant, the court, administrator's name, address, occupation and relationship to the deceased appear, with the names of next of kin entitled to a share in the estate, which may be lacking in the grant itself. Underneath are set out itemised legacy amounts, their stipulated purposes, names of

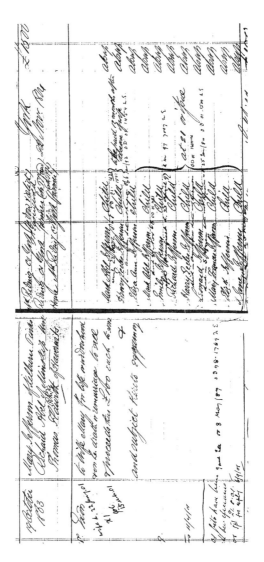

Figure 15 Leonard Jefferson's death duty entry, 1864. Although he died in 1864, duty did not become payable until after his widow's death on 22 January 1901, when only two of their eight children were still alive. (Reproduced by permission of the Public Record Office, Kew)

beneficiaries and the degree of kinship of each to the deceased, any contingency or succession of interest, whether the gift was absolute or an annuity, and if the latter, age of each annuitant, and finally the values and rates of duty payable, the amounts and dates they were received. Unfortunately many of the entries are heavily abbreviated, especially pertaining to consanguinity and type of legacy, but a free Public Record Office information leaflet offers guidance on how to interpret these.

The death duty registers were kept open for fifty years to allow any contingent interests to vest, for example division of sale proceeds of property left to the widow on her death or remarriage, whereupon duty was assessed on the sale price, as apportioned out among the surviving recipients. Reversionary registers compiled after 1853 contain details of trusts and settlement deeds drawn up outside wills, showing successive transfer dates and names of lineal heirs to property on which succession duty fell due. As this might happen over a considerable time, relevant marriages, deaths and changes of residence were noted.

The registered entries thus go further than the actual wills, for instance they track changes of address, dates of death or remarriage of widows, names of children born after the will was drafted, posthumous issue who were to benefit, children's married names, dates of death, domiciles abroad, names of grandchildren taking a dead parent's share in the estate, and where relevant were annotated with cryptic registration references to death duty entries for the widow and children. The registers can be tapped to settle exact degrees of kinship, find out what became of beneficiaries by the time the register was closed or whilst waiting for their gift to vest, and to eliminate or confirm a named person as your forebear by his or her position in a particular family or continued survival beyond a certain date.

Because they are indexed centralised registrations of grants in disparate country courts, they may seem more easily accessible, but their limitation lies in their scope of coverage, summarising relevant clauses rather than the whole will, relating only to estates over the minimum tax threshold.

Government stockholders

Registers of Bank of England will abstracts, relating to transfer of ownership of Government stock between 1717 and 1845, are kept at the Society of Genealogists, to which there is a printed index for the years after 1807, earlier volumes containing integral personal name indexes. They record names and addresses of fundholders authorised to receive shares assigned to them according to testators' instructions. Sometimes an accompanying baptism certificate was filed if the beneficiary was a minor, or a burial certificate if appropriate. From 1810, the wills were invariably proved in the PCC, the only court recognised by the bank.

Registries of deeds

Other places where you may expect to find extracts or copies of wills include the registers and enrolled memorials of devises of land between 1709 and 1938, and 1709 and 1837 respectively, in the Middlesex Registry of Deeds, at the London Metropolitan Archives. The City of London was excluded, as was the City of York from similar Deeds Registries in Yorkshire, set up for the East Riding in 1707 and abolished in 1976, for the North Riding, 1735–1970, and for the West Riding between 1704 and 1970. Records of the first are held by East Riding of Yorkshire Council Archives and Records Service, Beverley, of the second at North Yorkshire County Record Office, Northallerton, and of the last at West Yorkshire Archive Service, Wakefield. A registry was also established for parts of the drained fens on the Bedford Level, whose records for the period 1649–1920 are in the County Record Office, Cambridge, though registration of conveyances and leases was often disregarded after 1860.

At each venue the registers are listed by year, under surname initial index of testators or vendors of freehold land, lessors of property let for twenty-one years or more, and mortgagees. The indexes reveal their forenames, names of the new owners, the parish, street or place where the property was situated, together with the registration reference. Some early registers have topographical indexes too, but there are no corresponding indexes of grantees. The actual registers briefly summarise details extracted from the will, conveyance, indenture of lease or mortgage deed, the memorials being a full transcript of the original document.

Dormant funds

The Court Funds Division of the Public Trust Office in London holds moneys of which no legal ownership has yet been determined, and the accounts have been dormant for five years. There is a printed nominal index of persons in whose names sums have been lodged, or their specific beneficiaries, available on the premises and at The Family Records Centre. Documentary proof is required from anyone asserting status as next of kin, but as most amounts are under £250 the cost of verifying entitlement may well exceed the sum claimed.

16

TRACKING ESTATES ELSEWHERE IN THE BRITISH ISLES, IRELAND AND UNITED STATES OF AMERICA

Nominally, the Channel Islands are part of the diocese of Winchester, but on Jersey wills were proved locally in the Ecclesiastical Court of the Dean of Jersey until 25 May 1949, and thereafter in the Probate Registry, at the Royal Court of Jersey, St Helier. Real estate could not be willed before 1851, and it was common for subsequent wills of personalty and realty to be separately drawn up. Wills in which land was devised are filed and recorded in the Public Registry, also at the Royal Court of Jersey.

Original and enrolled copies of wills are indexed from 1660 up to 1964, at the Probate Registry, including later wills bequeathing both personalty and realty, with discrete calendars of administration grants between 1848 and 1964. Neither Registry is open to the public, but searches can be undertaken for you, the fee depending on the time expended.

Indexed original and registered copy wills and administration grants of personal estate on Guernsey, Alderney, Sark, Herm and Jethou proved in the Ecclesiastical Court of the Bailiwick of Guernsey from 1660 to the present day, are held by the Bureau des Connetables, St Peter Port. Guernsey wills dating from 1841 onwards, in which only land was devised, are kept at the Royal Court of Guernsey, St Peter Port. Land devised by will on Alderney since 1949 is registered at the island's Court House, together with a few earlier wills and intestacies relating to land, though none before 1946, as all previous records were destroyed during the War. Land on Sark is not disposable by will, descending instead to the next heir as far as the fifth degree of kinship (the common ancestor being the great-great-great-grandparent), then to the Seigneur. A widow always has a right to dower on a third of it. No land can be disposed of by will on Herm or Jethou.

Estates held in England and Wales

In all cases where Channel Islanders held property in England or Wales before 1858, their wills were taken for probate to the Prerogative Court of Canterbury, later ones being lodged at the Principal Probate Registry in London.

Isle of Man

The two ecclesiastical courts alternately serving the Island for parts of each year up to 1873 were the Consistory Court of Sodor and Man, whose testamentary records begin in 1600, and the Archdeaconry Court of Man, with probate material from 1631. The Consistory Court then continued alone until 1884, being succeeded in 1885 by the High Court of Justice. Records up to 1910 are in the Manx National Heritage Library, the Manx Museum, Douglas, after which you need to consult the Deeds and Probate Registry, at the General Registry, Douglas. The indexes to wills, administration grants and inventories up to 1949, commencing in 1659 and 1631 respectively, can also be seen on microfilm at the Society of Genealogists in London, and at family history centres of the Church of Jesus Christ of Latter-day Saints.

Estates held on the mainland

Until 1858 the Prerogative Court of York had superior jurisdiction over the Northern Province, including the diocese of Sodor and Man, the Prerogative Court of Canterbury having ultimate power of probate, so look at lists and indexes of wills proved there and in local ecclesiastical courts for property owned by Manx people on the mainland. From 1858 you can find wills and administration grants of English and Welsh estates of Manx people in the yearly printed indexed calendars of the Principal Probate Registry in London. Wills of property left in Scotland or Ireland were administered using their probate frameworks, which are now described.

Scotland

Up to 1823, testaments relating to personalty were produced by executors for confirmation (*testament testamentar*) at the commissariot within whose boundaries a person died. Commissary court demarcations were identical to those of Medieval dioceses, though bishops had ceased to have jurisdiction once the Crown took over in 1560. The chief commissariot in Edinburgh dealt with personal estates valued at £50 or more, and also received testaments of Scots dying overseas leaving property in Scotland. As in England and Wales, confirmation was a matter of conscience, so not every testament that was made was formally approved. A third of the personal estate passed automatically to the surviving widow, a third to the children, the remainder being freely disposable. If there was no widow, or no children, the estate was divided into half. If the deceased left neither, then all his personalty could be bequeathed as he wished. When a person died intestate, the commissariot appointed an administrator (*testament dative*), and the names of any surviving spouse and children were inserted in the court records.

Records of the commissariots up to 1823

All confirmed testaments and extant inventories of goods, chattels, tools, cash and debts emanating from the commissariots have been deposited in the Scottish Record Office, in Edinburgh. Printed indexes to testaments confirmed in the Commissariot of Edinburgh from 1514 until 1800, and for the other commissariots from the sixteenth century or later up to the same year, have been produced by the Scottish Record Society. There are typescript indexes of later confirmations to 1823. A list of start-dates can be found in *Probate Jurisdictions: Where to Look for Wills*, edited by J Gibson. The indexes themselves may contain valuable details about family relationships, abodes and occupations.

The sheriff courts

In 1823, the commissariots were abolished and succeeded by sheriff courts, the chief of which is in Edinburgh and which confirms testaments of people dying 'furth of Scotland' leaving personal property there.

The parameters of the sheriff court districts roughly correspond to those of counties, though some were later enlarged. A list of districts and constituent parishes can be ascertained from the current *Scottish Law Directory*. Most of the sheriff court registers and original confirmed testaments, testamentary deeds and inventories are filed in separate series in the Scottish Record Office, after retention by the appropriate sheriff court for between ten to fifteen years following confirmation.

There are three consolidated printed indexes to surviving inventories in *Personal Estates of Defuncts*, covering the sheriff courts of the Lothians, 1827–65, Argyll, Bute, Dumbarton, Lanark and Renfrew, 1845–65, and for the rest of Scotland between 1846 and 1867. Yearly calendars of confirmations and inventories for the whole of Scotland since 1876 are available not only at the Scottish Record Office, but up to 1935 in many local record offices and libraries too.

Inventories are useful, though only prolific since the early nineteenth century, because they give date of death and before civil registration of deaths began in 1855, where burial registers are defective they may be the sole source about a person's demise.

Disputed testaments and bona vacantia

Contested testaments were settled by the commissariots, passing on appeal to the Commissary Court of Edinburgh, and finally to the Court of Session. After 1830, the Commissary Court no longer exercised power of appeal. Full indexes to diocesan cases up to 1800 and for the Commissariot of Edinburgh have been published, all the original papers being housed in the Scottish Record Office.

Enquiries about Scottish estates in the Crown's hands as *bona vacantia* for want of heirs, are dealt with by the Queen's and Lord Treasurer's Remembrancer, in Edinburgh.

Services of heirs (retours)

The testaments contain no reference to heritable land before 1868. In the Scottish Record Office, however, are filed by county numerous services of heirs (or retours) relating to defined parcels of land inherited on the deaths of landholders, once the heirs' rights to them had been established which might be several years later. A brieve of succession was firstly sent out of Chancery to the county sheriff so that he could summon sworn jurors to enquire into what lands the owner actually possessed within the sheriffdom's confines when he died, and to obtain proof as to the next heir. Their verdict was then 'retoured' to Chancery and the heir issued with a certified copy of the 'retour' ratifying his entitlement. Personal name and topographical indexes of services of heirs from about 1544 until 1699 have been printed county by county in *Inquisitionum ad Capellam Domini Regis Retornatarum ... Abbreviato*, with decennial indexes running thereafter up to 1859, after which they are annual. The indexes before 1860 frequently contain abbreviated dated summaries of the original documents, specify the heir's exact relationship to the previous owner, plus the latter's date of decease, but later indexes omit deaths.

To 1747, regality courts exempt from control of the local sheriffdoms, also retoured services of heirs, and most of their records are in the Scottish Record Office.

Sasines

Registers of sasines from 1599 (excluding burghs before 1926) record an heir's or grantee's taking actual possession (seisin) of his land, once he had been served with his retour from Chancery. There are three series of registers, all of which are in the Scottish Record Office: a secretary's register for every county or district, 1599–1609, a particular register for each, and a general register relating to sasines of lands held in more than one district or county, both covering the period 1617–1871. Thus some entries may be duplicated. A general register is still kept today, and since 1926 has included burgh sasines. Only inherited land was dealt with by retours and sasines until leases of thirty-one years or more became registrable after 1857.

The retours and sasines are in Latin until about 1680, except for the period 1653–60. The first two sets of registers of sasines are only partly indexed, though there is a complete nominal and topographical index to the general register at the Scottish Record Office. There are printed county abridgements of registered entries from 1781, with corresponding personal and place-name indexes, although there is a gap in the latter series between 1830 and 1872. Similarly indexed annual minute books of abridgements from 1868 have been circulated to each county sheriff clerk. The registers may allude to previous dated land transactions within the family extending back several generations or into collateral branches, and name tenants and other kinsfolk besides the present heir.

Fifteenth- and sixteenth-century sasines were recorded in Latin in notarial protocol books, many of which were filed with burgh archives, and a number have been published. Instruments of sasine from the same period may occasionally surface amongst family archives, the Scottish Record Office being their chief depository.

Burgh sasines

Individual burgh protocol books to 1689 and later burgh registers of sasines to 1925 have been lodged in the Scottish Record Office, and are partially indexed. These include other registered deeds as well.

Registries of deeds

Besides the notarial protocol books, and a sixteenth-century register of acts and decreets of the Court of Session to 1581, another place where you might find testaments, marriage contracts, trusts and settlements recorded for preservation or for execution is the Register of Deeds, instituted by the Court of Session in Edinburgh in 1554. The first series of registers covers the period 1554–1657, the second (in three sections) 1661–1811, and the third extends from 1812 to the present. You can inspect these at the Scottish Record Office using printed indexes up to 1694, then manuscript indexes for 1750 and 1751, which become continuous from 1770 onwards. Minute books of the missing years, on the same premises, contain brief chronological entries of registrations.

From the seventeenth century to 1809 local commissariots, and regality courts to 1747, maintained their own registries of deeds, as do their successor sheriff courts today. The records of the first two have been deposited in the Scottish Record Office, and are indexed, those of the sheriff courts are kept by sheriff clerks.

Tutors, curators and guardians

Brieves of tutory and brieves of idiotry or furiosity concern appointments made by Chancery of tutors-at-law (and curators after 1696) for minors under twenty-one or after 1585 for mentally incapacitated people, when the deceased father had failed to nominate anyone. The nearest kinsman aged twenty-five or more on the paternal line acted as guardian of the estate, the mother becoming the child's physical guardian. From 1672 an inventory of the child's personal possessions was required from the tutor-at-law on taking up his responsibility. At fourteen a male minor (a female minor at twelve) could apply to Chancery to administer the property himself or appoint a curator of his choosing, as in England and Wales, but from 1696 curators were appointed in the same way as tutors-at-law. Indexed services *de tutela* to 1699 have been published with the retours described above, and there is a general index to later tutorships and curations, 1700–1897, at the Scottish Record Office.

Estates in England

Scots leaving property over the border in England had their wills proved in the appropriate ecclesiastical court before 1858, and afterwards you can trace their wills and administration grants in the annual alphabetical calendars of the Principal Probate Registry.

Dormant funds

Unclaimed funds are held for seven years by the Accountant of the Court of Session before being transferred to the Queen's and Lord Treasurer's Remembrancer in Edinburgh, to whom any enquiries should be sent.

—————————— Ireland ——————————

Up to 1858, wills of Irish people were proved in diocesan consistory courts. As diocesan and county boundaries were invariably not coincident, a person might own possessions in several dioceses. When personalty exceeding £5 in more than one diocese was involved the superior Prerogative Court of Armagh was utilised, but where property in the other diocese totalled less than this authority vested in the consistory court serving the district where the bulk of the estate lay. There were also a few peculiar courts outside this two-tier hierarchy.

How to find out what exists

In 1922 all original local probates and administration grants prior to 1858 housed centrally in Dublin, and most office copies registered there in will and grant books, were destroyed by fire, plus the records of the civil Principal Probate Registry established in Dublin in 1858, and original local wills up to 1903 which had been transferred from district probate registries. A list of surviving material is included in *Probate Jurisdictions: Where to Look for Wills.*

Copies of wills and administration grants

You can still examine will copies transcribed into locally kept district registry books and administration grant books from 1858. Surviving incomplete copies in will books of the Principal Probate Registry for 1874, 1878, 1891 and 1896, and copy administration grant books for 1878, 1883, 1891 and 1893, are available at the National Archives of Ireland in Dublin, and complete will books for the districts of Armagh, Belfast and Londonderry from 1858 onwards are at the Public Record Office of Northern Ireland in Belfast, indexed up to 1900.

Original and registered copy wills and administrations since 1904 are held by the National Archives of Ireland, though those filed or registered in Belfast, Londonderry and many in Armagh are in the custody of the Public Record Office of Northern Ireland. Wills proved more recently than twenty years ago are retained by district registries before transfer to the National Archives of Ireland, whilst those for the northern counties are kept for ten years by the Probate and Matrimonial Office in Belfast.

Indexes to wills and administrations before 1858

In the National Archives of Ireland, surviving indexes to wills and to administration bonds in each pre-1858 court give an indication of what was lost. Some of these have been published, including indexes to wills proved in the Prerogative Court between 1536 and 1810, and Dublin diocesan grants from 1270 until 1858. There are gaps for most courts before the mid-eighteenth century, and many probates stem only from the preceding century. The alphabetically listed wills and yearly surname initial-indexed administration bonds usually give the testator's or intestate's full name, address, year of probate or administration bond, and often his occupation.

Complete printed alphabetical annual union calendars of wills and administrations from 1858 onwards can be found at both the National Archives of Ireland and Public Record Office of Northern Ireland, to which there is a consolidated index for the period 1858–77. Until 1917, the calendars extend over all of Ireland, thereafter the calendars are distinct for the twenty-six southern counties and six northern counties. They contain references to will and grant book copies, which are complete from 1922. Because the calendars divulge the deceased's name, address, occupation, his date and place of death, date and place of probate or administration grant, and the name, address and relationship to him of his executors or administrators, and the value under which his effects were sworn, they reveal a modicum of genealogical information, though the original material before 1904 has now largely disappeared. In the case of administration grants, the names of all entitled next of kin are recorded in the calendars.

Betham's pedigrees and abstracts

In the early nineteenth century, Sir William Betham compiled sketch pedigrees from his notebooks of genealogical abstracts of almost all the wills proved in the Prerogative Court of Armagh up to 1800, administration grants up to 1802, and wills proved in the Kildare Consistory Court before 1827. His Prerogative Court notebooks of will abstracts can be accessed at the National Archives of Ireland via the published index mentioned earlier, whilst the alphabetically listed administration grants and alphabetical sketch pedigrees are at The Genealogical Office, in Dublin, to which later amendments and additions were made.

These abstracts, and an ever increasing collection of other card-indexed extant will and grant book copies, transcripts, and abstracts of wills and administrations before 1858 accumulated by the National Archives of Ireland, can also be seen on microfilm at the Public Record Office of Northern Ireland, which also holds an unannotated copy of Betham's sketch pedigrees. Betham's will abstracts are available on microfilm at the Society of Genealogists in London, and the College of Arms, also in London, has photostats of his indexed annotated sketch pedigrees, though this is not open to the general public. Other concentrations of will abstracts may be found in the National Library, and in the libraries of the Representative Church Body, Royal Irish Academy, and Trinity College, all in Dublin.

Death duty registers

Inland Revenue registers of Irish will abstracts and administrations in all its courts relating to estates attracting death and other duties between 1828 and 1839, are deposited in the National Archives of Ireland, the information contained in them being similar to that in English and Welsh death duty registers. The indexes, originally compiled in London, run on to 1879, and yield the names and addresses of the deceased and his executors or administrators, the date and place of probate or administration grant, and when the original wills and majority of the registers themselves no longer exist, these entries at least tell you approximately when or the latest date at which a person was dead, his last whereabouts and who were his legal representatives. Extant registers will of course give precise date of death, detail legacies, names and kinships of recipient beneficiaries or next of kin.

Estates in England, Wales and Scotland

Wills of Irish people leaving property in England or Wales before 1858 were proved in the Prerogative Court of Canterbury, Prerogative Court of York, or local diocesan court having jurisdiction over their personal goods. The indexes to London and North Country courts are particularly worth scanning, because of the heavy influx and two-way traffic of Irish through northern ports, or long-term Anglo-Irish family association with the mainland. Where property was held in both Ireland and England, double probates were granted.

Incomplete copies of abstracts of PCC and some other local wills of liable estates filed in the Death Duty Office in London between 1821 and 1857, and indexes covering 1812–57 have been transferred to the Public Record Office of Northern Ireland, the full contents of the original or registered copies being accessible among the PCC archives at The Family Records Centre in London, or local repository holdings of diocesan records. From 1858 onwards you can find details of London-filed Irish probates and administration grants to 1876 at the end of the yearly alphabetical calendars of the Principal Probate Registry in London, and thereafter incorporated into the main index, some of which duplicate Irish registrations. Where original wills and administrations were destroyed in Dublin, this source may be an effective substitute. Copies of the calendars are widely dispersed as described earlier.

Testaments of Irish people leaving personalty in Scotland were confirmed in the commissary or sheriff courts outlined above.

The Registry of Deeds

You can read at the National Archives of Ireland and at the National Library, in Dublin, published *Abstracts of Wills at the Registry of Deeds*, edited by PB Phair and E Ellis, which relate to enrolments between 1708 and 1832 at the Registry in Dublin to protect devises of land against future disputes. The volumes name and index each testator, beneficiary and witness, whilst the indexed books of office transcripts and original witnessed memorials (transcripts of the original deeds), at the Registry, contain full details of will provisions, sales, rent charges, pre-nuptial marriage settlements, leases of three years or more, or for specified lives, and mortgages. Transcripts and memorials of leases for lives supply the names and ages of people nominated by the lessee at the time the agreement was signed, and because they were often his children or close relatives, they are a valuable indicator of family composition and survival at a specific date. Leases for nine hundred years or for lives renewable in perpetuity were common in Ireland, making the land virtually freehold.

From about the mid-nineteenth century their genealogical value decreases as other more comprehensive sources become available, and as registration was never compulsory, the registers contain only a selection of actual conveyances registered to prove evidence of legal title should any challenge arise.

There is an alphabetical grantors' index from 1708, but although the surname of the first grantee or lessee, register volume, page or memorial number are recorded, no property locations are mentioned until counties were included from 1834. The lands index, running from 1708 until 1947, is arranged under counties, corporate towns and cities, and then by initial letter of townland until 1828 when the counties were subdivided into baronies, then townlands. As with the English registries, there is no index to grantees. Microfilm copies of both indexes are in the National Library, Dublin, and the Public Record Office of Northern Ireland, where microfilm copies of the cited memorial books can also be inspected. If you find the task of searching these indexes too outfacing you may be able to find the whereabouts and descent of a family's land during the nineteenth century from the tithe applotment books, Primary Valuation and Valuation Office Books, described in Chapter 8, all of which have surname indexes.

Land Commission records

Nineteenth-century and some earlier wills deposited with the Irish Land Commission as proof of ownership of smallholdings by vendors intending to sell to occupying tenants with the help of public subsidies, are kept by the National Archives of Ireland, to which there is a card index of testators in the National Library.

Dormant funds

Unclaimed funds in all Ireland before 1921 and subsequently in the southern counties, are held by the Accountant of the Courts of Justice in Dublin, those for the six northern counties by the Accountant General, Belfast, to whom any enquiries should be addressed.

—— United States of America ——

In many ways, the probate procedure adopted by British colonial America imitated that of England and Wales. It has been estimated that between twenty-five and forty per cent of the American male populace and less then ten per cent of females left wills which were proved. Wills of personalty can still be made by males on reaching fourteen, and by females at twelve (though eighteen is the minimum legal age in Connecticut, Massachusetts and Virginia, eighteen for males and sixteen for females in the state of New York, and twenty-one for Vermont residents). Land can only be devised by will at twenty-one. Similar age limits of fourteen and twelve qualify a person to act as executor, though in Massachusetts, Missouri and Rhode Island the minimum age is seventeen, eighteen in Mississippi.

What happens when no will is found

On intestacy, in most states a widow becomes entitled to a third of her husband's estate as her dower, and the balance is distributed evenly among their children, any dead child's share going *pari passu* to his or her offspring. In some states, the eldest son has double the share allotted to each of his siblings. If the deceased was unmarried then the parents are deemed next of kin. By 1811, realty descended on intestacy to the legal next of kin, on the universal repeal of the colonial laws of inheritance by primogeniture under which freehold land automatically devolved on the eldest son, but entailed land continued to descend as provided for under the terms of the original settlement deed. In certain states, on intestacy property owned independently by a couple when they married and any subsequently inherited by either party belongs solely to that person, whilst any they purchased or owned jointly vests entirely on the survivor. In others a widow's right of dower contrasts with her husband's claim to all property in her ownership on their marriage and any she later inherited so long as they have a surviving child who will ultimately be heir. If not, then he too is entitled only to third. Thus the laws of probate and intestacy varied according to when and where a person resided, especially in relation to realty.

Probate records

Probate packets and case files are lodged in county courthouses set up in every state from early colonial times, where they remain today, alongside will books into which probated wills were copied, and invalid unregistered, unindexed wills which were separately stored. The original probate papers and will books are indexed. Abstracts and incomplete transcripts of many colonial wills and administrations have been published, but these are of varying quality and reliability, so you should not solely rely on them to distil or accurately reproduce every genealogical detail in the original, nor on the will books alone, as transcription errors may be found.

What you can expect to find

The files or packets are stuffed with original signed and attested wills, the executors' petitions for letters testamentary for probate or those of administrators seeking letters of administration of an intestate's estate, executors' and administrators' bonds, probate inventories, preserved copies of newspaper and other public notifications of pending probate, guardians' bonds, petitions to the court for changes of guardianship initiated by minors, interim annual estate accounts filed by executors and administrators, final financial statements, division documents listing all the beneficiaries and their addresses, and their dated, signed receipts for specific gifts or estate portions thereby discharging the executors or administrators from further liability. Because a sequence of dated and autographed documents was generated by and kept together for each probate or administration grant, where one batch of papers is missing, unclear or deficient, the content of the rest may overlap or be more instructive.

Tracing a death

Dates of death may be elicited from the probate papers or indexed will books, or may otherwise by deduced from the date when probate was applied for, since it was in most states obligatory between thirty and ninety days after demise. The document itself was then produced to the court to be validated, the witnesses appearing personally to certify its authenticity before the executor was authorised to act. Occasionally however, the verification stage occurred whilst the testator was alive, or probate was granted to him so that he could control transfer of part of his estate during his lifetime. The will book copy was invariably written up between thirty and ninety days after death.

Procedure leading to probate

Petitions for letters testamentary were often presented orally at the county court, and written up in a probate minute book, though some courts insisted on full dated documentary particulars from the executors, incorporating the names and addresses of the petitioner and deceased, the latter's date of death and estimated values of his realty and personalty, the names and abodes of the witnesses who attested his signature on the will, the names, ages, domiciles and precise relationship to him of all devisees and legatees.

If the defunct was intestate, the nearest kinsman petitioned for a grant of letters of administration, and provided similar particulars about the heirs. Because the spouse ranks first in order of precedence as next of kin, followed by the children, the parents, grandparents, siblings, uncles and aunts, nephews and nieces, great-uncles and – aunts, first cousins, then the chief creditor, you can determine the proximate living relative at the time of death, though there might be regional variations.

The executor or administrator, once formally approved by the court, lodged a dated and signed bond as a guarantee of proper performance of his duties, a relative or friend serving as surety in a sum equal to the estate value, to safeguard the interests of the heirs against misconduct. The bond was redeemed once final distribution took place, and their liability ended.

Inventorying personal property

The court assigned three independent appraisers to inventory the deceased's personal possessions (including, up to the last century, number, names and values of any slaves), for return within ninety days, in order to protect the estate from excessive claims, and the heirs from fraud or theft.

Maintenance allowances were set aside during the probate process for named dependants, such as the wife's dower and towards the children's annual upkeep and education, which might be defrayed by sales of certain articles with the court's sanction. Periodic estate accounts were lodged from time to time to show the purpose of administrative expenditure and sums received.

Looking after minors or incapacitated heirs

A nominated guardian (tutor, curator, conservator or receiver, depending on where the person lived) was formally charged by the will or county court with management of the estate of minor orphaned males under twenty-one, females until eighteen, or mentally or physically incompetent persons. An 'orphan' might actually still have one living parent, who was usually appointed. The guardian signed a bond undertaking faithful execution of his responsibility, backed up by a surety in a sum equivalent to the child's quantified share in the estate. Boys on attaining fourteen, and girls at twelve could petition the court for its approval of a guardian proposed by them, and a further similar bond was pledged by the successor and his guarantor. The dated applications divulge the names and current ages of the minors, the names of their nominee and deceased parent.

Advertising probate and filing estate accounts

At this stage notices of pending probate were posted before final probate accounts were submitted to the court, enumerating total estate administration costs, disbursements, expenses and income, and quantifying the balance left to be apportioned according to the deceased's instructions or under the law of intestacy. Embodied in them are names of indebted or creditor relations, friends and associates.

Distribution of the assets

The division documents are useful because they give an intimation of death dates or new married names of beneficiaries since the will was drawn up, and the widow's remarriage. Their signed receipts record their comparative legacies, and indicate their standard of literacy.

Sharing out the land, and original land grants

You may find consequent property partitions among estate heirs enrolled in land entry books in local land offices of the appropriate state and county. These, original and copies of wills, bills of sale of slaves, deeds, gifts, leases and releases, patents and grants of land in state-land states (of which there were twenty, including all thirteen original states), marriage settlements, quitclaims of future rights, and mortgages, are kept with other land office papers and deeds in state archives or libraries, town or county offices. Where original material has been lost, these are a worthy substitute.

Manorial copyhold was virtually unknown in the American colonies. Records of federal land grants after about 1800 in the thirty public-land states, private land claims and military bounty land applications are held by the National Archives in Washington, DC, and in National Archives Regional Archives. Leases were not usually recorded. Sometimes the books contain wills found nowhere else.

Using the indexes

The means of reference to the land entry books is generally by alpha-, initial- or first three letter-index under the surname of the first seller, grantor or testator, running chronologically by date of recording, frequently with a companion set of indexes organised under the name of the first buyer, grantee, devisee or heir. Sometimes there is a tract index, arranged under the nomenclature of the land involved.

Each index gives both first-named contracting parties, the land's identity, and the date the conveyance was registered, which might be some years after the agreement was implemented. If your ancestor was a joint vendor or purchaser, his name may therefore not appear in the indexes, nor are the indexes a complete directory of every entry. Because there was no union system of inheritance among the colonies or over time, you may also find it difficult to sort out a person's exact kinship to the deceased without recourse to other documents. As neighbouring county and state boundaries were adjusted or extended, you may need to consult the indexes and books of several, depending on the period and area involved, but they can prove invaluable in tracking people's movements within a county or state or across country.

Deed books

Many deed books up to at least the Civil War, 1861–65, state, county and city land deeds have been microfilmed by the Genealogical Society of Utah in Salt Lake City, but not the cumulative indexes to them. You can hire copies for use in family history centres and branch libraries of the Church of Jesus Christ of Latter-day Saints using the Family History Library Catalog on FamilySearch.

The book enrolments specify a named property's exact location, bounded by natural features such as rocks and creeks, trees and man-made artefacts, giving compass bearings and measured distances, which are often sketched or demarcated on an accompanying survey map or town plan. Names of current tenants, previous proprietors, and of neighbouring occupiers of plots on which the property abutted, may also be set out. If the new owner was an immigrant or the tract was being granted for the first time, the name given to the property might signal where the settler originally came from.

Estates held in England and Wales and a bridge over the Atlantic

Many early settlers, armed military and naval personnel in the colonies or dying elsewhere overseas left possessions in England or Wales, wills or grants of letters of administration of their estates and probate inventories being filed in the Prerogative Court of Canterbury, and listed under 'Parts' rather than by individual county or country. Entries of wills and administrations taken from the act books are arranged in *American Wills and Administrations in the Prerogative Court of Canterbury, 1610–1857*, by PW Coldham, alphabetically by testator's or intestate's surname and forename, giving last place of residence and details of death, the name of the executor or administrator, and citing the whereabouts of any known printed abstract or transcript of the dated will or grant. There is an index of ships and of place-names, which is helpful if you want to find compatriots or other contemporary settlers leaving property at the same place of provenance.

Sometimes colonial wills were proved not only in the colonial county court, but in this court too for reasons of security or in expectation of future litigation, and if the county records have subsequently been destroyed, so the loss may be mitigated somewhat. The English grant might however come some years after the colonist's death.

Filed PCC warrants for probate and administration grants, surviving from 1660, may be trawled for precise dates and places of death. A limited probate or administration grant restricted it to time or place, for example final distribution of assets within twelve months, or within England only.

Dated probate inventories, though indexed under the surname and forename of the deceased, exist only in any quantity in the Prerogative Court after 1660, but they demonstrate the widespread practice of borrowing and lending among overseas merchants and traders, name kinsfolk, agents and associates in England and abroad, the whereabouts of migrants' houses and warehousing of trading stock, and approximate market values of their goods.

Indexes to Scottish confirmations of testaments and Irish probates of wills should also be scanned for references to property left there by emigrants or travellers abroad.

Settlers with London connections

American Wills proved in London, 1611–1775, also compiled by PW Coldham, concentrates on probates in the Bishop of London's Consistory Court relating to local estates of people dying overseas, nominally part of his diocese. Organised under year, the date of probate or administration grant, names of the deceased, his principal legatees, executor or administrator, and a short summary of the document are recorded, to which there is a comprehensive personal name index, plus indexes to ships and places.

Freemen of the city

If the status of the deceased was that of a citizen and merchant, tradesman or craftsman, it is likely that a record of his admission as a city and livery company freeman can be traced. Extant freedom registers of the City of London date from 1681, those of some livery companies from the fifteenth century, records of the former up to 1940 being held at the Corporation of London Records Office, and of the latter for the most part being on deposit in the Guildhall Library nearby. If freedom was by virtue of servitude the apprenticeship bindings registers of the appropriate company will detail the person's paternity or guardianship and place of residence at the time of binding-out, if it was by patrimony, then the father would himself have been free of the company at the time the person was born, so you might be able to track the family's association with that company over several generations. Colonial merchants maintained similar links with other cities and ports such as Southampton and Bristol. Wills of contemporary city, company or guild freemen, or burgesses may mention kinsfolk, friends, business partners or agents overseas, from which you may be able to fix where they came from and when, and where they were at a particular date.

If your family had a coat of arms

An ancestor described as a gentleman or 'armiger' may have been granted or inherited a coat of arms or have his lineage recorded in one of the thousands of pedigrees compiled during the periodic county by county heraldic visitations of England and Wales between 1530 and 1689. The heralds or their deputies enquired into and regulated the display and entitlement to coats of arms, a by-product of which were the numerous registers of narrative and tabular family trees based on information and muniments furnished by the gentry. Many allude to relatives overseas, especially in Virginia, so it is worth looking for published versions cited up to 1975 in the guides by Marshall, Whitmore and Barrow, or requesting a prepaid search of the more reliable original official records at the College of Arms in London.

Tracking people with unusual surnames

If your surname is unusual probate lists and indexes of the Prerogative and other local courts of the era, county marriage indexes and the IGI will reveal where it was particularly prevalent, and by patient examination of wills of people of the same surname you may succeed in finding an otherwise elusive transatlantic link. *A Dictionary of English and Welsh Surnames, with Special American Instances*, by CW Bardsley, may prove helpful too.

American Loyalists to the British Crown

Abstracts of wills submitted as evidence by petitioners for compensation, allowances or pensions from the British Crown for their loyalty or practical help and resulting loss of possessions during and after the Revolutionary War, 1775–83, bear testimony to what they surrendered or left behind. Two series of indexed files of these, between 1776 and 1835, are in the Public Record Office, Kew, but microfilmed copies of them are widely available. A selection of extracts from original memorials and papers has been published in *American Loyalist Claims*, by PW Coldham.

By their nature retrospective, the memorials, evidence and depositions of witnesses for the claimants comprise not only wills, but marriage settlements and land deeds from previous generations in support of the applications, which relate to people and places much earlier in the eighteenth century. They almost invariably contain a meticulous inventory valuing the claimants' lands, houses and their contents, listing crops, fruit trees, timber, livestock and slaves at the time they fled or were driven out compared with pre-War values, so that compensation could be reckoned accordingly. Names, relationships and ages of dependants are also disclosed. Such claim papers help recreate a vivid portrait of colonial life, and where wills and deeds no longer exist, at least you have a partial summary of them, and can learn what became of the family, whether returning to England, escaping into Canada or elsewhere.

Some other sources for tracing origins of immigrants

Once you have found wills of immigrants you might be able to trace their origins from customs or immigration passenger lists, naturalisation papers, or service records of military and naval personnel.

Look first for their names in *Passenger and Immigration Lists Index, 1538–1900*, by PW Filby and various co-editors. These volumes consist of an alphabetical string of personal names, with the dates and places or ships in which they appeared in numbered books. The author's name and full title of each numbered publication is found in the endpapers. Names of certain people recur again and again, because their personal details were taken from a variety of sources. Always check the publication for more information and the context in which the name was found, and if possible look also at the cited original archives to ensure nothing was missed out and there were no transcription errors.

Regular runs of customs' passenger lists start only in 1820, and are arranged by month, year and port of arrival, to which there are indexes. The musters give the name, age, occupation, country of embarkation and ultimate destination of every passenger, and details of deaths during the voyage.

Indexed immigration passenger lists, commencing when the customs' lists ceased in the 1890s, also include birthplace and last place of residence, and sometimes the name and address of a relative in the country of origin. These may be inspected on microfilm in the National Archives, in Washington, DC, and at its regional branches. *The Morton Allen Directory of European Passenger Steamship Arrivals* lists by year, the steamship company, name and date of arrival of each vessel at the ports of New York, 1890–1930, and Baltimore, Boston and Philadelphia, 1904–26.

Naturalisation papers contain dates and places of birth of petitioners, their current nationality, and indicate whether the dated applications were successful. The original records are kept by the appropriate National Archives Regional Archives from about 1790 onwards up to 1950. Prior to 1906, naturalisation could be conferred by the states themselves, so some applications will be filed in state rather than federal archives. Duplicates of all naturalisations from 26 September 1906 to date are held by the Immigration and Naturalisation Service (INS), Washington, DC, to whom written requests for information may be sent. Colonial grants have been published in *Naturalizations in the American Colonies, 1740–1772*, edited by MS Giuseppi.

Extensive service records and pension papers of soldiers and sailors are held by the National Archives in Washington, DC, of which its Regional Archives have microfilm copies relating to military personnel and defectors from British regiments and Hessian mercenaries during the Revolutionary War. They contain details about age, birthplace, date of enlistment and discharge as well as rank and career.

Summing up

Read carefully, wills can be used not only for their intrinsic value but as a gateway to other sources, especially about the places of provenance of people born outside the United States.

17

FRED KARNO'S ARMY

Fred Karno

Fred Karno began his working life as Frederick John Westcott, a plumber in Nottingham, where he had moved with his parents John and Emma and younger brother Frank around 1871. The 1881 census index of Nottinghamshire shows that the family lived at Careys Place. Frederick was by then fifteen, and was apparently born at Exeter in Devon, Frank, then eleven, was born at Salisbury in Wiltshire, and John, aged ten, and Mark, two, were natives of Nottingham. By 1881 Emma was thirty-four, so she was nineteen when her first son was born. Like her husband, her senior by four years, Emma originally came from Exeter. Emma called herself Emily Westcott (formerly Barden) when she registered Frederick's birth at Exeter on 23 April 1866. The confinement took place at her home in Paul Street on 26 March, and she gave her husband's occupation as cabinet maker, but by 1881 John was describing himself as a french polisher.

Young Fred goes on the stage

Within a year of the 1881 census, their eldest child had made his debut as Leanaro, the lady acrobat, at the Crown and Cushion free and easy, Nottingham. He quickly proved his versatility on the trapeze, miming short comic sketches and clowning, before enlisting in a circus troupe bound for a tour of Germany and the Low Countries. By 1889, when he married at twenty-three, he was a seasoned traveller, appearing in music halls up and down the country using London as his springboard. His wedding took place on 15 January, at the Register Office, Lambeth, south of the River Thames, and he gave out his employment as that of a gymnast, living at 14 Little Canterbury Place, a short walking distance from his bride's home at 118 Kennington Road. Edith Cuthbert's professed age was twenty-one, the daughter of John Cuthbert, a journeyman rope manufacturer.

Soon after his marriage, Fred and two other acrobats were asked to deputise for 'The Three Carnos' at the Metropolitan, Edgware Road, and were so well received that they continued to perform there for a month before securing a season's booking at the Westminster Royal Aquarium, billed under the dangerously similar title of 'The Three Karnos'. In the mid-1890s the Three Karnos were but a segment of his 'Fred Karno Fun Factory', an operation based in Camberwell, which he crammed with all the accumulated scenery, props and costumes for the various companies of speechless comedians he sent on engagements to act out his comic pieces, pantomimes and sketches. One of the locals, Charlie Chaplin, recalled first seeing and being deeply impressed by 'Early Birds' which he watched from a gallery seat as a teenager in 1903, while waiting for his half-brother Sydney's delayed return from sea, and his mother languished in the local lunatic asylum. Before long both Charlie and Sydney were on Karno's payroll.

Fred forms his Army and meets his Waterloo

Quite when Fred assumed the name of Karno is uncertain, though it has been claimed that he changed his name by deed poll in 1914 (*Fred Karno, Master of Mirth and Tears*, by JP Gallagher). If so, it was not formally enrolled in the records of the Supreme Court of Justice in London. By then he had traversed America, establishing an international reputation as a showman and theatre manager for his companies of slapstick comedians. His most famous sketch of the absurd ('Mumming Birds') was renamed 'A Night in an English Music Hall' for the benefit of his New York audience, where it ran for nine years from 1905.

Charlie Chaplin's and Stan Laurel's first trip to America in September 1910 was as part of Karno's troupe, Stan briefly understudying for Charlie. In 1913, to provide more scope for his sense of the burlesque, Karno leased Tagg's Island, situated in the Thames near Hampton

Court, sinking £70,000 of his own money into the construction of 'Karsino', a fun palace which served dinners and other entertainments to paying guests, who first had to bear the cost of being ferried across the river. His troupe came to be known during the Great War of 1914-18 as 'Fred Karno's Army', a military byword for anything farcical, ridiculous or inept. But for him the War proved a financial catastrophe, as few people came to the island, and before long he was embroiled in protracted and costly litigation over the lease. In May 1928 the hotel, its fixtures and fittings, the dancing pavilion and the river craft were calculated at being worth no more than £1,850, and he was declared a bankrupt. An immensely long list of his assets and liabilities is on deposit in the Public Record Office at Kew.

Two women in Fred Karno's life

Fred Karno died at Parkstone, in Dorset, on 17 September 1941, aged seventy-five, his widow, Marie Theresa Karno being granted probate of his will on 29 October, as his sole beneficiary and executrix. His total effects amounted merely to £42 7s 4d. When the will was drawn up on 15 January 1934, he was living in a flat in Charing Cross Road, London, and he referred to his former name of Westcott. This date would have been the forty-fifth anniversary of his wedding to Edith Cuthbert, but Marie Moore had become his second wife on 16 June 1927, exactly three weeks after Edith's death on 27 May at Leigh-on-Sea, in Essex.

The index of deaths for the June quarter of 1927 professed Edith Blanche Westcott's age as fifty-six, placing her birth about 1871, confirmed by the index entry in the March quarter of 1870. To assert that she was twenty-one when she married in 1889 thus stretched the truth somewhat, since she was actually a minor and would have required parental consent to the match. Edith's own will, though composed on 10 December 1926, was not proved until 8 September 1927, several months after her widower's remarriage. The probate registrar appointed her son and her sister as administrators because she had nominated the two witnesses as executors, which was disallowed. Her total effects were £353 18s 3d, none of which went to Fred. It is clear that it was a holograph will, being an artless, misspelt and poignant summary of her worldly possessions, and of whom she wanted to favour. It hints at a once-luxurious lifestyle. Her sister Florence Entwistle was left her fur black coat, all her feather cushions, two pictures, curtains, draperies and household linen, and was to share the table plate and cutlery with Edith's son, Leslie Karno Westcott. Leslie was bequeathed her large photograph in the drawing room, on condition that an exact copy was made and presented to her niece, Dora McCreesh. Dora, in turn, was to have the Sheffield silver tea tray. Another sister, Mary Mosley, was given a brown trimmed fur coat and any other clothing selected for her by Florence. Six sheets, two large blankets, six pillow cases, a bedspread, two large towels, six tea towels, four pairs of lace curtains, three table cloths (one coloured), two large feather pillows, a pair of heavy curtains, all her underclothing and any dresses found useful to her were reserved for Louise Karno Westcott, whose precise relationship was not stated, but the items would have gone a long way to starting a first home. Various pieces of jewellery, rugs, pictures, a Spode soup tureen and eight plates, a tea service, fruit servers and fish servers, fur articles and a gold brocaded eiderdown were destined as tokens to her friends. Half the sale proceeds of her furniture and remaining effects were to go to Leslie, the other half being equally shared by her sister Florence, and grandchildren Edith Patricia Karno Westcott, Frederick Karno Westcott and Kenneth Douglas Westcott, the granddaughter receiving the piano. Mrs Queenie Karno Westcott was left Edith's pearls and brilliants, and the will concluded with the significantly cryptic and meaningful bequest 'To my husband Fred Karno my wedding ring'. And who can be surprised? It was not for nothing that he was renowned for his love of the absurd, and it is a relief to know that he would not have received his gift in time for his second wedding.

An early Karno recruit: Charlie Chaplin

Charlie Chaplin's published autobiography opens with his birth on 16 April 1889, at 8 o'clock in the evening, at East Lane (East Street), in Walworth, South London. Alas, it would seem the birth was not registered by either parent, though *The Magnet*, published on 11 May, announced the birth of 'a beautiful boy' on 15 April to the wife of Mr Charles Chaplin (née Miss Lily Harley). Neither the boy's name nor birthplace was mentioned, nor even his mother's real name.

Charles Chaplin, Charlie's father, who was a professional singer, had married Hannah Harriet Hill at St Paul's Church, Walworth, on 22 June 1885, as from 57 Brandon Street where the nineteen-year-old bride had previously been delivered of an illegitimate son, Sydney John Hill, on 16 March. Charles Chaplin and his new wife parted company about 1891, soon after his return from New York; she then bore another son, to another successful music hall singer, 'Leo Dryden' (otherwise George Dryden Wheeler), on 31 August 1892. Charles remained in the vicinity, close to his brother Spencer, who was a publican, and kept up a tenuous link with his spouse, not always at his own choosing.

Family misfortunes

Hannah was a vaudeville actress, performing as Lily Harley, but the strain of trying to earn enough money to support herself and her young family from her dwindling stage bookings and any extra income she could bring in from nursing and dressmaking soon took its toll on her health, culminating in periodic bouts in the local workhouse or infirmary from 1895. In 1894, aged five, Charlie had stood in for her when her voice gave way on stage at Aldershot in Hampshire. By the time of her first admission to St Saviour's Union Workhouse, her youngest child (by 'Leo Dryden') had been spirited away by his father. On 19 June 1896 the clerk to the Board of Guardians wrote to the Local Government Board in Whitehall to report the admission to the workhouse of her two eldest sons, owing to the father's absence and the destitution and illness of the mother. It was decided the boys should stay together and that their father be ordered to contribute twelve shillings a week for their upkeep. He was described in the correspondence, in the Public Record Office at Kew and in London Metropolitan Archives, as 'a Music Hall Singer, able-bodied and ... in a position to earn sufficient to maintain his children'. It was proposed to send the boys to Hanwell School, and by 1 July the father had acquiesced.

Admissions and discharges of pupils recorded in the religious creed and general register of the school at Hanwell, in Central London School District (in the latter repository), reveal that they had already been taken there on 18 June on the instructions of the same clerk.

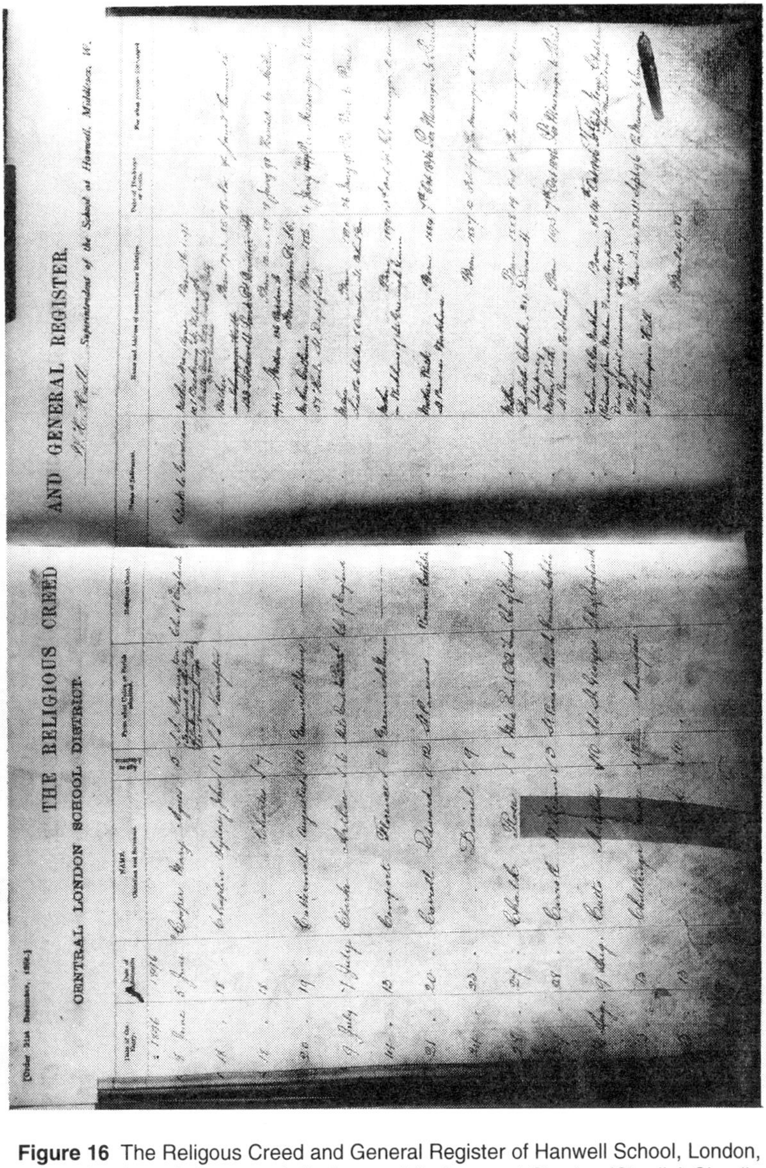

Figure 16 The Religous Creed and General Register of Hanwell School, London, 1896, showing admisson and discharge of Sydney and Charles (Charlie) Chaplin as pupils. Their birth dates are included. (Reproduced by permission of the Greater London Record Office)

Sydney was discharged on 18 November to join the *Exmouth*, a naval training ship moored at Grays, in Essex, where workhouse boys of his age could opt to be sent. The particulars about Charles show he was discharged from the school and handed to his mother on 18 January 1898. The register recorded her address by 26 October 1897 as in Oakden Street, Kennington Road, Surrey.

His father, meanwhile, frequently passed his days with his brother Spencer, who ran several public houses in the Lambeth area. It was Spencer who averted his arrest for maintenance arrears of £44 8s in 1897. Charles absconded that December and a warrant was issued for his arrest to enforce a Board decision that he should take the boys into his care. When apprehended, he settled the fine and requested that Hannah should take responsibility for them.

Charlie's autobiography paints a graphic picture of the grim conditions he and his brother experienced at the school while all this was going on. Throughout his childhood he was shunted in and out of a variety of local schools depending on the Union where the family lodged. He spent three months with his father from September 1898 when his mother was an inmate of Cane Hill Lunatic Asylum, sharing two rooms with his four-year-old half-brother and Louise, the boy's mother, as well as his elder half-brother, Sydney. Charles and Louise were apparently quarrelsome and Charles sought consolation in alcohol, an occupational hazard, since many music halls had evolved from drinking establishments.

Men at the bar

Charles and Spencer Chaplin's father was also named Spencer, and he traded as a butcher at least until Charles married in 1885, but when he died on 29 May 1897, at sixty-three, he too was a licensee, managing the Devonport Arms, Devonport Mews, in Radnor Place, Paddington, Middlesex. His short will, made eleven days before he expired, directed that his son Charles should carry on the business for twelve months during which he was 'to find a home for Mrs Machell' (a person mentioned without any further comment or explanation of her status, although a Lucy Mackhill and her husband lodged with Spencer Chaplin in 1881). He was to then sell up, dividing the proceeds with his siblings unless an amicable arrangement could be reached amongst them. As the effects totalled £1,259 when probate was granted on 2 September, this must have eased Charles Chaplin's financial situation somewhat, although this did not prevent his disappearing act three months later. He himself succumbed within four years, a victim of his predilection for the bottle. The death certificate shows that when he died in St Thomas's Hospital on 9 May 1901, it was his widow H Chaplin, of 16 Golden Place, Chester Street, Lambeth, who was the informant next day, rather than his regular companion, Louise, and his occupation was described as 'comedian of Lambeth'. He was merely thirty-seven, and was buried in a pauper's grave in Tooting Public Cemetery.

One of the hostelries Charles patronised was the Queen's Head, at 46 and 48 Broad Street, about half a mile away from from his rooms at 289 Kennington Road. The 1891 census return records that it was occupied by nine people on the night of Sunday 5 April. His brother Spencer W Chaplin was at its head, labelling himself a licensed victualler of thirty-five, born at Ipswich, in Suffolk.

The Suffolk connection

Seven years Spencer's junior, Charles Chaplin was born on 18 March 1863, at 22 Orcus Street, Marylebone, Middlesex, to Spencer Chaplin and his wife Ellen Elizabeth (formerly Smith), and they were married by licence on 30 October 1854, in the church of St Margaret, Ipswich. The parish register recorded them both as minors, and Spencer's father as Shadrach Chaplin, an innkeeper. Spencer applied to the Archdeaconry Court of Suffolk for the licence on 27 October, gave his parish as St Margaret and his age as nineteen, the same as his bride, asserting that parental consent had been obtained on both sides.

The 1851 census returns of Ipswich have been indexed, so that Spencer and his father were quickly found, at Carr Street, in the parish of St Margaret. Shadrack (*sic*) Chaplin was by then a master brewer aged forty, supporting his wife Sophia, forty-three, and five children, the eldest of whom was sixteen-year-old Spencer. Shadrack himself was born at Finborough, in Suffolk, his offspring at Ipswich, but his wife originated from Tunstall, in Staffordshire. Perhaps they had met through a connection with the brewing industry. By the time he died in Ipswich on 2 April 1893, aged seventy-nine, Shadrach had become a bootmaker, leaving a widow, Susannah, fourteen years his junior, who survived him but one day. Susannah Eyres was widowed by the time that they married at Crown Street Congregational Chapel, Ipswich, on 25 August 1872, when Shadrach was fifty-eight. Shadrach volunteered his occupation then as a commercial traveller, and that of his deceased father Shadrach as a farmer. Possibly Shadrach added a few years on to his age in 1851 to close the six-year gap with his older first spouse; why a few years were not knocked off her age instead seems slightly unchivalrous.

Although the March 1992 edition of the International Genealogical Index for Suffolk includes the marriage of Shadrach Chaplin and Sophia Hancock on 29 April 1834, at St Margaret, Ipswich, none of their children's baptisms are indexed, nor do they appear in the original parish registers of that parish between 1836 and 1856, but as Shadrach's second marriage was in a Congregational Chapel it may be that the family was briefly nonconformist. Unfortunately the baptism registers of the chapel survive only from 1876.

The Great Finborough Chaplins

As Shadrach Chaplin was apparently born about 1811 or 1814, at Finborough, the parish registers were scanned for his baptism in the absence of any entry on the IGI. The registers of Great Finborough commence in 1558, and are on microfiche at the three branches of Suffolk Record Office. According to his baptism entry on 8 April 1814, Shadrach was born on 15 January, the second of six children of Shadrach Chaplin, a shoemaker, and his wife Elizabeth. Shadrach had two younger brothers named Meshech and Abednego. The published 1851 census index of Ipswich was used to track down Abednego Chaplin to his home in Butter Market, in the parish of St Lawrence, where he worked as an ironmonger. His young wife Jane, and his parents, Shadrach and Elizabeth Chaplin, were also in the house. Like his son, sixty-five-year-old Shadrach, a retired farmer, was a native of Great Finborough, his wife coming from Buxhall, the parish next door. (Incidentally the printed index wrongly ascribed Shadrach's age as sixty-eight, illustrating the importance of checking the original document.)

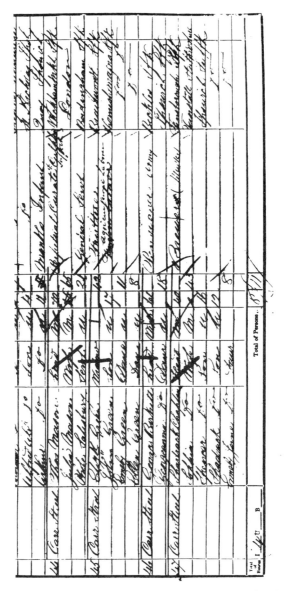

Figure 17 Census return, Ipswich, Suffolk, 1851, showing Shadrack (*sic*) Chaplin, his first wife and children. His son Spencer was Charlie Chaplin's grandfather. (Reproduced by permission of the Public Record Office, London)

Shadrake (*sic*) Chaplin and Elizabeth Wilden were married at Buxhall on 29 August 1809, after banns, and their daughter Philippa's baptism followed four months later at Great Finborough, on Christmas Day, when the mother's maiden name was spelt as Wilding.

Extracting all the Great Finborough Chaplin and variant baptisms to 1883, marriages to 1840 and burials before 1900, it was possible to construct a family tree spanning two further generations before any break. Daniel, Shadrach's older brother, born in 1779, was succeeded as a thatcher by his own son Daniel, and grandson Charles, who was still carrying on his craft in 1878 when his last known child was baptised there, some sixty-four years later. Daniel and Shadrach's youngest brother was baptised Meshech in 1788, and they were all the progeny of George and Susanna Chaplin (née Bacon).

As the microfiche were difficult to decipher, a microfiched heavily abbreviated transcript proving no better, the original parish registers were produced by the Record Office in Ipswich, a sad reminder that microforms can be a poor substitute. They were clearly written, easily read, less of a strain on the eye, and carefully handled, the pages could be swiftly turned, making the search more enjoyable, and the likelihood much less of missing or misinterpreting anything. I was able to flick backwards and forwards through the volumes to see if their contemporaries chose similar Biblical names for their children. It was a simple matter to note any gaps in recording, which in this instance included marriages between 1634 and 1643, 1645–90 and 1695, baptisms between 1634 and 1640, 1643, 1645, 1648, 1650–51, 1654–69, 1671, 1680, 1682–85, and 1687–88, which may help explain why I have been unable to extend the pedigree earlier than the marriage of John Chaplin and Elizabeth Burman in 1728, though Caleb and Elizabeth Chaplin had three daughters baptised there, the first on 14 April 1695, her day of birth. John and his wife Elizabeth did not name any of their four known sons Caleb, nor was he mentioned in the Suffolk IGI. Whilst there might be continuity of surname there is so far no evidence connecting the two families, nor any proven link with the Thomas Chaplin who was married at Great Finborough in 1609. Alas there are no bishop's transcripts or register bills for the missing years.

When Great Finborough church was rebuilt in 1875, many of the gravestones in the churchyard were uprooted to create a pavement around it. About 1892, Charles Partridge of Stowmarket, in Suffolk, copied down a hundred and fifty-two surviving inscriptions, and although six of the headstones commemorated nineteenth-century Chaplins, none was dated any earlier.

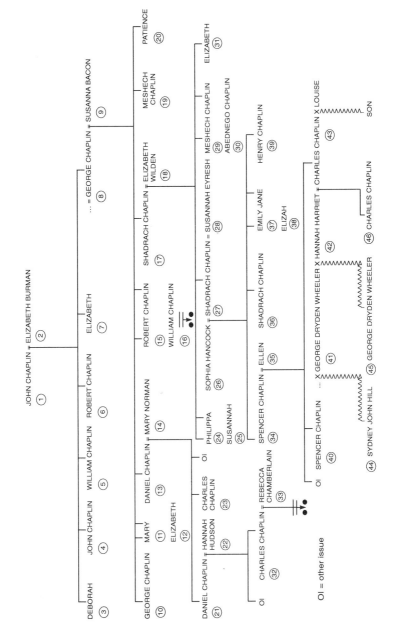

Figure 18 Chaplin Family tree

Key:

1. of Great Finborough, co. Suffolk, 1728, parish constable, 1744, 1746, overseer of the poor, 1768, 1773, churchwarden, 1774, bur 12 Oct 1787, Great Finborough.

2. marr 11 July 1728, Great Finborough afsd., after Banns.

3. bap 15 Dec 1728, Great Finborough, afsd.

4. bap 22 Nov 1730, Great Finborough, afsd.

5. bap 25 Dec 1732, Great Finborough, afsd.

6. bap 15 June 1734, Great Finborough, afsd.

7. bap 6 June 1737, Great Finborough, afsd.

8. of Great Finborough, afsd., farmer, 1771-1819, bap there 24 May 1741, parish constable, 1781-1809, overseer of the poor, 1809, died 12, bur 19 May 1819 Great Finborough, afsd., aged 78, M.I., will dd 13 May, pr 30 Sept 1819.

9. marr 8 Sept 1771, Great Finborough, afsd., after Banns, named executrix in husband's will, 1819, died 6, bur 10 April 1827, Great Finborough, aged 78 or 80, M.I.

10. bap 20 June 1773, Great Finborough, afsd.

11. bap 10 Sept 1775, Great Finborough, afsd., named in father's will, 1819.

12. bn 25 Apr, bap 17 May 1777, Great Finborough, afsd., received into the church 14 Sept 1783.

13. of Great Finborough, co. thatcher, 1802-50, there bn 8 Jly, bap 10 Aug 1779, and received into the church, 14 Sept 1783, aged c60 in 1841, died 22, bur 28 Feb 1850, Great Finborough, aged 70, M.I.

14. of Ipswich, co. Suffolk, 1852, marr 9 Dec 1802, Great Finborough, afsd., after Banns, aged c60 in 1841, died 7, bur 12 May, 1852, Great Finborough, aged 71, M.I.

15. bn 15 Mch, bap 29 Aug 1781, Great Finborough, afsd., received into the church 14 Sept 1783.

16. bn 2 Aug, bap 14 Sept 1783, Great Finborough, afsd., named in father's will as deceased, 1819.

17. of Great Finborough, afsd., 1809-19, Butter Market, Ipswich, afsd., 1851, shoemaker, 1814-22, retired farmer, 1851, bap 21 May 1786, Great Finborough, named in father's will, 1819, aged 65 in 1851, dead by 1872.

18. (WILDING) of Buxhall, co. Suffolk, there marr 29 Aug 1809, after Banns, aged 67 in 1851.

19. of Hadleigh Road, Great Finborough, afsd., farmer, 1841, bap 3 Aug 1788, Great Finborough, overseer of the poor, 1828, 1840, 1847, aged c50 in 1841, exectr of father's will, 1819, died 20, bur 25 Aug 1849, Great Finborough, aged 61, M.I.

20. bap 21 Jly 1793, Great Finborough, afsd., named in father's will, 1819.

21. of Village Green, Great Finborough, afsd., thatcher, 1841, bap 2 Jne 1803, Great Finborough, parish constable, 1851, 1855-61, aged c35 in 1841.

22. Banns read at Great Finborough, afsd., 8,15 Dec 183-, aged c30 in 1841, died 8, bur 13 Dec 1878, Great Finborough, aged 69, M.I.

23. bap 22 Apr 1821, Great Finborough, afsd., parish constable, 1850, 1854, 1862-64, 1868, nominated but not chosen as overseer of the poor, 1869, parish clerk 1872, Rate Collector and Assistant Surveyor, 1875, Surveyor, 1876, aged c20 in 1841.

24. bap 25 Dec 1809, Great Finborough,afsd.

25. bap 5 Jne 1812, Great Finborough, afsd.

26. bn c1808, Tunstall, co. Stafford, marr 29 Apr 1834, St. Margaret Ipswich, afsd., after Banns, aged 43 in 1851.

27. of Carr Street, Ipswich, afsd., 1851, and Old Cattle Market, Ipswich, 1881, master brewer, 1851, innkeeper, 1854, commercial traveller, 1872, bootmaker, 1881-87, bn 15 Jan, bap 8 Apr 1814, Great Finborough, afsd, aged 67 in 1881, died 2 Apr 1893, at Ipswich, aged 79, will dd 19 Feb 1887, Admon 12 May 1893.

28. dau of the late SAMUEL ROBIN-SON, labourer, deceased, marr 2nd, 25 Aug 1872, Crown Street Congregational Chapel of the Independents, Ipswich, died 3 Apr 1893, aged 65, Admon 5 May 1893.

29. bap 20 Apr 1817, Great Finborough, afsd.

30. of Butter Market, Ipswich, afsd., ironmonger, 1851, bap 6 Feb 1819, Great Finborough, afsd., aged 31 in 1851.

31. bap 12 May 1822, Great Finborough, afsd.

32. of Great Finborough, afsd., thatcher, 1873, bap 4 Jne 1846, Great Finborough.

33. Banns read at Great Finborough, afsd., 3, 10, 17 Dec 1871.

34. of St. Margaret, Ipswich, afsd., 1854, Orcus Street, Marylebone, co. Middx, 1863, Rillington Place, co. Middx, 1881, The Devonport Arms, Devonport Mews, Radnor Place, co. Middx, 1897, butcher, 1854-63, unemployed, 1881, public house manager, 1897, bn c1835, Ipswich, aged 16 in 1851, died 29 May 1897, aged 63, will dd 18 May 1897, Admon 2 Sept 1897.

35. dau of WILLIAM SMITH, dealer, marr 30 Oct 1854, St Margaret, Ipswich, afsd., by Licence, dead by 30 Mch 1851.

36. bn c1839, Ipswich, afsd., aged 12 in 1851.

37. bn c1843, Ipswich, afsd., aged 8 in 1851.

38. bn c1845, Ipswich, afsd., aged 6 in 1851.

39. bn c1849, Ipswich, afsd., aged 2 in 1851.

40. of Northcote Hotel, Battersea Rise, London, 1881, Queens Head, Lambeth, co. Surrey, 1891, manager to a publican, 1881, licensed victualler, 1891, bn c1856, Ipswich, afsd., aged 25 in 1881.

41. (LEO DRYDEN), music hall singer.

42. (LILY HARLEY) of Southwark, 1881, Brandon Street, Walworth, 1885, Oakden Street, Kennington Road, 1898, all co. Surrey, Golden Place, Chester Street, Lambeth, afsd., 1901, mantle machinist, 1881, dau of CHARLES HILL, bootmaker, marr 22 Jne 1885, St. John Walworth, after Banns.

43. of Northcote Hotel, Battersea Rise, afsd., 1881, Brandon Street afsd., 1885, Albert Street, Newington, co. Surrey, 1891, Lambeth, afsd., 1901, barman, 1881, professional singer, 1885, music hall singer, 1891, comedian, 1901, bn 18 Mch 1863, Orcus Street, Marylebone, afsd., died 9 May 1901, St Thomas's Hospital, Lambeth.

44. bn 16/17 Mch 1885, Brandon Street, afsd.

45. (WHEELER DRYDEN), bn 31 Aug 1892.

46. (CHARLIE CHAPLIN) bn 12/15/16 Apr 1889.

Stuck with the Chaplins

Percival Boyd's Marriage Index, covering 489 out of 504 Suffolk parishes, drawing on printed copies rather than original parish registers, failed to yield the wedding of Caleb between 1676 and 1750, but this may be explained by defective recording during the relevant period. The wedding between Jn Chaplin and Mary Jourdaine was noted in 1680 at Buxhall. The microfiche copies of the parish registers, 1588–1740, disclosed that the couple were both resident at Great Finborough when they married on 15 May 1680, but no children were recorded for them among subsequent baptisms at either place, or at Little Finborough. As there are gaps in the Great Finborough registers throughout that decade this may be significant. At Buxhall John Chaplin and his wife Bridget had six offspring baptised between 1697 and 1706, including Daniel, but no John, and Thomas and Elizabeth Chaplyn produced at least one son Thomas, and two daughters from 1676 until 11 March 1683/4, almost five months after the father's burial on 28 October 1683. No trace was found of these two marriages in Boyd's Index nor the IGI of Suffolk.

Indexes to wills proved in the local probate courts serving this part of Suffolk contained various references to the surname from 1660 until 1857, but not to Caleb or any Chaplin at Great Finborough, Buxhall or proximal parishes, before George Chaplin's will was proved at the Archdeaconry Court of Sudbury on 30 September 1819. Caleb's will was not proved in the superior Prerogative Court of Canterbury between 1741 (his year of burial at Great Finborough) and 1755.

The Chaplins take up community service

The contents of Great Finborough parish chest have been deposited at Suffolk Record Office in Ipswich. The inventory lists vestry minute books from 1684 until 1915, a book containing poor rates and overseers' disbursements between 1742 and 1800, summary churchwardens' accounts, 1755–76, and summary highway surveyors' accounts, 1754–67, and three volumes of overseers' accounts from 1800 until 1835.

The first book of vestry minutes records annual appointments of parish officers; the family's first chronicled call to duty was the election of John Chapling (*sic*) as constable on 27 March 1744, three years after Caleb's death. A long catalogue of the Chaplins' more or less continuous service to the parish can be traced down five generations to the signature in the vestry minute book of Charles Chaplin as church-warden in April 1912. Charles Chaplin was obviously a valued member of the community, for on 11 May 1887 he was elected one of the parish committee with Robert Chaplin to help plan arrangements for a festival with a roast beef dinner and plum pudding, and a tea afterwards, to cele-brate Queen Victoria's Golden Jubilee.

As an overseer of the poor in 1768 and 1773, John Chaplin recovered all his necessary outgoings from the poor rates, which he fixed each half year with the vestry's approval. The amounts varied, and from 17 April until 4 October 1742 it was set at elevenpence-halfpenny in the pound, levied on each householder's rent. He himself had a property worth £9 then and another valued at £5. The fluctuating scale of half-yearly payments can be tracked via the overseers' rate books, his son George being first listed as a contributor for rent of £5 in October 1769.

The overseers' disbursements show that at Easter 1751, John Chaplain (*sic*) was paid 3s 6d for clothing 'for ye girl Whittum', and a further £1 4s for Sarah Boor's board for twenty-four weeks. His third account, for unspecified services, came to fifteen shillings, making his total receipts £2 2s 6d for the half year, while he himself contributed seven shillings in poor rates. A later overseers' book records that a boy was boarded-out with his son George Chaplin for a year on 2 September 1807 funded by the parish rates, and in 1827 George's youngest son Meshech had a girl balloted to him, having been taken from the Hundred House (workhouse) into the homes of other parish householders during the previous two years.

It seems bizarre that at one end of the nineteenth century and even as late as 1890, rural Suffolk Chaplins should be involved in dispensing poor relief, whilst in the depths of teeming Lambeth their distant cousins were dependent upon it.

—————— Trouper Stan Laurel ——————

When Fred Karno's troupe of comedians set sail for Canada en route to America in September 1910, young Stanley Jefferson was taken aboard as Charlie Chaplin's understudy. His father, a notable theatre manager, had engineered his passage but the contract did not last long, as Stan found it impossible to survive on his pay of twenty dollars a week, which Karno refused to increase, so he made his own way back to England from Colorado Springs. After an unsuccessful interlude trying out different acts, he took up typing, until Fred Karno's manager offered him a place on the tour at a higher salary. Chaplin announced his withdrawal, Stan taking over his part, and the show opened to great acclaim at the Hippodrome in West Ealing, London. Chaplin watched it several times and decided he would join in after all, so Stan was placed back in the chorus. Nonetheless he was one of the troupe when it went again to America, and this time he stayed behind, combining forces with other former members of the company, and exacting a brand of revenge with his pioneering Charlie Chaplin impersonations. In 1918 he became part of a duo called 'Stan and Mae Laurel', before eventually going into films, teaming up with Oliver Hardy in 1926.

Stanley Jefferson becomes Stan Laurel

Arthur Stanley Jefferson, thenceforward known as Stan Laurel, was born on 16 June 1890, at Foundry Cottages, Ulverston, in Lancashire. His parents were Arthur Jefferson, a comedian, and Margaret (formerly Metcalfe), who already had another son, George Gordon. When the 1891 census was taken on the night of 5 April, neither the baby nor his parents were in Ulverston, but George Metcalfe, a master shoemaker, aged fifty-four, was living at 3 Foundry Street with his wife Sarah, fifty-nine, and their grandson George G Jefferson, a schoolboy of six. True to form, only the child's first forename was written in full, but he was undoubtedly Stan's elder brother.

Arthur Jefferson's mysterious past

Their parents were married on 19 March 1884, at Holy Trinity Church, Ulverston, Arthur Jefferson describing himself as an unmarried man of twenty-one, a comedian domiciled in Manchester, Lancashire, and the son of a solicitor, Frank Jefferson. Margaret, his bride, was a year older and her father George was then a watchmaker.

According to *Laurel before Hardy*, by J Owen-Pawson and B Mouland, Margaret (or Madge) was a singer, and had first encountered Arthur when he worked at a theatre in Ulverston known as Spencer's Gaff.

They acted together all over the North of England, generally leaving their young brood behind in Ulverston with the Metcalfes or with Madge's married sister Sarah Shaw. Beatrice Olga was born in December 1894, at Bishop Auckland, in Co. Durham, where Arthur leased and managed the Old Theatre Royal, Sydney Everitt was born on 30 April 1899, in North Shields, in Northumberland, but died as an infant, and finally Edward Everitt arrived in April 1901. By 1905 the family was reunited and living at Rutherglen, Glasgow, in Scotland, Arthur having secured the post of manager of The Metropole Theatre. Madge died in Glasgow in December 1908, and on 14 November 1912 Arthur took a second wife, Venetia Matilda Robinson, a widow aged forty, in a ceremony at St George's Hanover Square, Middlesex. Arthur gave out his own age as fifty, and his profession as a theatrical proprietor. George Gordon Jefferson and her own son Henry H Robinson were two of the witnesses, the register entry curiously identifying Arthur's father as the late Christopher Jefferson, gentleman (deceased). By 1922, he was back in Bishop Auckland running the theatre he had first left in 1895; now he faced severe competition from the cinema, so in 1925 he migrated to London to try and improve his luck, living out his final years at the Lincolnshire public house home of his married daughter.

Arthur Jefferson died on 15 January 1949, at the Plough Inn, Barkston, in Lincolnshire, apparently aged ninety-three, having made his will on 7 October 1947, the same year that Laurel and Hardy paid him a visit. Beatrice was left everything, unless she predeceased him, whereupon his son Stanley Jefferson (professionally known as Stan Laurel) was to be sole beneficiary. His total assets were £203 3s 11d when the will was proved on 11 February 1949. The *Grantham Journal*, issued on 21 January 1949, reported his age as ninety-four. Arthur's second wife had died on 23 January 1941, willing Arthur the diamond engagement ring he had given her, his furniture in their house at 49 Colebrooke Avenue, Ealing, £100, and the income from £1,000 invested for his lifetime.

A gravestone inscription in Barkston Cemetery notes that Arthur was born in 1862, but alas not his actual birthday. This year is more consistent with his own assertion than his death certificate and obituary (1855 or 1856). Unfortunately there is no contemporary parish magazine for Barkston which might have added more to his biography.

The quest for Arthur

A search was made of the consolidated indexes of births registered in England and Wales between 1859 and 1867, starting with 1862 and then yearly steps either side. There were six entries of Arthur Jefferson, four with this as the first forename, and three unnamed 'Male' registrations. Two of the six were registered at Thirsk and Hull, in Yorkshire and one at Ely in Cambridgeshire, in 1863, and another at Darlington in Co Durham, in 1862.

The North Country 1881 census indexes were culled on microfiche for Lancashire, Yorkshire, Durham, Northumberland, Cumberland and Westmorland, in the hopes of picking up Arthur's whereabouts before Manchester at the time of his marriage, and the births, baptisms and parentage of the above infants. The Lancashire index revealed that an Arthur Jefferson, a single man of seventeen, was boarding with Mrs Julia Kair, a merchant's wife, at 6 Jassall Street, Charlton upon Medlock, Manchester. He was described as a canvasser (coal) and his given birthplace was Birmingham, in Warwickshire. Presumably Arthur was employed in making coalbags at one of the local factories. There were two entries in Yorkshire, one Arthur L Jefferson, a twenty-year-old bookbinder and ruler, was the son of Leonard Jefferson, a confectioner in York, whose birth was registered in the York district in the last quarter of 1861, and the second, Arthur Wilberforce Jefferson, an ironmonger's assistant of fifteen, born at Skidby in the same county, had his birth registered at Beverley in 1865. Arthur Jefferson, son of William, a joiner, and his wife Hannah, was an apprentice joiner of eighteen living at Darlington, his birthplace. His birth was registered there in 1862, and he was baptised on 7 December 1862, at St Cuthbert, Darlington. No trace was found of the Cambridgeshire child in the 1881 census index of that county, but the birth certificate itself revealed that Arthur Jefferson was born on 6 June 1863, at Ely, son to George Jefferson, a house painter, and May Ann (formerly Watson). What became of the family is unknown, but in the first quarter of 1864, an Arthur Jefferson's death was registered at Ely.

Arthur Jefferson in 1891

As an actor, it is likely that Arthur was itinerant, and he may have boarded in Manchester for short seasonal periods only before moving on. However, several addresses were known for him in the 1890s at

Bishop Auckland, and the 1891 census returns of the town disclosed that he and Madge were then visitors of Sarah Barker, who kept a lodging house at 15 High Tenters Street. Madge was thirty by then, from Hawes, in Yorkshire, and Arthur, a theatrical manager and two years younger, was a native of Birmingham, like the other lodger, John Price, a sixty-six year old comedian. Next door were the Thorns, another theatrical family, the father, Thomas, apparently being Arthur's partner in the lease on the Old Theatre Royal from 1889, though he bought himself out in 1891. His wife Florence was a professional actress, and their son Francis a scenic artist.

Of the 1881 Census indexes searched so far, only the Lancashire entry of Arthur Jefferson, aged seventeen, gave an identical birthplace, the only Jefferson in the county to be born in Birmingham.

Scanning indexes

The 1881 census index of Warwickshire was then gleaned for Arthur, Frank or Christopher Jefferson, needless to say without success, and so was the International Genealogical Index of this county, of its neighbours Worcestershire and Staffordshire, and of Lancashire, Westmorland, Cumberland, Northumberland and Durham. Tantalisingly, in Warwickshire, Frederick Forrest Jefferson's marriage to Eliza Salt was recorded on 2 May 1859, at Aston iuxta Birmingham, and on 5 December the same year she gave birth to a son Arthur, at Park Lane, Aston Manor. Her husband's occupation was given as a journeyman bronzer. By 1881 they had vanished from the country.

As a William Henry Jefferson's birth was registered at Birmingham in the June quarter of 1863, a copy of the certificate was obtained in case it was endorsed with a different baptismal name. There was no evidence of this. Unfortunately, neither this child nor his parents, Alfred and Tamar, appeared in the 1881 census index of Warwickshire.

The IGI of Yorkshire, on the other hand, recorded the baptisms of Arthur, son of William Thrush Jefferson and his wife Margaret, on 2 October 1859, at Northallerton, and of Arthur, son of Eliza Ann Jefferson, on 10 May 1864, at Kilburn. The birth certificate of this child announced his arrival on 8 July 1863, at Kilburn Parks, the home of his mother, who registered the birth at Thirsk, without naming the father. The other Yorkshire birth certificate in 1863 was that of Arthur, son of William Jefferson, a marine fireman, and his wife Sarah (formerly Marshall), born on 11 August at their house in Siminsons Gallery, Little Queen Street, Hull.

Looking for a solicitor

The annual printed *Law Lists* were searched for the name and workplace of Frank or Francis Jefferson between 1855 and 1884, but unsurprisingly, nothing was forthcoming, though they elicited a William Thrush Jefferson, a Northallerton solicitor, and John Ingleby Jefferson, attached to the same firm from 1877. Indexes at the Public Record Office at Kew, to enrolled articles of clerkship failed to yield any Frank or Francis Jefferson from 1856 until 1875. As William's name disappeared from the *Law List* after 1891, a glimpse at the Principal Probate Registry indexed calendars of wills revealed that he died on 13 April that year, his executors being his three sons, including John Ingleby Jefferson, the solicitor. No mention was made in his will of a son Arthur, but it contained directions for his estate to be sold and divided equally among all his children, grandchildren taking their parent's share if any should predecease the testator. The register of death duty wills for 1891 showed no son called Frank, but noted the demise of William's son Arthur on 15 April 1892. His will, made on 15 June 1891, in England, described him as a gentleman of Chicago, Illinois, as well as of Northallerton, and referred only to an infant daughter. Thus he could be eliminated as Stan's father, who married in 1884 and sired children at the turn of the century.

And turning up a farmer

The 1871 census return of Kilburn Parks produced the household of Mary Jefferson, a fifty-two-year-old widowed farmer of two-hundred and forty acres, but no daughter Eliza Ann or grandson Arthur. The returns of neighbouring villages were inspected, and at Thirkleby Arthur Jefferson, a schoolboy aged seven, native of Kilburn, was found staying at the farm of his uncle William Manfield and his wife Emily. On the night of the 1881 census, Emily and her two daughters were lodging with her mother, Mary Jefferson, at her house in Castle Terrace, Thirsk, but Arthur was gone.

The Yorkshire IGI places Emily's baptism at 27 November 1842, at Kilburn, and that of her sister Eliza Ann, on 3 November 1838, at Ainderby Steeple, some ten miles away. Both were children of Leonard and Mary Jefferson (née Abel), and his will was drawn up on 19 October 1863, three months after his illegitimate grandson's birth, but he was not a beneficiary. After disposing of specific gifts, the remainder of Leonard's estate, which was valued under £1,500, was to be sold and divided equally among his children on reaching twenty-one, any grandchildren taking a deceased child's portion. The death duty register duly noted the final distribution in May 1901, after his widow Mary's death, Leonard himself having succumbed in October 1864. Eliza Ann and her brother Leonard had died in the meantime at unknown dates in America, and another son in South Africa, so their shares as overseas residents would have been exempt in any event, and as the sums apportioned to the three surviving children were less than £18 apiece, no duty was payable. What became of Arthur, Eliza Ann's son, is unknown, but the consolidated death indexes from 1871 up to 1884 failed to yield his name, so he is likely to have lived until then.

The trouble with Arthur

As Arthur Jefferson consistently gave his year of birth as about 1862 or 1863, the likeliest candidates whose births were registered are the Kilburn, Darlington, Hull and York namesakes, none of whose fathers' or mothers' names were perpetuated by Stan's father for his own children, nor was Frank or Christopher the acknowledged father, or any solicitor or gentlemen involved. None of the names of the Kilburn family reappeared in the comedian's. There is always the possibility that the birth was unregistered, he was born later or earlier than put out, he never knew his real paternity, or we should discount Arthur Jefferson as his real name. What later became of Arthur Jefferson, last known of at Kilburn Park, in 1871, aged seven, and Arthur Jefferson in Chorlton upon Medlock, in 1881, aged seventeen? Where was Arthur Jefferson living before 1884, when he was domiciled in Manchester?

Bobby Baxter, the unknown factor

Not once does a published account refer to visits or any kind of

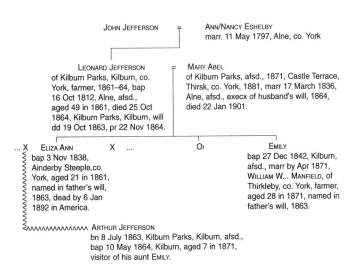

George Gordon Jefferson
bn c. 1885, Ulverston, afsd., aged 6 in 1891

Arthur Stanley Jefferson
(Stan Laurel), bn 16 June 1890,
Foundry Cottages, Ulverston, afsd.,
bap 3 Jan 1895, Bishop Auckland,
afsd.

OI = Other issue

Figure 19 Pedigree of the Jeffersons. The Jefferson grandfather of Stan Laurel is so far unknown.

FRANK JEFFERSON ₸ ...
solicitor, 1884.

CHRISTOPHER JEFFERSON ₸ ...
gentleman, dead by
14 Nov 1912.

MARGARET (MADGE) ₸
dau of GEORGE METCALFE,
of Ulverston, co. Lancaster,
watchmaker and bootmaker,
marr 19 March 1884, Holy
Trinity, Ulverston, by Licence,
died 1 Dec 1908, Craigmillar
Road, Langside, Cathcart, .
co. Renfrew, aged 50.

ARTHUR JEFFERSON =
of Manchester, co. Lancs,
1884, Foundry Cottages,
Ulverston, 1890, High
Tenters Street, Bishop
Auckland, co. Durham,
1891, Craigmillar Road,
Langside, afsd., 1908,
Culross Street, London,
1912, The Plough Inn,
Barkston, co Lincoln,
1947, comedian, 1884–90,
theatrical manager, 1890–91,
theatrical proprietor, 1912,
bn c. 1855–63, Birmingham,
co. Warwick, aged 21 in 1884,
28 in 1891, died 15 Jan 1949,
The Plough Inn, Barkston, bur
Barkston, M.I., will dd 7 Oct
1947, pr 1 Feb 1949.

VENETIA MATILDA
of Drayton House,
Colebrooke Avenue,
West Ealing, co. Middx,
widow of ... ROBINSON,
1912, dau of RICHARD
WILLIAM PARREY, retired
merchant, marr 2nd
14 Nov 1912, St.
George Hanover Square,
London, by Licence,
died 23 Jan 1941,
Montpelier Nursing
Home, Ealing, aged 68,
will dd 25 July 1933,
pr 17 June 1941.

⊤
⊥•

BEATRICE OLGA
of The Plough Inn,
Barkston, afsd., 1947,
bn ... Dec 1894, South
View, Bishop Auckland
afsd., bap 3 Jan 1895,
Bishop Auckland, named
in step-mother's will,
1933, execx of father's
will, 1949.

SYDNEY EVERITT JEFFERSON
bn 30 Apr 1899, Dockwray
Square, North Shields,
co. Northumberland.

EDWARD EVERITT JEFFERSON
bn 1 Apr 1901, Dockwray
Square, North Shields,
afsd.

contact with other Jeffersons, and no Jefferson was a register signatory at Arthur and Madge's wedding in 1884. The Grantham press obituary said that Arthur first performed on stage as 'Bobby Baxter', and an Arthur John Baxter was born to William Robert Baxter and his wife Amy (formerly Wildsmith) and baptised on 17 March 1862 at St Martin, Birmingham. No trace was found of any of them in the 1881 census index of Warwickshire.

A collection of red herrings?

Each of Arthur's boys' second names were also surnames, Gordon, Stanley and Everitt, the last of which was used twice, in 1899 and 1901. This was also the surname of Allen Edward Everitt, a Birmingham artist who died in 1882. Alas, his will, made in 1880, casts no light, as his new wife Frances was his sole beneficiary. Births registered under the surname of Everitt between 1860 and 1863 included a male child, born on 16 November 1861, at Nelson Street West, Birmingham, the son of Edward Everitt, a journeyman electro-plater, but no forename was inserted. By 1881 the father was still living in Birmingham, apparently with a different wife, and more children, but no son of twenty. The IGI of Warwickshire likewise conceded nothing. The death of an unnamed male Everitt was however recorded in the index for the March quarter of 1862 at Birmingham and it is probably the same baby, as baptismal names were entered in the birth registrations in due course on information furnished by the officiating minister. In this instance nothing had been added.

A self-made man

It seems that Arthur Jefferson was not only a comedian, but reinvented his past as well. It is fitting that he should claim Birmingham as his birthplace, for it was then the manufacturing centre of the British Empire. Not every family tree has roots deeper than the parents' generation.

18

CALLED TO ACCOUNT: WRITING UP YOUR FAMILY'S HISTORY

When I was ten years old I wrote my autobiography, and reading through it now I can vividly relive how it felt to grow up in a Lakeland village of the 1950s. It stirs memories of the long forgotten goings-on which punctuated my short existence. Some day I hope others in my family will peruse that fresh and innocent account, when most of my life lay uncharted ahead of me, and my personal values and perceptions of the world were still being moulded.

When and where do you begin?

One of the obvious and most pleasurable ways of bringing the past alive in a personal context is to write up your family's history. When should you start? It is never too soon, for the longer you delay it, the more material you will have to negotiate, and the less inclined you will be to tackle and unravel it all. Writing up your story concentrates the mind wonderfully, and draws your attention to points of uncertainty or spurious family connections which need sorting out before you take it any further. Older relatives may still be around to help resolve some of these problems, pepper your story with anecdotes and photographs, and lend encouragement.

Who is it for?

Decide first for whom the text is designed: is it for your own delectation, for your descendants, all known kinsfolk or a wider audience? Is it for private circulation only, or publication? Have a look at other people's writings, for you will readily see which grip you. By adopting a similar approach, scribbling an unvarnished and flowing narrative, you will soon warm to your task, and your text move at a cracking pace, which you can edit later. Two evocative and most enjoyable books are *The Simple Annals*, by P Sanders, which traces his family from seventeenth-century Stansted Mountfitchet, in Essex, to London and its suburbs, and *Hannah, The Complete Story*, by H Hauxwell with B Cockroft, recounting life in the Yorkshire Dales, and describing Baldersdale inhabitants, family networks and histories in house order. You may have your own favourites you want to imitate.

From present to past or fast forward?

You could begin by explaining the possible etymology and distribution of your surname and its variants with the help of a map plotting out its incidence over time and place, followed by a potted proven history of the family from earliest times. You may however prefer to act as storyteller, working back from the present day. This has the advantage of carrying your readers with you on your quest, sharing in your discoveries and disappointments, and you can continue to add to the narrative without detriment to earlier sections. Try not to let your script get out of hand, by running on for ever, so fix a structure and stick to it.

The essentials

Do you want the work to contain personality profiles of individual members, confine it to your direct ancestors, or widen the story to say something about their life and times in the community? In any event, bear in the mind the following points:

- Always date and identify yourself in your composition, do not miss out your own story, and draw on the reminiscences of living relations, taking care not to cause any offence by what you write and who you quote. If in any doubt about the truth you can always preface a statement by 'it is alleged', 'supposedly', or 'it is said', because you do not want to alienate family goodwill or risk being sued for libel.
- Reveal what happened when, how and why, rather than

cataloguing what and where, but avoid getting bogged down in minutiae or making false assumptions. Tell enough to make the story succinct and places identifiable.

- Resist the temptation to express personal opinions and judgements about people's actions and attitudes, remembering that you exist in a different environment or era.

- You can pad out your text with contemporary writings of other locals or briefly quote from the chronicled experiences of individuals of similar backgrounds or employment to make it more lively and immediate. Be careful though not to use huge chunks of someone else's prose, and that you are not contravening copyright regulations, as published works are protected until the death of the copyright owner plus seventy years.

- Always acknowledge your sources by inserting a sequential number in superscript immediately after the appropriate word, phrase or sentence, and cite the full title, authorship, edition, year of publication and page reference from which the quotation or information was taken. This enables the reader to follow the argument further and expresses your appreciation of someone else's work.

- Numbered explanatory footnotes may be placed at the bottom of the page, end of the chapter, or at the conclusion of your story, enumeration perhaps starting afresh with every new chapter in case you decide to alter their order later. Be sparing with them, as it can be a maddening experience ploughing through material dotted with countless footnote references.

Adding pictures

- Include regular, accurate, clear and simple family trees, illustrations, diagrams and pictures to break up the narrative and keep the reader abreast with your story so far, but always ensure they are relevant to their place in the text, sufficiently sharp or legible, and that they enhance rather than conflict with or detract from their context. Acknowledge their derivation, dating and identifying people in any photograph.

- The explanatory caption should quote any document reference and its provenance (for which repositories are usually happy to grant reproduction permission, using a standard form of words of acknowledgement).

- A map of the area described is another important adjunct, especially for a reader unfamiliar with it, and you can shade in places mentioned in the text. Do not neglect to give compass bearings.

Editing your script

- You must consider text length, final layout and presentation. It is very helpful to have an independent and sympathetic outsider read a copy of your typewritten or word-processed double-spaced narrative, whose constructive suggestions about its strengths and weaknesses and where it might be pruned to make it more punchy or clear will spare you any later embarrassment.
- You may have to rewrite the introduction which is always the worst part anyway, so leave this until last if you can. Discussion with a reliable friend at this stage is preferable to cruel uninformed criticism heaped on you when it is too late to rectify the situation.
- Never pass original drawings or photographs to anyone else before they go to the printer, in case of loss or damage; use photocopies if necessary.
- When you are happy with your script type it up or put it onto computer disk, leave it a week or two, and come back to it anew, for it is amazing what you will find you have omitted or misconstrued. You can now do fine-tuning and final editing, moving the text around if it is on computer.

How are you going to publish?

You may want to restrict circulation to a few bound photocopies or produce a regular newsletter to subscribing family members. This means you have to keep up your promise, find enough interesting items to capture and hold their attention and maintain its quality, which can prove a time-consuming commitment.

If you intend to publish or present your story in a polished and professional style, have adequate computer software, and a high-quality printer, a desktop publishing course will inspire confidence, and teach you technical expertise in deciding page size, number of lines per page, text layout and alignment, fonts and typesizes, and enable you to practise and perfect design skills. Study other published family histories for guidance on ways of making your book look attractive and appealing. A professional printer will demonstrate samples of different paper qualities and weights, so that you avoid using any with ink bleed-through. He will advise on colour compatibilities, weight of card or paper for the cover, whether it would be better gloss or matt, and the type of binding appropriate to your estimated number of pages. Canvassing the experience and expertise of others is vital as mistakes on technical points can prove costly. For instance, how best can your particular illustrations be reproduced, and at what cost? You may have to reduce their number or opt for black and white only, thereby eliminating certain items.

Using a professional printer

You can submit the text camera-ready, with crop-marks as a guide to page size, which keeps the cost down, but if you have no inclination or aptitude for home publishing, you might select a local printer to do the work for you. You can produce your text on a disk from which the printer can prepare the artwork for you, but always check and retain a marked-up copy of printer's proofs, making sure the layout, page-lengths, alignment and overall appearance are consistent and as you intended, there are no spelling errors or missing lines, and ask to see the final corrected proofs. Photographs and illustrations should be clean and accurately reproduced, the right way up and right way around, correctly numbered and captioned.

Check that your software is compatible with the printer's, as otherwise a charge may be imposed to convert your disk. A printout (hard copy) of files on your disk will illustrate what the text looks like and any conversion coding errors can be instantly spotted. Always keep an updated back-up disk in case of gremlins.

And the cost

The cost of publication will be governed by text length, number and type of illustrations, paper quality, number of jacket colours and print-run. The more copies you have printed the more cost-effective it becomes, but you must be realistic and balance definite and likely demand with what you can afford and may be lumbered with to store.

By casting around for prepaid subscriptions you can estimate how many volumes you need to sell to recoup your initial cost. Relatives might be enticed by the offer of a special pre-publication price discount, which will help towards paying your bill, but you will have to convince them their investment is worthwhile. Obtain quotations for print-runs of a hundred, two-hundred and fifty, five hundred and a thousand from several printers. These are bound to vary, as some specialise in print-runs lower than two thousand and will offer a better price than printers producing bulk runs. You then need to compute the unit cost per copy, dividing the total sum by the number of copies to be printed, multiplying this between three to five to reach a competitive selling price, thus taking into account permission fees, free presentation, review or publicity volumes on which you can make nothing, advertising, postage, packing and any hidden unforeseen extras, and which will yield a profit rather than a nasty loss.

Marketing, promotion and delivering the goods

Decide how you wish to market your product, as storing spare copies indefinitely will not only prove inconvenient, take up space, but result in their eventual deterioration before you can recover your outlay. Before committing yourself financially approach likely outlets in the area with which your family was associated or where members were prominent to enquire if they will exhibit and sell some stock, but be sure you agree on written trade terms in advance. They are in business and so are you, and not all authors are good at self-promotion. You could draft a flyer for local distribution and display, compose a short item for the press, or publicise your forthcoming book via the family history society to solicit advance orders.

Once customers have paid their dues they will expect the book to be delivered promptly. Printers usually hold their quotations firm for a month or so, and when you know your print-run (trying to avoid the need for a small reprint which would be expensive), you can submit the text in the agreed form. Printing may be turned round in as little as ten days, but may take up to a month, depending on the input you expect from the printer, his current workload, speed of proof-reading and time taken over corrections, so do not make promises you cannot keep. Make sure in advance the probable time lag, and add a fortnight for unknown eventualities. Planning publication to coincide with a special family event or Christmas is more likely to kindle demand, provided you give sufficient warning and can meet the deadline.

Ensuring permanent preservation and publicity

Lodge a copy of your work with the relevant county record office, local studies library, family history society and the library of the Society of Genealogists in London, and put your name and dated address inside if you would welcome feedback. You can request reviews by sending copies to journals with a large circulation such as *Family Tree Magazine, Genealogists' Magazine*, and that of the family history society, plus the local newspaper. Remember that the more free copies you distribute the lower your profit will be, but it can be an effective way of boosting sales and spreading awareness of your literary efforts.

And finally . . .

The more sound and accurate printed and circulated family histories there are the more family historians and others interested in the past can utilise them to compare individual and community experiences in time and place, and thus add to our knowledge and cultural heritage.

You can build on what you have learned by pursuing clues in the records tapped so far about your forefathers' occupations, abodes, movements, social and economic status into the rich plethora of further archives at your disposal. Your family history may then broaden into a history of the community.

Tracing your ancestry is a constant learning process, for a family's history is never complete, and it is much more fun reconstructing it for yourself. Now go to it.

APPENDIX 1

A checklist of questions to ask your family

Always write names in capital letters so they can be easily picked out. The why and how questions should provide fuller answers than the what, when or where type, as they often explain motives for people's actions.

1 Full name. Are any of these nicknames? How was the nickname acquired? Are the names in the correct order?
2 Relationship to you.
3 Name of his/her father.
4 How long ago or when and where did the father die and where was he buried? Include the county (place-names are frequently duplicated so be sure which one is appropriate).
5 Name of his/her mother.
6 How long ago or when and where did the mother die and where was she buried?
7 Date and place of the subject's birth, including the county.
8 Place in the family (eg eldest child, younger child)?
9 Full names of any brothers and sisters. Are any of these nicknames? Why? How much older/younger was each of them and date and place of birth if known? Which was the subject's and parents' favourite, and why?
10 Are they still alive? If not how long ago or when and where did they die and where are they buried? If still alive where are they now, or last known to be and when?
11 Religious denomination: where did the subject go to church/chapel?

12 Where did the subject go to school? How old was he/she when schooling started/ended? Did he/she go to university or other place of further education? When, where and what qualifications were gained?

13 Where does the subject live? Where has he/she lived before and the dates of each? Why did he/she move?

14 Occupation now and name and address of employer? How big an organisation? When did the job start and did he/she gain promotion? How did he/she get the job? What kind of training or qualifications were obtained?

15 What other jobs has he/she done? Dates of the various employments and name and address of employers. Why did he/she change jobs?

16 Which job was most enjoyable? Why?

17 What clubs and associations does he/she belong to? Does he/she serve on any committees? What are his/her hobbies?

18 Who did he/she marry? How and where did they meet and how long before they were married?

19 When and where did he/she marry? At what age? Was this the only marriage? If not when and where did he/she marry again? Is the first partner still alive? When and how did the first marriage end? Were there any children by each marriage? Who are they and when and where were they born? Are they all still alive?

20 Does he/she own any property? Where? Was it inherited or purchased? When, and from whom?

21 Has he/she a family Bible? If not does he/she know of someone in the family who has? Who did it originally belong to?

22 Did he/she serve in the armed forces? When and where? What rank, regiment, ship or squadron? Has he/she any campaign medals? Where are they and what do they commemorate? Was he/she wounded or taken prisoner, and if so when and where?

23 Did he/she ever work or live abroad/ Why, when and where? When and why did he/she return?

24 Has anyone researched the family's history before?

And about family members who are deceased

25 How long ago or when and where did the subject die? Where is he/she buried?

26 Did he/she leave a will?

APPENDIX 2

Abbreviations commonly used in compiling pedigrees

bn	born	wid	widow
bap, bp	baptised	dd	dated
co.	county	cod.	codicil
afsd.	aforesaid	pr	(will) proved
m, marr	married	Admon	(letters of)
o.t.p., b.o.t.p.	of this parish, both		administration
	of this parish	Inv.	Inventory
By Lic.	married by licence	o.i.	other issue
ML	Marriage Licence	.⋎.	unnamed issue
coelebs, unm	unmarried	dau	daughter
fl.	flourished	s and h	son and heir
temp.	in the time of	coh.	coheiress
c.	about	M.I.	monumental
d	died		inscription
b, bur	buried		
ob	obiit (died)		
obs.p., d.s.p.	died without issue		
d.s.p.m.	died without		
	male issue		
o.b.s.p. legit,	died without		
d.s.p. legit.	legitimate		
	offspring		
obvp, dvp	died during		
	father's lifetime		

USEFUL ADDRESSES

Before visiting any of the repositories, first write or telephone to check on current address, opening times, fees and search regulations.

Bedford Level Deeds Registry
Cambridgeshire Archives Service
County Record Office
Shire Hall
Castle Hill
Cambridge CB3 0AP
Tel: 01223–317281

The Bodleian Library
Department of Western Manuscripts
Broad Street
Oxford OX1 3BG
Tel: 01865–277158

The Borthwick Institute of Historical
  Research
St Anthony's Hall
Peasholme Green
York YO1 2PW
Tel: 01904–642315

British Association for Cemeteries in
  South Asia
76 ½ Chartfield Avenue
Putney
London SW15 6HQ
[excludes war graves]

The British Library
Great Russell Street
London WC1B 3DG
Tel: 0171–412 7000
Reader admissions 0171–412 7677
[Scheduled to move to 96 Euston Road,
  London NW1 2DB in 1997, with all the
  following departments except (d)]

(a) Department of Manuscripts
    The British Library
    Great Russell Street
    London WC1B 3DG
    Tel: 0171–412 7513/7514

(b) The Map Library
    [address as (a)]
    Tel: 0171–412 7700/7747

(c) National Sound Archive
    29 Exhibition Road
    London SW7 2AS
    Tel: 0171–412 7440/7430

(d) Newspaper Library, British Library
    Colindale Avenue
    London NW9 5HE
    Tel: 0171–412 7353

(e) Oriental and India Office Collections
    197 Blackfriars Road
    London SE1 8NG
    Tel: 0171–412 7873

British Record Society
The Secretary
College of Arms
Queen Victoria Street
London EC4V 4BT

British Telecommunications Archives
GO9 Telephone House
2–4 Temple Avenue
London EC4Y 0HL
Tel: 0171–822 1002
[Holds a historical telephone book
collection from 1880.]

Catholic Record Society
The Secretary
12 Melbourne Place
Wolsingham
Co. Durham DL12 3EH

Church of Jesus Christ of Latter-day
Saints [see The Genealogical Society of
Utah]

City Business Library (Corporation of
London)
1 Brewers Hall Gardens
London EC2V 5BX
Tel: 0171-638 8215

College of Arms
The Officer in Waiting
Queen Victoria Street
London EC4V 4BT
Tel: 0171–248 2762

Commonwealth War Graves Commission
2 Marlow Road
Maidenhead
Berkshire SL6 7DX
Tel: 01628–34221

Corporation of London Records Office
PO Box 270
Guildhall
London EC2P 2EJ
Tel: 0171–332 1251

The Court Funds Division
Public Trust Office
24 Kingsway
Stewart House
London WC2B 6LE
Tel: 0171–269 7000

Dr Williams's Library
14 Gordon Square
London WC1H 0AG
Tel: 0171–387 3727

Duchy of Cornwall
The Solicitor
10 Buckingham Gate
London SW1E 6LA
Tel: 0171–834 7346

Duchy of Lancaster
The Solicitor
Lancaster Place
Strand
London WC2E 7ED

East Riding Registry of Deeds
East Riding of Yorkshire Council
    Archives and Records Service
The Archivist
County Hall
Champney Road
Beverley
East Yorkshire HU17 9BA
Tel: 01482–885005/7

The Family Records Centre (see also
    Office for National Statistics, and
    Public Record Office)
Myddleton Place
Myddleton Street
Islington
London EC1R 1UW
(for further details, telephone
    0181-392 5300)

Federation of Family History Societies
The Administrator
The Benson Room
Birmingham and Midland Institute
Margaret Street
Birmingham B3 3BS

Federation of Family History Society
    (Publications) Ltd
2–4 Killer Street
Ramsbottom
Bury
Lancs BL0 9BZ
Tel: 01706–824254

The Genealogical Society of Utah
British Isles Family History Service Centre
185 Penns Lane
Sutton Coldfield
West Midlands B76 1JU
Tel: 0121–384 2028
[for details of local family history centres
of the Church of Jesus Christ of Latter-
day Saints]

Guildhall Library
Aldermanbury
London EC2P 2EJ
Tel: 0171–332 1863

Guild of One-Name Studies
The Secretary
Box G
14 Charterhouse Buildings
Goswell Road
London EC1M 7BA

House of Lords Record Office
House of Lords
London SW1A 0PW
Tel: 0171–219 3074

The Huguenot Society of Great Britain
and Ireland
Huguenot Library
University College, London
Gower Street
London WC1E 6BT
Tel: 0171-380 7094

The Institute of Heraldic and
Genealogical Studies
79–82 Northgate
Canterbury
Kent CT1 1BA
Tel: 01227–768664

Lambeth Palace Library
London SE1 7JU
Tel: 0171–928 6222

Laurel and Hardy Museum
The Curator
4c Upper Brook Street
Ulverston
Cumbria LA12 7LA
Tel: 01229–582292

London Metropolitan Archives
40 Northampton Road
London EC1R 0HB
Tel: 0171–332 3824

The National Organisation for the
Counselling of Adoptees and Parents
(NORCAP)
112 Church Road
Wheatley
Oxford OX33 1LU
Tel: 01865–875000

The National Register of
Archives/Manorial Documents Register
Royal Commission on Historical
Manuscripts
Quality House
Quality Court
Chancery Lane
London WC2A 1HP
Tel: 0171–242 1198

North Riding Deeds Registry
The Archivist
North Yorkshire County Record Office
County Hall
Northallerton
North Yorkshire DL7 8AF
Tel: 01609–777585
[Situated at Malpas Road, Northallerton]

Office for National Statistics (see also
The Family Records Centre)

(a) Adoption/Overseas/Postal
Applications Sections
Office for National Statistics
General Register Office
Smedley Hydro
Trafalgar Road
Southport
Merseyside PR8 2HH
Tel: 0151–471 4800
[For priority service 0151–471 4524,
fax 0151–471 4368 quoting
credit/debit card details.]

(b) Census Division
Office for National Statistics
Segensworth Road
Titchfield, Fareham
Hants PO15 5RR
Tel: 01329–813429 (for 1901 Census
searches)

(c) Office for National Statistics
   Queries Section
   PO Box 2
   Southport
   Merseyside PR8 2JD
   Tel: 01704–563563 ext. 4392 or
   0151–471 4800

Preservation Equipment Ltd
Shelfanger
Diss, Norfolk IP22 2DG
Tel: 01379–651527
[For archival storage systems, see also
   Secol Ltd]

Principal Registry of the Family Division
Somerset House
Strand
London WC2R 1LP
Tel: 0171–936 6940 (Divorce Registry)
Tel: 0171–936 7000 (Principal Probate
   Registry)

(a) (for postal copies of wills)
   The Chief Clerk
   Probate Subregistry
   Duncombe Place
   York YO1 2EA

The Public Record Office
Ruskin Avenue
Kew
Richmond
Surrey TW9 4DU
Tel: 0181-876 3444

The Religious Society of Friends
The Library
Friends House
Euston Road
London NW1 2BJ
Tel: 0171–387 3601
[Closed from March 1997 until
   approximately March 1998.]

The Royal Commission on Historical
Manuscripts (see The National Register
of Archives)
Secol Ltd
Howlett Way
Thetford
Norfolk IP24 1HZ
Tel: 01842–752341
[For archival storage systems, see also
   Preservation Equipment Ltd]

Society of Antiquaries of London
Burlington House
Piccadilly
London W1V 0HS
Tel: 0171–734 0191 or 0171–437 9954

Society of Genealogists
14 Charterhouse Buildings
Goswell Road
London EC1M 7BA
Tel: 0171–251 8799, library 0171-250 0291

The Treasury Solicitor (BV)
Treasury Solicitor's Department
Queen Anne's Chambers
28 Broadway
London SW1H 9JS
Tel: 0171–210 3046

Ushaw College Library
Ushaw College
Durham DH7 9RH

Westminster (Roman Catholic) Diocesan
   Archives
16a Abingdon Road
London W8 6AF
Tel: 0171–938 3580

West Riding Deeds Registry
The Archivist
West Yorkshire Archive Service
Wakefield HQ
Newstead Road
Wakefield
West Yorkshire WF1 2DE
Tel: 01924 295982

Wales

Association of Family History Societies of
   Wales
c/o JB Rowlands
18 Marine Terrace
Aberystwyth
Dyfed SY23 2AZ

Glamorgan Record Office
County Hall
King Edward VII Avenue
Cathays Park
Cardiff CF1 3NE
Tel: 01222–780282

National Library of Wales
Department of Manuscripts and Records
Aberystwyth
Dyfed SY23 3BU
Tel: 01970–628816

Channel Islands

Channel Islands Family History Society
The Hon. Secretary, Mrs S Payn
PO Box 507
St Helier
Jersey JE4 5TN
[Research Room, 22 Hilgrove Street,
   St Helier]

Alderney

The Court House
Alderney

Guernsey

Bureau des Connetables
St Peter Port
Guernsey
Tel: 01481–721732 (Wills of personalty
   only)

The Greffe
HM Greffier
The Royal Court House
St Peter Port
Guernsey GY1 2PB
Tel: 01481–725277
[Write first to Priaulx Library with
   genealogical enquiries.]

Island Archives Service
29 Victoria Road
St Peter Port
Guernsey GY1 1HU
Tel: 01481–724512

Priaulx Library
Candie Road
St Peter Port
Guernsey GY1 1UG
Tel: 01481–721998

La Société Guernesiaise
Candie Gardens
St Peter Port
Guernsey GY1 1UG
Tel: 01481–725093

Jersey

Jersey Archives Service
Jersey Museum
The Weybridge
St Helier
Jersey JE2 3NF
Tel: 01534–617441

Jersey States Library
Jersey Library
Halkett Place
St Helier
Jersey JE2 4WH
Tel: 01534–59991

The Judicial Greffe
The Royal Court of Jersey
No 16 Hill Street
St Helier
Jersey
[For copies of wills.]

Probate Registry/Public Registry
The Royal Court of Jersey
Burrard House
Don Street
St Helier
Jersey JE2 4TR
Tel: 01534–50200

Société Jersiaise
The Librarian
The Museum
9 Pier Road
St Helier
Jersey JE2 4UW
Tel: 01534–30538

The Royal Court of Jersey (see The
    Judicial Greffe and Probate Registry)
The Superintendent Registrar
10 Royal Square
St Helier
Jersey JE2 4WA
Tel: 01534–502335

Isle of Man

The General Registry (includes the Deeds
    and Probate Registry)
The Chief Registrar
The Registries
Deemsters Walk
Bucks Road
Douglas
Isle of Man IM1 3AR
Tel: 01624–685242

Isle of Man Family History Society
c/o The Secretary
5 Selborne Drive
Douglas
Isle of Man
Tel: 01624–622188

Manx Museum Library/Manx National
    Heritage Library
Manx Museum and National Trust
Kingswood Grove
Douglas [Isle of Man] IM1 3LY
Tel: 01624–675522

Scotland

Adoption Counselling Centre and
  Adoption Contact Service
Family Care/Birth Link
21 Castle Street
Edinburgh EH2 3DN
Tel: 0131–225 6441

General Register Office for Scotland
New Register House
Edinburgh EH1 3YT
Tel: 0131–334 0380, fax: 0131–314 4400
  (quoting credit number)

HM Court of the Lord Lyon
New Register House
Edinburgh EH1 3YT
Tel: 0131–556 7255

The National Library of Scotland
Department of Manuscripts
George IV Bridge
Edinburgh EH1 1EW
Tel: 0131–226 4531

National Register of Archives (Scotland)
Scottish Record Office
West Register House
Charlotte Square
Edinburgh EH2 4DF
Tel: 0131–556 6585

Queen's and Lord Treasurer's
  Remembrancer
Crown Office
5/7 Regent Road
Edinburgh EH7 5BL

The Scottish Association of Family
  History Societies
The Secretary
51/3 Mortonhall Road
Edinburgh EH9 2HN
Tel: 0131-667 0437

Scottish Genealogy Society
Library and Family History Centre
15 Victoria Terrace
Edinburgh EH1 2JL
Tel: 0131–220 3677

Scottish Record Office
Historical Search Room
HM General Register House
Princes Street
Edinburgh EH1 3YY
Tel: 0131–556 6585

and

West Register House
Charlotte Square
Edinburgh EH2 4DF
Tel: 0131–556 6585

Ireland

The Accountant of the Courts of Justice
The High Court of Justice
Dublin

Council of Irish Genealogical
  Organisations
186 Ashcroft
Dublin 5

The Genealogical Office/Clans of Ireland
  Office
2 Kildare Street
Dublin 2
Tel: 003531–6618811

General Register Office
Joyce House
8–11 Lombard Street East
Dublin 2
Tel: 003531–6711000

Irish Genealogical Project
c/o Department of the Taoiseach
Government Buildings
Merrion Square,
Dublin 2

Irish Manuscripts Commission
73 Merrion Square
Dublin 2

Land Valuation Office
6 Ely Place
Dublin 2
Tel: 003531–6763211

National Archives of Ireland
Bishop Street
Dublin 8
Tel: 003531–4783711

National Library of Ireland
2/3 Kildare Street
Dublin 2
Tel: 003531–6618811

Religious Society of Friends Historical
    Library
Swanbrook House
Morehampton Road
Donnybrook
Dublin 4
Tel: 003531–6683684

The Registry of Deeds
Henrietta Street
Dublin 1
Tel: 003531–6733300

Representative Church Body Library
Braemor Park
Rathgar
Dublin 14
Tel: 003531–4923979

Royal Irish Academy
16 Dawson Street
Dublin 2
Tel: 003531–6762570

The Superintendent Registrar's Office
Eastern Health Board
Ground Floor
Joyce House
8–11 Lombard Street
Dublin 2

Trinity College Library
Manuscripts Department
College Street
Dublin 2
Tel: 003531–7021189

Northern Ireland

The Accountant General
Royal Courts of Justice, Ulster
Chichester Street
Belfast 1

Belfast Central Library
Irish and Local Studies Department
Royal Avenue
Belfast BT1 1EA
Tel: 01232–243233

General Register Office of Northern
    Ireland
Oxford House
49–55 Chichester Street
Belfast BT1 4HL
Tel: 01232–252000

Linen Hall Library (Belfast Library and
    Society for Promoting Knowledge)
17 Donegall Square North
Belfast BT1 5GD
Tel: 01232–321707

The Presbyterian Historical Society of
    Ireland
Room 220
Church House
Fisherwick Place
Belfast BT1 6DW
Tel: 01232–322284

The Probate and Matrimonial Office
Royal Courts of Justice, Ulster
Chichester Street
Belfast 1
Tel: 01232–235111

Public Record Office of Northern Ireland
66 Balmoral Avenue
Belfast BT9 6NY
Tel: 01232–661621

Religious Society of Friends Library
Ulster Quarterly Meeting
Friends Meeting House
Railway Street
Lisburn
Co. Antrim BT28 1XG

Ulster Historical Foundation and Ulster
 Genealogical and Historical Guild
Balmoral Buildings
12 College Square East
Belfast BT1 6DD
Tel: 01232–332288

———— United States of America ————

Civil Reference Branch (NNRC)
National Archives
Washington, DC 20408
[For births, marriages and deaths of
 American citizens overseas more than
 seventy-five years ago]

and

Department of State
Washington, DC 20520
[For births, marriages and deaths of
 American citizens overseas less than
 seventy-five years ago]

Family History Library of the Church of
 Jesus Christ of Latter-day Saints
35 North West Temple Street
Salt Lake City
UT 84150

The Immigration and Naturalization
 Service (INS)
Washington, DC 20536

Library of Congress
10 First Street SE
Local History and Genealogy Section
Washington, DC 20540–5554

National Archives and Records
 Administration
National Archives Building
Pennsylvania Avenue
Between 7th and 9th Streets
Washington, DC 20408
[Will supply details about 13 current
 National Archives Regional Archives]

National Society of Daughters of the
 American Revolution
1776 D Street, NW
Washington, DC 20006–5392

Newberry Library
60 West Walton Street
Chicago
IL 60610–3380

New England Historic and Genealogical
 Society
101 Newbury Street
Boston
Mass 02116–3087

The New York Genealogical and
 Biographical Society
122 East 58th Street
New York
NY 10022–1939

University Microfilms

(a) 300 N Zeeb Road
    Ann Arbor
    MI 48103–1500

(b) 683 Williamsburg Ct NE
    Concord
    NC 28025–2537

University Microfilms International Inc.

(a) 811 S Waco Street
    Weatherford
    TX 76086–5341

(b) Mound City
    MO 64470

(c) Shawnee Mission
    KS 66200

Select Bibliography

Books mentioned in the text
*Indicates US or other sources overseas

Atkins, PJ, *The Directories of London*, 1677–1977, 1990

Bardsley, CW, *A Dictionary of English and Welsh Surnames, with Special American Instances*, 1901, reprinted 1988

Barrow, GB, *The Genealogist's Guide: an index to printed British pedigrees and family histories*, 1950–1975, 1977

Bentley, EP (ed.), *The Country Courthouse Book*, 1995

Berko, RL and Sadler S, *Where to Write for Vital Records of Births, Deaths, Marriages and Divorces including forms for obtaining these and other Vital records*, 1989

Besse, J, *A Collection of the Suffering of the People called Quakers for the Testimony of a Good Conscience from … 1650 to … 1689*, 2 vols. 1753

Burchall, MJ (ed.), *National Genealogical Directory*, annual 1979–86, continued under Caley, IL, (ed.), 1987–93

Burek, D (ed.), *Cemereries of the United States: A Guide to Contact Information for United States Cemeteries and Their Records*, 1995

Burek, DM (ed.), *Encyclopedia of Associations* [in North America], 15th edn 1997

Burke's Family Index to Burke's Landed Gentry and Burke's Peerage and Baronetage (1826–1876), 1976

Burns, Rev T, *Church Property* (The Benefice Lectures), 1905

Camp, AJ (ed.), *An Index to the Wills Proved in the Prerogative Court of Canterbury 1750–1800*, 6 vols. 1976–92

Cerny, J and Elliott E, *The Library: A Guide to the LDS Family History Library*, 1988

Chaplin, C, *My Autobiography*, 1964, reprinted 1979

Cheney, CR, *Handbook of Dates for Students of English History*, 1945, reprinted 1981

*Coldham, PW, *American Loyalist Claims, Audit Office Series 13, bundles 1–35, and 37*, 1980

*Coldham, PW, *American Wills and Administrations in the Prerogative Court of Canterbury, 1610–1857*, 1989

*Coldham, PW, *American Wills proved in London, 1611–1775*, 1992

Cole, J and Church R, *In and around Record Repositories in Great Britain and Ireland* (3rd edition 1992, 4th edition forthcoming 1997)

Colwell, S, *Dictionary of Genealogical Sources in the Public Record Office*, 1992

Craig, FWS, *Boundaries of Parliamentary Constituencies 1885–1972*, 1972

Culling, J, *An Introduction to Occupations, a Preliminary List*, 1994

de Breffny, B, *Bibliography of Irish Family History and Genealogy*, 1974
DeMaggio, JA and Kirby, DM (eds.), *Directory of Special Libraries and Information Centers* [in North America], 15th edn 1992

*Eakle, A and Cerny J, *The Source: A Guidebook of American Genealogy*, 1984
Estcourt, EE and Payne JO (eds.), *The English Catholic Non-Jurors of 1715...*, [1885], facsimile edn 1969

Family Tree Magazine, monthly, 1984–1900: *A Guide to Published Arrival Records*, 3 vols. 1981, annual supplements, 1982–
Federation of Family History Societies, *Family History News and Digest*, half-yearly, 1977
Ferguson, JPS, *Scottish Family Histories*, 2nd edn 1986
*Filby, PW (camp.), *Directory of American Libraries with Genealogy and Local History Collections*, 1988
*Filby, PW, *Passenger and Immigration Lists Bibliography 1538–1900: being a guide to published lists of arrivale in the United States and Canada*, 2nd edn 1988
*Filby, PW and Meyer, MK, *Passenger and Immigration Lists Index 1538–*
Foster, J and Sheppard J, *British Archives – a Guide to Archive Resources in the United Kingdom*, 3rd edn 1995

Gallagher, JP, *Fred Karno, Master of Mirth and Tears*, 1971
Gandy, M (ed.), *Catholic Missions and Registers 1700–1880*, 6 vols 1993
Gandy, M (ed.), *Catholic Parishes in England, Wales and Scotland*, an Atlas, 1993
*Genealogical Society of Utah, *A General Index to Census of Pensioners for Revoltionary or Military Service, 1840,* 1841, reprinted 1965
Gibson, J, *Bishops' Transcripts and Marriage Licences, Bonds and Allegations: Guide to their Location and Indexes*, 3rd edn 1991
Gibson, J, *The Hearth Tax, other later Stuart Tax Lists and the Association Oath Rolls*, 2nd edn 1996
Gibson, J, *Probate Jurisdictions: Where to Look for Wills*, 4th edn 1994, updated 1997
Gibson, J, *Quarter Sessions Records for Family Historians: A Select List*, 4th edn 1995
Gibson, J, *Unpublished Personal Name Indexes in Record Offices and Libraries*, 2nd edn 1987, reprinted with Addenda 1988
Gibson, J and Dell, A, *Protestation Returns 1641–42 and Other Contemporary Listings*, 1995
Gibson, J and Hampson, E, *Census Returns 1841–1891 in Microform*, 6th edn 1994
Gibson, J and Hampson, E, *Marriage, Census and Other Indexes for Family Historians*, 6th edn 1996
Gibson, J and Medlycott, M, *Local Census Listings, 1522–1930: Holdings in the British Isles*, 2nd edn 1994

Gibson, J, Medlycott, M and Mills, D, *Land and Window Tax Assessments*, 1993
Gibson, J and Peskett, P, *Record Offices: How to Find Them*, 7th edn 1996
Gibson, J and Rogers, C, *Coroners' Records in England and Wales*, 2nd edn 1997
Gibson, J and Rogers, C, *Electoral Registers since 1832; and Burgess Rolls*, 2nd edn 1990
Gibson, J and Rogers, C, *Poll Books c. 1696–1872: A Directory to Holdings in Great Britain*, 3rd edn 1994
Gibson, J and Rogers, C, *Poor Law Union Records (in England and Wales)*, 4 vols, 1993, the last of which is *Gazetteer of England and Wales*, compiled from *Guide to Local Administrative Units of England*, by FA Youngs, jr, 1981, 1991, and the 1851 Census population tables for Wales (Parts 1 and 2, 2nd edn 1997)
*Giuseppi, MS (ed.), *Naturalizations in the American Colonies, 1740–1772*, 1921, Huguenot Society, vol xxiv
Gordon, A, *Candie for the Foundling*, 1992
Grenham, J, *Tracing Your Irish Ancestors: the Complete Guide*, 1992
Grieve, HEP, *Examples of English Handwriting 1150–1750*, 1954, 5th impression 1981
Griffith, Sir Richard, *Primary Valuation of Ireland*, 1848–64
Groome, F, *Gazetteer of Scotland*, 6 vols 1882–85
Guildhall Library Research Guide 2: *The British Oversea, A guide to births, marriages and deaths of British persons overseas before 1945*, 3rd revised edn 1994
Guild of One Name Studies, *Register of One-name Studies*, 11 edn 1995

Hauxwell, H with Cockroft, B, *Hannah, The Complete Story*, 1991
Hawgood, D, *Internet for Genealogy*, 1996
Helferty, S and Refaussé R (eds.), *Directory of Irish Archives*, 2nd edn 1993
Henderson, SPA and AJW, *Directory of British Associations and Associations in Ireland*, 12th edn 1994–95
Houston, J, *Index of Cases in the Records of the Court of Arches at Lambeth Palace Library 1660–1913*, 1972
Humphery-Smith, CR (ed.), *The Phillimore Atlas and Index of Parish Registers*, 2nd edn 1995
Hurley, B, *The Book of Trades or Library of Useful Arts*, 1811, 2 vols 1977
Hurley, B, *The Book of Trades or Library of Useful Arts, 1818*, 1994

Ifans, D (ed.), *Cofresti anghydffutfiol Cymru Nonconformist registers of Wales*, 1994

Jacobus, DL, *Index to Genealogical Periodicals*, 1952, reprinted 1978
Johnson, KA and Sainty, MR (eds.), *Genealogical Research Directory, National and International*, annual 1981–
Journal of the Association for the Preservation of the Memorials of the Dead [in Ireland], 1888–1934

Kain, RJP and Oliver RR, *The Tithe Maps of England and Wales*, A cartographic analusus and country-by-country catalogue, 1995

Kaminkow, MJ (compiler and ed.), *A Complement to Genealogies in the Library of Congress: A Bibliography*, 1981

*Kaminkow, MJ (ed.), *Genealogies in the Library of Congress: A Bibliography*, 2 vols. 1972, 4th printing 1978, with Supplement 1972–76, 1977, and printing 1978

Kelly's *Handbook to the Titled, Landed and Official Classes*, 1874–

Kemp, TJ, *International Vital Records Handbook*, 3rd edn 1994

Lewis, S, *Topographical Dictionary of Ireland*, 1837

The Local Historian (formerly *The Amateur Historian*, 1954–)

The Local History Magazine, 1984–

Local Population Studies, 1968–

MacLysaght, E, *Bibliography of Irish Family History*, 1982

Marker, IJ and Warth, KE (eds), *Surname Periodicals, A World-wide Listings of One-Name Genealogical Publications*, 1987

Marshall, GW, *The Genealogist's Guide*, 1903, reprinted 1980

Martin, CT, *The Record Interpreter, a collection of abbreviations, Latin words and names used in English historical manuscripts and records*, 1910, reprinted 1994

Milward, R, *A Glossary of Household, Farming and Trade Terms from Probate Inventories*, 3rd edn 1991

Mitchell, B, *Guide to Irish Parish Registers*, 1988

The Morton Allen Directory of European Passenger Steamship Arrivals, 1931

Mullins, ELC (ed.), *Texts and Calendars: an Analytical Guide to Serial Publications*, 1958, reprinted with correction 1978

Mullins, ELC (ed.), *Texts and Calendars II: an Analytical Guide to Serial Publications 1957–82*, 1983

Munby, LM, *How Much is That Worth?* 2nd edn 1996

Municipal Year Book and Public Services Directory, 1996

National Archives Trust Fund Board, *Guide to Genealogical Research in the National Archives*, 1985

National Inventory of Documentary Sources in the United States, Part 1: Federal Records, Index, 1985, Part 2: Manuscripts Division, Library of Congress, 1983

Newington-Irving, NJN (ed.), *Directories and Poll Books, including Almanacs and Electoral Rolls, in the Library of the Society of Genealogists*, 1995

Newington-Irving, NJN (ed.), *Will Indexes and Other Probate Material in the Library of the Society of Genealogists*, 1996

Nichols, EL, *Genealogy in the computer age: understanding FamilySearch*, revised edn 1994

Nichols, EL, *The International Genealogical Index*, 1992 edition, 1995

Nikolic, M, *Genealogical Microform Holdings in Scottish Libraries*, 2nd edn 1994

Norton, JE, *Guide to National and Provincial Directories of England and Wales, excluding London, published before 1856*, 1950

Owen, DB, *Guide to Genealogical Resources in the British Isles*, 1989

Owen-Pawson, J and Mouland, B, *Laurel before Hardy*, 1984

Phair, PB and Ellis, E, *Abstracts of Wills at the Registry of Deeds* [Dublin], 3 vols 1954–88

Phillimore, WPW and Fry, EA, *Index to Changes of Name, 1760–1901*, 1905, reprinted 1986

Price, VJ, *Regsiter Offices of Births, Deaths and Marriages in Great Britain and Northern Ireland*, 2nd edn 1993

Ramscar, J, *Associations and Professional Bodies of the United Kingdom*, 1996

Raymond, SA, *British Genealogical Bibliographies: Occupational Sources for Genealogists*, 1992, 2nd edn (1996)

Raymond, SA, *British Genealogical Periodicals: A Bibliography of their Contents*, vol 1 *The Ancestor; Collectanea Topographica et Genealogica: Topographer and Genealogist*, 1991, vol 2 *The Genealogist, Part 1 Sources, Part 2 Family Histories, Pedigrees, Biographical Notes and Obituaries*, 1991 vol 3 *Miscellanea Genealogica et Heraldica: Part 1 Sources, Part 2 Family Histories*, 1993

Raymond, SA, *British Genealogy in Miscellaneous Journals: Supplement 1*, 1994

Return of Owners of Land of One Acre and Upwards in England (excluding the Metropolis), and Wales 1873, 2 vols 1875

Return of Owners of Land or One Acre and Upwards in Ireland, 1876

Return of Owners of Land of One Acre and Upwards in Scotland, 1872–3, 1874

Reynard, KW and JME (eds.), *The ASLIE Directory of Information Sources in the United Kingdom*, 8th edn 1994

Richards, M, *Welsh Administrative and Territorial Units*, 1969

Routh, G, *Occupations of the People of Great Britain 1801–1981*, 1987

Royal Commission an Historical Manuscripts, *Record Repositories in Great Britain: A geographical directory*, 9th edn 1991, 3rd impression (with revisions) 1994

Sanders, P (*The Simple Annals, The History of an Essex and East End Family*) 1989

Schürer, K and Anderson SJ (eds.), *A Guide to Historical Datafiles Held in Machine-Readable Form*, 1992

Scottish Association of Family History Societies, *The Parishes, Registers and Registrars of Scotland*, 1993

Shaw, G and Tipper, A, *British Directories: a Bibliography and Guide to Directories published in England and Wales (1850–1950) and Scotland (1773–1950)*, 1988

*Shell, TK, *Directories in Print*, 1996
Society of Genealogists, *Computers in Genealogy*, quarterly 1981–
Society of Genealogists, *Genealogists' Magazine*, quarterly 1925–
Society of Genealogists, *A List of Parishes in Boyd's Marriage Index*, 6th edn
1987, corrected reprint 1994
Society of Genealogists, *Marriage Licences: Abstracts and Indexed in the
Library of the Society of Genealogists*, 4th edn 1991
Society of Genealogists, *Monumental Inscriptions in the Library of the Society
of Genealogists*, Part 1 *Southern England*, 1984, Part 2 *Northern England,
Wales, Scotland, Ireland and Overseas*, 1987
Society of Genealogists, *Parish Copies in the Library of the Society of
Genealogists*, 11th edn 1995
Society of Genealogists, *The Trinity House Petitions: A Calendar of the
Records of the Corporation of Trinity House*, London, in the Library of the
Society of Genealogists, 1987
Spear, DN, *Bibliography of American Directories Through 1860*, 1961
Stevenson, D and WB (eds.), *Scottish Texts and Calendars: an Analytical
Guide to Serial Publications*, 1987
Stuart, D, *Latin for Local and Family Historians*, 1995
Stuart, M, *Scottish Family History, A guide to works of reference on the
history and genealogy of Scottish families... To which is prefixed an essay on
How to write the history of a family, by Sir James Balfour Paul*, 1930

Tate, WE (ed.), *A Domesday of English Enclosure Acts and Awards*, 1978
Thomson, T (ed.), *Inquisitionum ad Capellam Domini Regis Retornatarum, quae
in publicis archivis Scotiae adhuc servantur [Retours]*, 3 vols. 1811–16, 1900
The Times Tercentenary, *Handlist... of English and Welsh Newspapers,
Magazines and Reviews 1620–1920*, 1920
Thomson, TR, *Catalogue of British Family Histories*, 3rd edn 1980 with
Addenda
Turner, G Lyon, *Original Records of Early Nonconformity under Persecution
and Indulgence*, 3 vols 1911–14

Victoria County History, 1900–

Wagner, AR, *English Genealogy*, 3rd edn 1983
Whitaker's Almanack, annually 1869– (includes details of learned societies,
associations, universities, schools etc)
Whitmore, JB, *A Genealogical Guide. An index to British pedigrees in
continuation of Marshall's Genealogist's Guide*, 1953
Who's Who 1897–1996: One hundred years of biography, 1996
Williams, CJ and Watts-Williams, SJ (compilers), *National Index of Parish
Registers* vol 13 *Cofresti Plwyf Cymru / Parish Registers of Wales*, 1986
Willing's Press Guide, 122nd edn 1996, vol 1 United Kingdom vol 2 Overseas